RECORD PROFILES OF
BASEBALL'S HALL OF FAMERS

ALSO BY JOHN A. MERCURIO

Chronology of Major League Baseball Records
Chronology of Boston Red Sox Records
Chronology of New York Yankee Records

RECORD PROFILES OF BASEBALL'S HALL OF FAMERS

John A. Mercurio

PERENNIAL LIBRARY

Harper & Row, Publishers

New York • Grand Rapids • Philadelphia • St. Louis • San Francisco • London • Singapore • Sydney • Tokyo • Toronto

The photographs of the following players appear courtesy of the National Baseball Library, Cooperstown, New York: Grover Cleveland Alexander, Earl Averill, Dave Bancroft, Jacob Peter Beckley, Jesse Cail Burkett, John Dwight Chesbro, James Joseph Collins, John Gibson Clarkson, Tyrus Raymond Cobb, Roger Connor, Joseph Edward Cronin, William Arthur Cummings, Robert Pershing Doerr, Hugh Duffy, Urban Clarence Faber, Richard Benjamin Ferrell, Elmer Harrison Flick, Edward Charles Ford, Frank Frisch, James Francis Galvin, Clark Griffith, Robert Moses Grove, Jesse Joseph Haines, Rogers Hornsby, Miller James Huggins, Travis Calvin Jackson, Walter Perry Johnson, George Clyde Kell, Joseph James Kelley, George Lange Kelly, Ralph McPherran Kiner, Frederick Charles Lindstrom, Joseph Vincent McCarthy, Bill McKechnie, Satchel Paige, James Henry O'Rourke, Charles Herbert Ruffing, George Herman Ruth, Red Schoendienst, Samuel L. Thompson, Joseph Floyd Vaughn, John Peter Wagner, Rhoderick John Wallace, Edward Augustin Walsh, Harry Wright, Carl Yastrzemski, and Ross Middlebrook Youngs.

RECORD PROFILES OF BASEBALL'S HALL OF FAMERS. Copyright © 1990 by John A. Mercurio. All rights reserved. Printed in the United States of America. No part of this book may be used or reproduced in any manner whatsoever without written permission except in the case of brief quotations embodied in critical articles and reviews. For information address Harper & Row, Publishers, Inc., 10 East 53rd Street, New York, N.Y. 10022.

FIRST EDITION

Designed by M 'N O Production Services, Inc.

Library of Congress Cataloging-in-Publication Data

Mercurio, John A.
   Record profiles of baseball's hall of famers / John A. Mercurio.—1st ed.
     p. cm.
   Bibliography: p.
   ISBN 0-06-096448-0
   1. Baseball—United States—Records.   2. National Baseball Hall of Fame and Museum.   3. Baseball players—United States—Statistics.
I. Title.
GV877.M45   1990
796.357'64'0922—dc20

                                      89-45688

90 91 92 93 94 DT/MPC 10 9 8 7 6 5 4 3 2 1

Contents

PREFACE   ix

I. PLAYER RECORD PROFILES   1

Henry Louis Aaron	2	Edward Trowbridge Collins, Sr.	79
Grover Cleveland Alexander	4	James Joseph Collins	83
Walter Emmons Alston	7	Earle Bryan Combs	87
Adrian Constantine Anson	9	Charles Albert Comiskey	89
Luis Ernesto Aparicio	13	Roger Connor	92
Lucius Benjamin Appling	15	Stanley Anthony Coveleski	95
Howard Earl Averill	17	Samuel Earl Crawford	97
John Franklin Baker	19	Joseph Edward Cronin	100
Dave Bancroft	22	William Arthur Cummings	102
Ernest Banks	24	Hazen Shirley Cuyler	103
Jacob Peter Beckley	26	Jay Hanna Dean	105
Johnny Lee Bench	29	Edward James Delahanty	107
Charles Albert Bender	31	William Malcolm Dickey	109
Lawrence Peter Berra	34	Joseph Paul DiMaggio	111
James Leroy Bottomley	37	Robert Pershing Doerr	114
Louis Boudreau	39	Donald Scott Drysdale	116
Roger Bresnahan	41	Hugh Duffy	118
Louis Clark Brock	43	John Joseph Evers	120
Dennis Joseph Brouthers	45	William Ewing	122
Mordecai Peter Centennial Brown	48	Urban Clarence Faber	124
Jesse Cail Burkett	51	Robert William Andrew Feller	126
Roy Campanella	54	Richard Benjamin Ferrell	128
Max George Carey	56	Elmer Harrison Flick	129
Frank LeRoy Chance	59	Edward Charles Ford	131
John Dwight Chesbro	62	James Emory Foxx	134
Fred Clifford Clarke	64	Frank Francis Frisch	136
John Gibson Clarkson	68	James Francis Galvin	140
Roberto Walker Clemente	70	Henry Louis Gehrig	142
Tyrus Raymond Cobb	72	Charles Leonard Gehringer	146
Gordon Stanley Cochrane	77	Robert Gibson	148

Vernon Louis Gomez 150
Leon Allen Goslin 152
Henry Benjamin Greenberg 154
Clark Calvin Griffith 156
Burleigh Arland Grimes 159
Robert Moses Grove 161
Charles James Hafey 164
Jesse Joseph Haines 166
William Robert Hamilton 168
Stanley Raymond Harris 171
Charles Leo Hartnett 173
Harry Edwin Heilmann 175
William Jennings Bryan Herman 176
Harry Bartholomew Hooper 178
Rogers Hornsby 180
Waite Charles Hoyt 183
Carl Owen Hubbell 185
Miller James Huggins 187
James Augustus Hunter 190
Monford Merrill Irvin 192
Travis Calvin Jackson 194
Hugh Ambrose Jennings 195
Walter Perry Johnson 198
Adrian Joss 202
Albert William Kaline 204
Timothy John Keefe 206
William Henry Keeler 208
George Clyde Kell 210
Joseph James Kelley 212
George Lange Kelly 214
Michael Joseph Kelly 216
Harmon Clayton Killebrew 218
Ralph McPherran Kiner 220
Charles Herbert Klein 222
Sanford Koufax 224
Napoleon Lajoie 227
Robert Granville Lemon 231
Frederick Charles Lindstrom 233
Ernest Natali Lombardi 235
Alfonso Ramon Lopez 237
Theodore Amar Lyons 239
Cornelius Mack 241
Mickey Charles Mantle 244
Henry Emmett Manush 246
Walter James Vincent Maranville 248
Juan Marichal 251
Richard William Marquard 253
Edwin Lee Mathews, Jr. 255
Christopher Mathewson 257
Willie Howard Mays 260
Joseph Vincent McCarthy 263
Thomas Francis Michael McCarthy 265
Willie Lee McCovey 267
Joseph Jerome McGinnity 269
John Joseph McGraw 272
William Boyd McKechnie 275
Joseph Michael Medwick 277
John Robert Mize 279
Stanley Frank Musial 281
Charles Augustus Nichols 284
James Henry O'Rourke 286
Melvin Thomas Ott 288
Leroy Robert Paige 291
Herbert Jefferis Pennock 293
Edward Stewart Plank 295
Charles Gardner Radbourn 297
Harold Henry Reese 300
Edgar Charles Rice 302
Wesley Branch Rickey 304
Eppa Rixey 306
Robin Evan Roberts 307
Brooks Calbert Robinson, Jr. 309
Frank Robinson 311
Jack Roosevelt Robinson 313
Wilbert Robinson 315
Edd J. Roush 317
Charles Herbert Ruffing 319
Amos Wilson Rusie 321
George Herman Ruth 323
Raymond William Schalk 330
Albert Fred Schoendienst 332
Joseph Wheeler Sewell 334
Aloysius Harry Simmons 336
George Harold Sisler 338
Enos Bradsher Slaughter 340
Edwin Donald Snider 342
Warren Edward Spahn 344
Albert Goodwill Spalding 346
Tristram E. Speaker 348
Wilver Dornel Stargell 351
Charles Dillon Stengel 353
William Harold Terry 356
Samuel L. Thompson 358
Joseph Bert Tinker 361
Harold Joseph Traynor 364
Clarence Arthur Vance 367
Joseph Floyd Vaughan 369
George Edward Waddell 371
John Peter Wagner 373
Rhoderick John Wallace 377
Edward Augustin Walsh 379
Lloyd James Waner 382
Paul Glee Waner 384
John Montgomery Ward 386

Michael Francis Welch 390
Zachary Davis Wheat 392
James Wilhelm 394
Billy Leo Williams 396
Theodore Samuel Williams 397
Lewis Robert Wilson 400

George Wright 402
William Henry Wright 404
Early Wynn 406
Carl Michael Yastrzemski 408
Denton True Young 410
Ross Middlebrook Youngs 414

II. NON-PLAYER PROFILES 417

Albert Joseph Barlick 418
Edward Grant Barrow 418
James Bell 419
Morgan Gardner Bulkeley 421
Alexander Joy Cartwright 421
Henry Chadwick 422
Albert Benjamin Chandler 423
Oscar Charleston 424
John Bertrand Conlan 424
Thomas Henry Connolly 425
Raymond Dandridge 426
Martin DiHigo 427
William George Evans 428
Andrew Foster 428

Ford Christopher Frick 429
Joshua Gibson 430
Warren Crandall Giles 431
William Harridge 432
Cal Hubbard 433
Byron Bancroft Johnson 433
William J. Johnson 434
William Joseph Klem 435
Kenesaw Mountain Landis 435
Walter Leonard 437
John Henry Lloyd 437
Leland Stanford MacPhail, Sr. 438
George Martin Weiss 439
Thomas Austin Yawkey 440

III. ALL-TIME RECORDS LIST 441

All-Time Longevity List—Everyday Players 442
All-Time Longevity List—Pitchers 443
All-Time Longevity List—Managers 443
All-Time American League Batting and Fielding Records List 444
All-Time American League Unbroken Batting and Fielding Records List 444
All-Time National League Batting and Fielding Records List 444
All-Time National League Unbroken Batting and Fielding Records List 445
All-Time Major League Batting and Fielding Records List 445
All-Time Major League Unbroken Batting and Fielding Records List 446
All-Time All-Star Game Records List 446
All-Time All-Star Game Unbroken Records List 447
All-Time World Series Records List 447
All-Time World Series Unbroken Records List 447
All-Time League Leaders Batting Records List 448
All-Time League Leaders Composite Fielding Records List 449

All-Time Most Seasons Batting Over .300 List 449
All-Time Most Seasons Batting Over .300 List 450
All-Time Most Seasons Batting Over .300 Consecutively List 450
All-Time American League Pitchers Records List 451
All-Time American League Pitchers Unbroken Records List 452
All-Time National League Pitchers Records List 452
All-Time National League Pitchers Unbroken Records List 452
All-Time Major League Pitchers Records List 452
All-Time Major League Pitchers Unbroken Records List 453
All-Time All-Star Game Pitchers Records List 453
All-Time World Series Pitchers Records List 453
All-Time World Series Pitchers Unbroken Records List 453
All-Time Pitchers League Leaders List 454

All-Time Pitchers With Most
  20-Plus Wins Seasons List   454
All-Time Pitchers With Most Consecutive
  20-Plus Wins Seasons List   455
All-Time Pitchers With Most Wins Over
  Losses List   455
All-Time Pitchers Composite Records List   455
All-Time Pitchers Composite Unbroken
  Records List   456
All-Time Managers Records List   456
All-Time Managers Unbroken Records List   456
All-Time Club Records List   457
All-Time Unbroken Club Records List   457
All-Time Composite Records List by Position
  First Basemen   458
  Second Basemen   458
  Shortstops   459
  Third Basemen   459

Catchers   459
Outfielders   459
All-Time Composite Unbroken Records List
  by Position
  First Basemen   459
  Second Basemen   460
  Shortstops   460
  Third Basemen   460
  Catchers   460
  Outfielders   460
All-Time Composite Records List   460
All-Time Composite Unbroken Records List   462
Unbroken Outstanding Records By
  Non-Hall of Fame Members   463
  Season Records   463
  Career Records   463
  Title Records   463
  Highest Career Batting Average   464

IV. HALL OF FAME RULES AND MEMBERS   465

The National Baseball Hall of Fame
  Eligibility Rules   466

National Baseball Hall of
  Fame Members   467

BIBLIOGRAPHY   470

Preface

The Baseball Hall of Fame in Cooperstown, New York, has honored many players who never set a major league record. And several players who have set impressive records have not been inducted into the Hall. Still, most of the great players have set great records, even if some of these were broken later. When I saw that the records created by these legends weren't generally known or available (and sometimes the Hall of Fame passed questions they couldn't easily answer on to me), I decided to collect them all and put them in a book.

I have collected records in all the major categories, including years, games, and season, career, All-Star, and World Series records for pitching, batting, and fielding. The categories in batting include most at bats, hits, singles, doubles, triples, home runs, highest home run percentage, runs scored, RBIs, extra base hits, total bases, bases on balls, stolen bases, strikeouts, batting average, slugging average, pinch hit at bats, and pinch hits. The categories in pitching include most years, games, starts, games completed, wins, losses, highest winning percentage, lowest ERA, innings pitched, hits allowed, bases on balls, strikeouts, shutouts, relief appearances, relief wins, relief losses, saves, relief wins plus saves, and relief wins without a loss. In fielding, for each position, the categories include most putouts, assists, errors, double plays, total chances, and highest fielding average.

It was easier for early players to set records than it was for later players, because there were no existing records to beat. The purpose of this book isn't to decide who was better than whom. Instead, the purpose is to preserve records and to celebrate some of the greatest people our national pastime has known.

EXPLANATION OF RECORD PROFILES

The "Record Profiles" contain five columns. From left to right, the first column is the date records were set. The second column is the description of the record, the third column is the actual record, the fourth column shows the number of years a record lasted before broken, and the last column signifies if a record is still unbroken.

For example, look at the first three records in Hank Aaron's profile. In 1966 he won his fourth RBI title, which tied the existing record. (Ties can also mean a player later tied that record.) In 1967 he set the record for most total bases titles with seven. This record lasted only one year, for in 1968 Hank won the title again, and no one has since won eight or more such titles.

The ranking of a player's career statistics is given in parentheses at the end of the profile, but only if the player's rank is within the top ten.

EXPLANATION OF TITLE RECORDS

When a player leads the league in any department, he has won a "title."

When a player has won more titles than any other player, he has set a record. This represents the category of title records.

1

PLAYER
RECORD PROFILES

Henry Louis Aaron
(Hank, Hammerin' Hank)
B. Feb 5, 1934
Mil–NL 1954–65, Atl–NL 1966–74, Mil–AL 1975–76

NUMBER OF RECORDS ESTABLISHED: 19

NATIONAL LEAGUE RECORDS

Season Batting Title Records

1966	Most RBI Titles	4		Tied
1967	Most Total Bases Titles	7	1	
1969	Most Total Bases Titles	8		Never Broken

Career Batting Records

Most Hits	3,771	11	
Most Runs Scored	2,107	11	
Most Home Runs	733		Never Broken
Most RBIs	2,202		Never Broken
Most Games Played	3,076	10	
Most Extra Base Hits	1,453		Never Broken
Most Total Bases	6,587		Never Broken
Most at Bats	11,628	10	

MAJOR LEAGUE RECORDS

Season Batting Title Records

| 1967 | Most Total Bases Titles | 7 | 2 | |
| 1969 | Most Total Bases Titles | 8 | | Never Broken |

Career Batting Records

Most Games Played	3,298	8	
Most at Bats	12,364	8	
Most Home Runs	755		Never Broken
Most Extra Base Hits	1,477		Never Broken
Most Total Bases	6,856		Never Broken
Most RBIs	2,297		Never Broken

SUMMARY

"Hammerin' Hank" Aaron hit the most home runs in baseball history. He drove in more runs than any other player. He is second in runs scored and at bats, and he is third in games played and base hits. He has the records to be considered one of the greatest players of all time.

There is a tendency to rate the old-time players as "great" a little more easily than it is modern players. But this tendency comes to a stop with Hank Aaron. What he accomplished under the more difficult conditions of modern-day pitching is as great as anything any player before him accomplished.

In order to break Aaron's home run record, a batter will have to average 38 homers per year for 20 years (or just over 30 home runs for 25 years)!

Aaron, in addition to his four home run titles, is a two-time hits and home run percentage champion, a four-time doubles and RBI king, and a three-time runs scored leader. He batted over .300 fourteen times, which earned him two more titles, and he slugged over .500 eighteen times and won four titles in that department.

Most of Aaron's career was in the outfield, but he also played first, second, and third base.

Aaron was welcomed into the Hall of Fame in 1982.

POSTSEASON AWARDS

1957 MVP

CAREER STATISTICS:

23 Years
Games 3,298 (3rd)
At Bats 12,364 (2nd)
Hits 3,771 (3rd)
Doubles 624 (8th)
Triples 98

Home Runs 755 (1st)
Home Run Percentage 6.1
Runs Scored 2,174 (2nd)
RBIs 2,297 (1st)
Bases on Balls 1,402
Stolen Bases 240

Strikeouts 1,383
Batting Average .305
Slugging Average .555
Pinch Hit At Bats 86
Pinch Hits 17

Grover Cleveland Alexander
(Pete)
B. Feb. 26, 1887, D. Nov. 4, 1950
Phi–NL 1911–17, Chi–NL 1918–26, StL–NL 1926–29, Phi–NL 1930

NUMBER OF RECORDS ESTABLISHED: 32

NATIONAL LEAGUE RECORDS

Season Pitching Records

1916	Shutouts	16	Tied

Season Pitching Title Records

1915	Complete Games Titles	3	1
	Innings Titles	4	1
1916	Complete Games Titles	4	1
	Innings Titles	5	1
	Shutout Titles	4	1
1917	Wins Titles	5	3
	Strikeout Titles	5	3
	Complete Games Titles	5	3
	Innings Titles	6	3
	Shutout Titles	5	2

4

Year	Record			
1919	Shutout Titles	6		Never Broken
1920	Wins Titles	6	40	
	Strikeout Titles	6	8	
	Complete Games Titles	6	41	
	Innings Titles	7		Never Broken
	ERA Titles	5		Tied

Career Pitching Records

	Total Games	696	35	
	Starts	598	35	
	Innings	5,189	35	
	Shutouts	90		Never Broken

MAJOR LEAGUE RECORDS

Season Pitching Records

Year	Record			
1916	Shutouts	16		Tied

Season Pitching Title Records

Year	Record			
1916	Innings Titles	5	1	
1917	Wins Titles	5	3	
	Innings Titles	6	3	
1920	Wins Titles	6	40	
	Innings Titles	7		Never Broken
	Complete Games Titles	6	41	
	ERA Titles	5	15	

WORLD SERIES RECORDS

Game Pitching Records

Year	Record			
1928	Earned Runs Allowed	8		Never Broken

4-Game Series Pitching Records

Year	Record			
1926	Saves	1	6	
1928	Total Games	2	10	

SUMMARY

"Pete" Alexander proved to the baseball world that he was destined for greatness in his first year, when he led the National League in wins with 28, completions with 31, innings pitched with 367, and shutouts with 7. Twenty years of toiling in the National League produced 32 outstanding records of which 8 remain unbroken. Alexander led the league in various pitching categories 44 times, the most in NL history.

Alexander was a six-time most wins king, a five-time ERA leader, a six-time completions champion, a seven-time innings leader, a six-time strikeout champ, and a six-time shutout leader. His 90 shutouts are the most in NL history, and he is second in the major leagues.

Alexander earned Hall of Fame honors in 1938..

CAREER STATISTICS:

20 Years
Wins 373 (3rd)
Losses 208
Winning Percentage .642
ERA 2.56
Total Games 696

Games Started 598
Games Completed 439
Innings 5,189
Hits 4,868
Bases on Balls 953
Strikeouts 2,199

Shutouts 90 (2nd)
Relief Appearances 98
Relief Wins 23
Relief Losses 17
Saves 31

Walter Emmons Alston

(Smokey)

B. Dec. 1, 1911, D. Oct. 1, 1984

StL–NL 1936
Manager: Bkn–NL 1954–57, LA–NL 1958–76

NUMBER OF RECORDS ESTABLISHED AS MANAGER: 2

NATIONAL LEAGUE WORLD SERIES CAREER RECORDS

1954–76 Most Series Won	4	Never Broken
1959–65 Most Cons. Series Won	3	Never Broken

SUMMARY

Walter Alston certainly didn't make the Hall of Fame because of his playing skills. He earned his nickname "Smokey" for his blazing fastball as a youngster. Though he was a slugger in the minors, he got only one at bat in the majors. He struck out.

When Walter Alston was hired by the Brooklyn Dodgers, the team had never won a world championship. A year later, they were the world champions. In his 23-year career with the Dodgers—during which he signed 23 one-year contracts—he led them to first place seven times and four times won the World Series.

In his seven World Series, Alston managed 40 games (fifth), won 20 (fifth), and lost 20 (third), and his .500 winning percentage ranks eighth.

7

In his career, he managed 3,657 games (sixth), won 2,040 (fifth), and lost 1,613 (eighth) for a .558 winning percentage. In addition to his seven pennants, he came in second eight times.

Alston managed such Hall of Famers as Pee Wee Reese, Duke Snider, Roy Campanella, Jackie Robinson, Don Drysdale, and Sandy Koufax.

Alston entered the Hall of Fame in 1983.

Adrian Constantine Anson
(Cap, Pop)
B. Apr. 17, 1852, D. Apr. 14, 1922
Chi–NL 1876–97
Manager: Chi–NL 1879–97, NY–NL 1898

NUMBER OF RECORDS ESTABLISHED AS PLAYER: 100

NUMBER OF RECORDS ESTABLISHED AS MANAGER: 20

TOTAL: 120

PLAYER RECORDS

Season Batting Records

1885	Most RBIs	114	1
1886	Most RBIs	147	1
1890	Most Bases on Balls	113	2

Season Batting Title Records

1877	Most Doubles Titles	1	1
1879	Most Batting Ave. Titles	1	2

1881	Most Batting Ave. Titles	2	7	
	Most Hits Titles	1	2	
1886	Most RBI Titles	2	2	
1888	Most RBI Titles	3	3	
	Most Batting Ave. Titles	3	4	
1891	Most RBI Titles	4		Tied

NATIONAL/MAJOR LEAGUE RECORDS*

Rookie Fielding Records—3B

1876	Most Putouts	135	5
	Most Assists	147	3
	Most Double Plays	8	2
	Most Total Chances	332	5
	Most Total Bases	4,109	20
	Most At Bats	9,108	10

Career Fielding Records—1B—1878–97

	Most Games Played	2,058	10	
	Most Putouts	20,761	10	
	Most Assists	945	10	
	Most Assists per Game	0.43	10	
	Most Errors	589		Never Broken
	Most Double Plays	1,189	10	
	Most Total Chances	22,299	10	

MANAGER RECORDS

National League Season Records

1880	Wins	67	5	
	Winning Percentage	.798		Never Broken
	Games Won Pennant By	15	22	
1885	Wins	87	1	
1886	Wins	90	6	

National League Career Records

	Years	20	34
	Games	2,296	9
	Wins	1,297	17
	Losses	957	9
	Pennants Won	5	34
	Cons. Pennants Won	3	42

* Anson played his entire career in the National League when there was no American League. Therefore, his National and Major League records are combined.

Major League Season Records

1880	Wins	67	4
	Winning Percentage	.798	4
	Games Won By	15	4

Major League Career Records

	Years	20	34
	Games	2,296	9
	Wins	1,297	9
	Losses	957	9
	Pennants Won	5	31
	Cons. Pennants Won	3	6

Season Fielding Records—1B

1879	Highest Fielding Ave.	.975	1	
1880	Highest Fielding Ave.	.977	4	
1881	Most Assists	43	3	
1884	Most Putouts	1,211	1	
	Most Assists	58	2	
	Most Double Plays	86	7	
	Most Total Chances	1,309	1	
	Most Errors	58		Never Broken
1885	Most Putouts	1,253	1	
	Most Total Chances	1,349	1	
1887	Most Assists	70	1	
1889	Most Putouts	1,409	2	
	Most Assists	79	2	
	Most Total Chances	1,515	2	
1891	Most Double Plays	86	1	

Season Fielding Records—3B

1876	Most Putouts	135	5
	Most Assists	147	3
	Most Double Plays	8	2
	Most Total Chances	332	5
1877	Highest Fielding Ave.	.883	1
	Most Double Plays	9	2

Career Batting Records

	Most Games Played	2,276	10
	Most Hits	3,041	20
	Most Singles	2,289	20
	Most Doubles	532	20
	Most Runs Scored	1,719	20

Most RBIs	1,715	20
Most RBIs per Game	0.75	1
Highest Batting Ave.	.334	3

SUMMARY

"Cap" Anson was one of baseball's first superstars. In 22 seasons he compiled 120 records and had a .334 batting average. In only two of those years did he fail to hit over .300. Three times he batted over .390.

Anson was the first major leaguer to rap out 3,000 hits and win four RBI crowns and three batting average titles.

He was also an excellent defensive player and 32 times was a leader in various fielding departments, more than any other player in baseball history. He played first, second, and third base and behind the plate. The last 12 years were only at first base. Anson was a player-manager for 19 of the 22 years he played.

Anson became a Hall of Famer in 1939.

CAREER STATISTICS:

22 Years
Games 2,276
At Bats 9,108
Hits 3,041
Doubles 532
Triples 124

Home Runs 96
Home Run Percentage 1.1
Runs Scored 1,719
RBIs 1,715
Bases on Balls 952
Stolen Bases 247

Strikeouts 294
Batting Ave. .334
Slugging Ave. .451
Pinch Hit At Bats 2
Pinch Hits 1

CAREER STATISTICS AS MANAGER:

20 Years
Games 2,296

Wins 1,297
Losses 957

Winning Percentage .575
First-place Finishes 5

Luis Ernesto Aparicio
(Little Looie)
B. Apr. 29, 1934
Chi–AL 1956–73

NUMBER OF RECORDS ESTABLISHED: 13

AMERICAN LEAGUE RECORDS

Season Fielding Records—SS

1963	Highest Fielding Ave.	.983	8

Season Base-Running Title Records

1961	Most Stolen Bases Titles	6	1
1962	Most Stolen Bases Titles	7	1
1963	Most Stolen Bases Titles	8	1
1964	Most Stolen Bases Titles	9	Never Broken

Career Fielding Records—SS

Most Games Played	2,581	Never Broken
Most Putouts	4,548	Never Broken
Most Assists	8,016	Never Broken

Most Double Plays	1,553	Never Broken
Most Total Chances	12,930	Never Broken

MAJOR LEAGUE RECORDS

Career Fielding Records—SS

Most Games Played	2,581	Never Broken
Most Assists	8,016	Never Broken
Most Double Plays	1,553	Never Broken

SUMMARY

In a brilliant 18-year career, "Little Looie" established 13 records, 9 of which remain unbroken. He led all shortstops 24 times in various fielding departments and won the Gold Glove award eight consecutive times from 1959 through 1966. When he retired in 1973, he had played the most games and made the most assists and double plays of any shortstop in major league history. These records still stand today.

Aparicio was also one of the great base runners. In his first nine years of play, he won nine consecutive stolen base titles, an American League record that has not been duplicated.

He ranks tenth on the all-time list in at bats and stolen bases.

Aparicio was welcomed into the Hall of Fame in 1984.

POSTSEASON AWARDS

1956 Rookie of the Year

CAREER STATISTICS:

18 Years	Home Runs 83	Strikeouts 742
Games 2,599	Home Run Percentage 0.8	Batting Ave. .262
At Bats 10,230 (10th)	Runs Scored 1,335	Slugging Ave. .343
Hits 2,677	RBIs 791	Pinch Hit At Bats 15
Doubles 394	Bases on Balls 736	Pinch Hits 3
Triples 92	Stolen Bases 506 (10th)	

Lucius Benjamin Appling
(Luke, Old Aches and Pains)
B. Apr. 2, 1907
Chi–AL 1930–50

NUMBER OF RECORDS ESTABLISHED: 7

AMERICAN LEAGUE RECORDS

Career Fielding Records—SS

Most Games Played	2,218	23
Most Putouts	4,398	23
Most Assists	7,218	23
Most Double Plays	1,424	23
Most Total Chances	12,259	23

MAJOR LEAGUE RECORDS

Career Fielding Records—SS

Most Games Played	2,218	23
Most Double Plays	1,424	23

SUMMARY

Before Luis Aparicio, Luke Appling was the White Sox's best shortstop. When he retired after 20 years, he had played more games at the position than anyone else in the history of the game. He participated in more double plays than any other player, and led the league in various categories 20 times. It was 23 years before Luis Aparicio could surpass Appling's accomplishments.

Appling was one of the best all-around shortstops in baseball. He had a lifetime batting average of .310 and was a two-time batting average champion. His best season was 1936, when he hit .388, with 204 hits.

Appling was voted into the Hall of Fame in 1964.

CAREER STATISTICS:

20 Years	Home Runs 45	Strikeouts 528
Games 2,422	Home Run Percentage 0.5	Batting Ave. .310
At Bats 8,857	Runs 1,319	Slugging Ave. .398
Hits 2,749	RBIs 1,116	Pinch Hit At Bats 49
Doubles 440	Bases on Balls 1,302	Pinch Hits 9
Triples 102	Stolen Bases 179	

Howard Earl Averill
(Rock)

B. May 21, 1902, D. Aug. 16, 1983

Cle–AL 1929–41

NUMBER OF RECORDS ESTABLISHED: 10

ALL-STAR GAME RECORDS

Game Batting Records

1933	Most Games Played	1	1	
1934	Most Games Played	2	1	
	Most Triples	1	44	
	Most Total Bases	5	3	
	Most Extra Base Hits	2		Tied
	Most RBIs	3	3	

Career Batting Records

	Most Games Played	2	1
	Most Doubles	1	1
	Most Triples	1	39
	Most Extra Base Hits	2	1

SUMMARY

Outfielder Earl Averill's induction into the Hall of Fame is based on his batting over .300 eight times during a fine 13-year career. His best season was 1936, when he smacked enemy pitchers around for a .378 batting average and led the league in hits with 232, in triples with 15 and had 39 doubles and 28 home runs. He scored 136 runs and drove in 126. He had a lifetime batting average of .318 and he slugged for .533.

Averill was a fielding leader five times. All his records were set in All-Star games.

He was voted into the Hall of Fame in 1975.

CAREER STATISTICS:

13 Years
Games 1,619
At Bats 6,358
Hits 2,020
Doubles 401
Triples 128

Home Runs 238
Home Run Percentage 3.7
Runs Scored 1,224
RBIs 1,165
Bases on Balls 775
Stolen Bases 69

Strikeouts 518
Batting Ave. .318
Slugging Ave. .533
Pinch Hit At Bats 73
Pinch Hits 22

John Franklin Baker
(Frank, Home Run)
B. Mar. 13, 1886, D. June 28, 1963
Phi–AL 1908–14, NY–AL 1916–22

NUMBER OF RECORDS ESTABLISHED: 41

AMERICAN LEAGUE RECORDS

Rookie Batting Records

1909	Most Triples	19		Tied
	Most Extra Base Hits	50	2	

Rookie Fielding Records—3B

1909	Most Assists	277	3

Season Batting Title Records

1914	Most Home Runs Titles	4	9

Season Fielding Records—3B

1910	Most Double Plays	34	11
1913	Most Putouts	233	14

| 1918 | Fewest Errors | 13 | 1 | |
| | Highest Fielding Ave. | .972 | 2 | |

Career Batting Records

| | Most Home Runs | 96 | 1 | |
| | Highest Home Run Percentage | 1.6 | 1 | |

Career Fielding Records—3B

	Most Games Played	1,648	2	
	Most Putouts	2,154	40	
	Most Assists	2,965	2	
	Most Double Plays	252	13	
	Most Total Chances	5,631	13	

MAJOR LEAGUE RECORDS

Season Fielding Records—3B

| 1910 | Most Double Plays | 34 | 8 | |

Career Fielding Records—3B

| | Most Double Plays | 252 | 5 | |

WORLD SERIES RECORDS

Game Batting Records

| 1911 | Most Home Runs | 2 | 15 | |

Game Fielding Records—3B

| 1911 | Most Putouts | 4 | | Tied |
| 1914 | Most Putouts | 4 | | Tied |

4-Game Series Fielding Records—3B

| 1914 | Most Putouts | 10 | | Never Broken |
| | Most Assists | 15 | | Never Broken |

5-Game Series Batting Records

1910	Most At Bats	22	6	
	Most Hits	9		Tied
	Most Runs Scored	6		Tied
1913	Most Hits	9		Tied
	Most Home Runs	1	2	

6-Game Series Batting Records

1911			
	Most Hits	9	6
	Most Home Runs	2	12
	Most Extra Base Hits	4	12
	Most Total Bases	17	12
	Most Runs	7	12
	Highest Batting Ave.	.375	6
	Highest Slugging Ave.	.708	12

6-Game Series Fielding Records—3B

1911	Most Putouts	10	25

Career Batting Records—1910–22

	Most Home Runs	3	10
	Most RBIs	18	10
	Most Extra Base Hits	10	10
	Highest Slugging Ave.	.538	10
	Most Series Played	6	10

Career Fielding Records—3B—1910–22

Most Putouts	36	Never Broken

SUMMARY

Frank "Home Run" Baker set 41 records, 15 of which were in the American League, 2 are major league marks, and 24 are in World Series competition. Eight of Baker's marks remain unbroken. He earned his nickname "Home Run" by hitting 2 home runs in the 1911 World Series.

Baker had a career batting average of .307, and he slugged .442. He was an outstanding all-around player who could hit and field with equal ability. He was a league leader ten times in various batting categories and led all third basemen in fielding departments 16 times.

Baker was inducted into the Hall of Fame in 1955.

CAREER STATISTICS:

13 Years	Home Runs 96	Strikeouts 182
Games 1,575	Home Run Percentage 1.6	Batting Ave. .307
At Bats 5,985	Runs Scored 887	Slugging Ave. .442
Hits 1,838	RBIs 1,013	Pinch Hit At Bats 23
Doubles 313	Bases on Balls 473	Pinch Hits 1
Triples 103	Stolen Bases 235	

Dave Bancroft

(Beauty)

B. Apr. 20, 1891, D. Oct. 9, 1972

Phi–NL 1915–20, NY–NL 1920–23, Bos–NL 1924–27, Bkn–NL 1928–29, NY–NL 1930
Manager: Bos–NL 1924–27

NUMBER OF RECORDS ESTABLISHED AS PLAYER: 11

NATIONAL LEAGUE RECORDS

Season Fielding Records—SS

1920	Most Assists	598	4	
1921	Most Double Plays	105	4	
1922	Most Total Chances	1,046		Never Broken

Career Fielding Records—SS

	Most Putouts per Game	2.5		Tied
	Most Assists per Game	3.5		Tied
	Most Double Plays	1,016	5	

MAJOR LEAGUE RECORDS

Season Fielding Records—SS

1920	Most Assists	598	4	
1921	Most Double Plays	105	2	
1922	Most Total Chances	1,046		Never Broken

Career Fielding Records—SS

	Most Putouts per Game	2.5		Tied
	Most Double Plays	1,016	5	

SUMMARY

Dave Bancroft was a slick-fielding shortstop who created 11 records. He was a league leader in various fielding categories 16 times.

Bancroft was also a respected hitter, with a lifetime batting average of .279. He batted over .300 six times, with a high of .321 in 1922, when he belted 209 hits, including 41 doubles.

Bancroft became a Hall of Famer in 1971.

CAREER STATISTICS:

16 Years	Home Runs 32	Strikeouts 487
Games, 1,913	Home Run Percentage 0.4	Batting Ave. .279
At Bats 7,182	Runs Scored 1,048	Slugging Ave. .358
Hits 2,004	RBIs 591	Pinch Hit At Bats 17
Doubles 320	Bases on Balls 827	Pinch Hits 3
Triples 77	Stolen Bases 145	

CAREER STATISTICS AS MANAGER:

4 Years	Wins 249	Winning Percentage .407
Games 615	Losses 363	First-place Finishes 0

Ernest Banks
(Ernie)

B. Jan 31, 1931
Chi–NL 1953–71

NUMBER OF RECORDS ESTABLISHED: 6

NATIONAL LEAGUE RECORDS

Rookie Fielding Records—SS

1954	Most Double Plays	105		Never Broken

Season Fielding Records—SS

1959	Highest Fielding Ave.	.985	12

MAJOR LEAGUE RECORDS

Season Fielding Records—SS

1959	Highest Fielding Ave.	.985	12

ALL-STAR GAME RECORDS

Game Batting Records

1959	Most Extra Base Hits	2	Tied
1960	Most Extra Base Hits	2	Tied

Career Batting Records

Most Doubles   3   Tied

SUMMARY

Ernie Banks enjoyed a fine 19-year career that saw him at shortstop for nine years and then 10 years at first base. A powerful home run hitter, Banks put 512 balls out of the park to land himself in the twelfth position on the all-time list.

Banks led the league in various batting departments seven times, all in the power-hitting areas. His 47 home runs in 1958 are the most hit by any shortstop in baseball history. During his nine years at shortstop, Banks hit 40 or more home runs five times. He won back-to-back RBI crowns in 1958 and 1959.

Banks was a fielding leader 21 times and showed he could play shortstop and first base with equal ability. He also appeared at third base and in the outfield.

Banks entered the Hall of Fame in 1977. He was the first National League player to win consecutive MVP Awards.

POSTSEASON AWARDS

1958 MVP
1959 MVP

CAREER STATISTICS:

19 Years	Home Runs 512 (12th)	Strikeouts 1,236
Games 2,528	Home Run Percentage 5.4	Batting Ave. .274
At Bats 9,421	Runs Scored 1,305	Slugging Ave. .500
Hits 2,583	RBIs 1,636	Pinch Hit At Bats 62
Doubles 407	Bases on Balls 763	Pinch Hits 14
Triples 90	Stolen Bases 50	

☆

Jacob Peter Beckley

(Jake, Eagle Eye)

B. Aug. 4, 1867, D. June 25, 1918

Pit–NL 1888–89, Pit–NL 1890, Pit–NL 1891–96,
NY–NL 1896–97, Cin–NL 1898–1903, StL–NL 1904–07

NUMBER OF RECORDS ESTABLISHED: 31

NATIONAL LEAGUE RECORDS

Season Fielding Records—1B

1891	Most Assists	87	1
1892	Most Putouts	1,523	12
	Most Assists	132	13
	Most Total Chances	1,691	13
1904	Most Putouts	1,526	1

Career Batting Records

	Most At Bats	9,527	10
	Most Triples	244	10
	Most Extra Base Hits	807	10
	Most Total Bases	4,158	10
	Most Games Played	2,386	14

26

Career Fielding Records—1B

Most Games Played	2,377		Never Broken
Most Putouts	23,709		Never Broken
Most Assists	1,315	4	
Most Assists per Game	0.58	4	
Most Double Plays	1,326	28	
Most Total Chances	25,505		Never Broken

MAJOR LEAGUE RECORDS

Season Fielding Records—1B

1891	Most Assists	87	1
1892	Most Assists	132	13
	Most Putouts	1,523	10
	Most Total Chances	1,691	13

Career Batting Records

Most Games Played	2,386	14
Most At Bats	9,527	9
Most Triples	244	10
Most Extra Base Hits	807	9
Most Total Bases	4,158	10

Career Fielding Records—1B

Most Games Played	2,377		Never Broken
Most Putouts	23,709		Never Broken
Most Assists	1,315	4	
Most Assists per Game	0.58	4	
Most Double Plays	1,326	28	
Most Total Chances	25,505		Never Broken

SUMMARY

What first baseman played in the most games, recorded the most putouts, and had the most total chances? Was it Lou Gehrig? No, it was Jake Beckley.

In the batting department, Beckley also had the most at bats, triples, extra base hits, and total bases and had played more games than any other player at the time of his retirement.

During his super 20-year career, he rang up 31 records, 6 of which have never been broken.

Beckley batted .300 or over 13 times, with a high of .343 as a rookie in 1888, and again in 1894. Beckley won back-to-back Triple Crowns in 1890 and 1891 and led the league in doubles in 1901. As a fielder he led in various categories 17 times.

Beckley was inducted into the Hall of Fame in 1971.

CAREER STATISTICS:

20 Years

Games 2,386

At Bats 9,527

Hits 2,931

Doubles 475

Triples 244

Home Runs 88

Home Run Percentage 0.9

Runs Scored 1,600

RBIs 1,575

Bases on Balls 616

Stolen Bases 315

Strikeouts 270

Batting Ave. .308

Slugging Ave. .436

Pinch Hit At Bats 4

Pinch Hits 2

Johnny Lee Bench

B. Dec. 7, 1947

Cin–NL 1967–83

NUMBER OF RECORDS ESTABLISHED: 6

NATIONAL LEAGUE RECORDS

Rookie Fielding Records—C

| 1968 | Most Putouts | 942 | Never Broken |
| | Most Total Chances | 1,053 | Never Broken |

Career Fielding Records—C—1967–83

| | Most Putouts | 9,260 | Never Broken |
| | Total Chances | 10,207 | Never Broken |

MAJOR LEAGUE RECORDS—C

Rookie Fielding Records

| 1968 | Most Putouts | 942 | Never Broken |
| | Total Chances | 1,053 | Never Broken |

SUMMARY

Johnny Bench is considered by many as the greatest catcher in baseball history. Not only did his 327 home runs as a catcher set a record, he had one of the strongest and most accurate throwing arms of all who wore the tools of ignorance.

Along with Pete Rose and Joe Morgan, Bench was an integral member of Cincinnati's "Big Red Machine."

He caught 2,158 games and slammed 2,048 hits and 381 doubles, scored 1,095 runs, and drove in 1,376. He led the league twice in home runs and three times was the RBI leader.

On the career all-time fielding list for catchers, Bench ranks second in putouts and total chances, fourth in games caught, and ninth in fielding average.

Bench was an All-Star 11 times, coming to bat 27 times and getting 10 hits. His 3 home runs rank third among all All-Star players. He is also sixth in hits, total bases, extra base hits, and RBIs. His .370 batting average places him in the ninth position, and his .703 slugging average earns him the seventh slot.

Bench won MVP Awards in 1970 and 1972.

Bench was inducted into the Hall of Fame in 1988.

POSTSEASON AWARDS

1970 MVP
1972 MVP

CAREER STATISTICS:

17 Years	Home Runs 389	Strikeouts 1,278
Games 2,158	Home Run Percentage 5.1	Batting Ave. .267
At Bats 7,658	Runs Scored 1,091	Slugging Ave. .476
Hits 2,048	RBIs 1,376	Pinch Hit At Bats 114
Doubles 381	Bases on Balls 891	Pinch Hits 22
Triples 24	Stolen Bases 68	

Charles Albert Bender

(Chief)

B. May 5, 1883, D. May 22, 1954

Phi–AL 1903–14, Bal–FL 1915, Phi–NL 1916–17, Chi–AL 1925

NUMBER OF RECORDS ESTABLISHED: 29

AMERICAN LEAGUE RECORDS

Rookie Pitching Records

1903	Strikeouts	127	1

Season Pitching Records

1906	Saves	3	1
1913	Games in Relief	26	4

Season Pitching Title Records

1906	Saves Titles	1	4
1910	Winning Percentage Titles	1	1
1914	Winning Percentage Titles	2	17

Career Pitching Records

Relief Games	96	2
Relief Wins	23	8
Relief Losses	14	2
Saves	18	2
Wins & Saves	41	2
Highest Winning Percentage	.649	27

WORLD SERIES RECORDS

Game Pitching Records

1905	Innings	9	2	
	Earned Runs Allowed	0		Tied
1910	Earned Runs Allowed	0		Tied
1911	Earned Runs Allowed	0		Tied

5-Game Series Pitching Records

1905	Fewest Hits Allowed	9	2
	Bases on Balls	6	3
1913	Fewest Bases on Balls	1	20

6-Game Series Pitching Records

1911	Total Games	3	48	
	Starts	3		Tied
	Complete Games	3		Tied
	Wins	2	6	
	Strikeouts	20		Never Broken
	Most Bases on Balls	8	7	

Career Pitching Records—1905–14

Wins	6	28
Total Games	10	15
Strikeouts	59	28
Most Series Played	5	17

SUMMARY

In a 16-year career, Chief Bender amassed 29 pitching records, 6 of which still stand today.

Playing for the Philadelphia Athletics from 1903 to 1914, he compiled a .649 winning percentage, which set a new American League record. His best season was in 1910, when he won 23 games and lost only 5. Bender tossed 3 shutouts, started 28 games, completed 25, and had a cool ERA of 1.58.

Bender won 210 games and lost 127 with 41 career shutouts. In the early days, there was little relief pitching, but the "Chief" did a lot of work from the bullpen. In his 459 games, he worked 124 in relief, winning 25, losing 16, and saving 24.

The "Chief" appeared in five World Series, and 17 of his 29 records were set in World Series competition. He starred in the 1911 World Series, setting six new records, and three of them still remain. When he had pitched in his last World Series game in 1914, Bender had the most wins, games, and strikeouts, and had participated in more World Series than any pitcher in baseball history.

His 6 wins now rank fifth, his ten games started fourth, his nine complete games second, his 85 innings pitched fourth, and his record of 59 strikeouts still sixth.

Bender became a Hall of Famer in 1953.

CAREER STATISTICS:

16 Years	Games Started 335	Shutouts 41
Wins 210	Games Completed 256	Relief Appearances 124
Losses 127	Innings 3,017	Relief Wins 25
Winning Percentage .623	Hits 2,645	Relief Losses 16
ERA 2.46	Bases on Balls 712	Saves 24
Total Games 459	Strikeouts 1,711	

Lawrence Peter Berra

(Yogi)

B. May 12, 1925

NY–AL 1946–65

Manager: NY–AL 1964, NY–NL 1972–75, NY–AL 1984

NUMBER OF RECORDS ESTABLISHED AS PLAYER: 20

AMERICAN LEAGUE RECORDS

Season Batting Title Records

1955	Most MVP Titles	3		Tied

Season Fielding Records—C

1958	Highest Fielding Ave.	1.000		Tied

Career Fielding Records—C

	Most Putouts	8,711	11	
	Most Total Chances	9,619	11	

MAJOR LEAGUE RECORDS

Season Batting Title Records

1955	Most MVP Titles	3		Tied

Season Fielding Records—C

| 1958 | Highest Fielding Ave. | 1.000 | | Tied |

Career Fielding Records—C

| | Most Putouts | 8,711 | 5 |
| | Most Total Chances | 9,619 | 5 |

WORLD SERIES RECORDS

7-Game Series Fielding Records—C

| 1952 | Most Putouts | 59 | 6 |
| 1958 | Most Putouts | 60 | 10 |

Career Batting Records—1947–63

	Most Games Played	75		Never Broken
	Most At Bats	259		Never Broken
	Most Hits	71		Never Broken
	Most Singles	49		Never Broken
	Most Doubles	10		Never Broken
	Most Runs Scored	41	1	
	Most RBIs	39	1	
	Most Total Bases	117	1	
	Most Extra Base Hits	22	1	
	Most Series Played	14		Never Broken

SUMMARY

Whoever first saw the resemblance between the short, squat Lawrence Berra and an Indian wise man was inspired. And Yogi had an inspired career, hitting more home runs than any previous catcher.

Yogi set ten World Series records, and six of them have never been broken. Only Mickey Mantle has surpassed the other four.

Berra was also a great defensive catcher. In his 19-year career, he led the league in various fielding departments 30 times, another major league record.

As a manager, he brought both the Yankees and the Mets to the World Series.

Yogi is well known for his colorful sayings, which somehow always seem to make more sense than you might think on first hearing them.

Berra was welcomed into the Hall of Fame in 1971.

POSTSEASON AWARDS

1951 MVP
1954 MVP
1955 MVP

CAREER STATISTICS:

19 Years

Games 2,120

At Bats 7,555

Hits 2,150

Doubles 321

Triples 49

Home Runs 358

Home Run Percentage 4.7

Runs Scored 1,175

RBIs 1,430

Bases on Balls 704

Stolen Bases 30

Strikeouts 415

Batting Ave. .285

Slugging Ave. .482

Pinch Hit At Bats 178

Pinch Hits 44

CAREER STATISTICS AS MANAGER:

6 Years

Games 914

Wins 478

Losses 434

Winning Percentage .524

First-place Finishes 2

James Leroy Bottomley
(Jim, Sunny Jim)
B. Apr. 23, 1900, D. Dec. 11, 1959
StL–NL 1922–32, Cin–NL 1933–35, StL–AL 1936–37
Manager: StL–NL 1937

NUMBER OF RECORDS ESTABLISHED: 3

NATIONAL LEAGUE RECORDS
Career Fielding Records—1B

Most Double Plays	1,457	1

WORLD SERIES RECORDS
6-Game Series Batting Records

1930	Most Strikeouts	9	50

7-Game Series Fielding Records—1B

1926	Most Putouts	79	Never Broken

SUMMARY

Jim Bottomley is a perfect example of an outstanding player who did not create many records. In his sensational 16-year career, "Sunny Jim" batted over .300 nine times and had a lifetime batting average of .310. He slugged an even .500.

Bottomley led the league in hits with 227 in 1925 and was a back-to-back doubles king in 1925 and 1926. He led the league in triples with 20, home runs with 31, and RBIs with 136 in 1928, the year he won the MVP Award. He also led the league in RBIs in 1926. He achieved his highest batting average his sophomore year, when he hit .371.

Bottomley was a sound-fielding first baseman who led the league in various fielding categories eight times.

Bottomley received Hall of Fame honors in 1974.

POSTSEASON AWARDS

1928 MVP

CAREER STATISTICS:

16 Years	Home Runs 219	Strikeouts 591
Games 1,991	Home Run Percentage 2.9	Batting Ave. .310
At Bats 7,471	Runs Scored 1,177	Slugging Ave. .500
Hits 2,313	RBIs 1,422	Pinch Hit At Bats 99
Doubles 465	Bases on Balls 664	Pinch Hits 27
Triples 151	Stolen Bases 58	

CAREER STATISTICS AS MANAGER:

1 Year	Wins 21	Winning Percentage .266
Games 80	Losses 58	First-place Finishes 0

Louis Boudreau

(Lou)

B. July 17, 1917

Cle–AL 1938–50, Bos–AL 1951–52
Manager: Cle–AL 1942–50, Bos–AL 1952–54, KC–AL 1955–57, Chi–NL 1960

NUMBER OF RECORDS ESTABLISHED AS PLAYER: 7

AMERICAN LEAGUE RECORDS

Season Fielding Records—SS

1943	Most Double Plays	122	1
1944	Most Double Plays	134	35
	Highest Fielding Ave.	.978	3
1947	Highest Fielding Ave.	.982	16

Career Fielding Records—SS

| | Highest Fielding Ave. | .972 | 29 |

MAJOR LEAGUE RECORDS

Season Fielding Records—SS

| 1944 | Most Double Plays | 134 | 26 |

Career Fielding Records—SS

Highest Fielding Ave.	.972	14

SUMMARY

One of baseball's finest-fielding shortstops, Lou Boudreau led the league in various fielding departments 18 times.

Boudreau could also hit. He had a lifetime batting average of .295 and was the batting average champion in 1944, when he belted 191 hits and batted .327. That same year he led the league in doubles with 45. He was a three-time doubles champion.

Lou won the MVP title in 1948 when he had a league-leading average of .355, with 199 hits, including 34 doubles, 6 triples, and 18 homers. That year he had a slugging average of .534. In addition, he scored 116 runs and drove in 106.

Boudreau became a Hall of Famer in 1970.

POSTSEASON AWARDS

1948 MVP

CAREER STATISTICS:

15 Years	Home Runs 68	Strikeouts 309
Games 1,646	Home Run Percentage 1.1	Batting Ave. .295
At Bats 6,030	Runs Scored 861	Slugging Ave. .415
Hits 1,779	RBIs 789	Pinch Hit At Bats 32
Doubles 385	Bases on Balls 796	Pinch Hits 6
Triples 66	Stolen Bases 51	

CAREER STATISTICS AS MANAGER:

16 Years	Wins 1,162	Winning Percentage .487
Games 2,404	Losses 1,224	First-place Finishes 1

Roger Bresnahan
(The Duke of Tralee)

B. June 11, 1879, D. Dec. 4, 1944

Was–NL 1897, Chi–NL 1898, Bal–AL 1901–02,
NY–NL 1903–08, StL–NL 1909–12, Chi–NL 1913–15
Manager: StL–NL 1909–12, Chi–NL 1915

NUMBER OF RECORDS ESTABLISHED AS PLAYER: 14

NATIONAL LEAGUE RECORDS

Season Fielding Records—C

| 1908 | Most Putouts | 657 | 3 | |
| | Most Total Chances | 809 | 1 | |

WORLD SERIES RECORDS

Game Batting Records

| 1905 | Most Runs Scored | 2 | | Broken in Same Series |
| | Most Bases on Balls | 2 | 4 | |

5-Game Series Batting Records

1905	Most Extra Base Hits	2	5
	Most Total Bases	7	5
	Most Bases on Balls	4	5
	Highest Slugging Ave.	.438	2
	Most Doubles	2	5

5-Game Series Fielding Records—C

1905	Most Putouts	27	3
	Most Assists	8	2

Career Batting Records

	Most Doubles	2	1
	Most Bases on Balls	4	4

Career Fielding Records—C

	Most Assists	8	4

SUMMARY

Roger Bresnahan is most famous for inventing shin guards. He was also a fine catcher, who paid his dues for 17 years in the early days of little or no protection.

Because of his clutch hitting talents, Bresnahan contributed 20 pinch hits during his career, when pinch hitters were rarely used. He batted over .300 four times, his best season coming in 1903, when he batted .350 for the New York Giants. He had rare speed for a catcher and stole 212 career bases. In 1903, he surprised everyone with 34 stolen bases.

Another of Bresnahan's qualities was his ability to read the strike zone. He walked 714 times in his career and was a league leader in bases on balls in 1908 with 83.

Bresnahan was voted into the Hall of Fame in 1945.

CAREER STATISTICS:

17 Years	Home Runs 26	Strikeouts 99
Games 1,430	Home Run Percentage 0.6	Batting Ave. .279
At Bats 4,478	Runs Scored 683	Slugging Ave. .378
Hits 1,251	RBIs 530	Pinch Hit At Bats 63
Doubles 223	Bases on Balls 714	Pinch Hits 20
Triples 71	Stolen Bases 212	

CAREER STATISTICS AS MANAGER:

5 Years	Wins 328	Winning Percentage .432
Games 774	Losses 432	First-place Finishes 0

Louis Clark Brock
(Lou)
B. June 18, 1939
Chi–NL 1961–64, StL–NL 1964–79

NUMBER OF RECORDS ESTABLISHED: 15

NATIONAL LEAGUE RECORDS

Season Base-Running Records

1974	Most Stolen Bases	118		Never Broken

Career Batting Records

	Most Strikeouts	1,730	2	

Career Base-Running Records

	Most Stolen Bases	938		Never Broken

MAJOR LEAGUE RECORDS

Season Base-Running Records

1974	Most Stolen Bases	118	8	

Career Batting Records

    Most Strikeouts   1,730   2

Career Base-Running Records

    Most Stolen Bases   938   Never Broken

WORLD SERIES RECORDS

Game Base-Running Records

1967	Most Stolen Bases	3		Tied
1968	Most Stolen Bases	3		Tied

7-Game Series Base-Running Records

1967	Most Stolen Bases	7		Never Broken
1968	Most Stolen Bases	7		Never Broken

7-Game Series Batting Records

1967	Most Runs Scored	8		Tied
1968	Most Hits	13		Tied
	Most Extra Base Hits	6	11	
	Most Total Bases	24	11	

Career Batting Records—1964–68

    Most Stolen Bases   14   Tied

SUMMARY

Lou Brock was one of baseball's greatest base stealers. Seven of his nine World Series records remain unbroken. But Brock was also a good hitter. He had 3,023 hits and turned in a .293 lifetime batting average. His 938 career steals are the most by any player who has ever stalked the base paths.

Lou Brock was a league leader in stolen bases eight times. He was also a league leader in at bats, doubles, triples, and twice in runs scored. He finished the season batting over .300 eight times, and his 10,332 at bats place him ninth on the all-time list.

Brock was inducted into the Hall of Fame in 1985.

CAREER STATISTICS:

19 Years	Home Runs 149	Strikeouts 1,730 (5th)
Games 2,616	Home Run Percentage 1.4	Batting Ave. .293
At Bats 10,332 (9th)	Runs Scored 1,610	Slugging Ave. .410
Hits 3,023	RBIs 900	Pinch Hit At Bats 125
Doubles 486	Bases on Balls 761	Pinch Hits 33
Triples 141	Stolen Bases 938 (1st)	

Dennis Joseph Brouthers
(Big Dan)

B. May 8, 1858, D. Aug. 2, 1932

Tro–NL 1879–80, Buf–NL 1881–85, Det–NL 1886–88, Bos–NL 1889, Bos–PL 1890, Bos–AA 1891,
Bkn–NL 1892–93, Bal–NL 1894–95, Lou–NL 1895, Phi–NL 1896, NY–NL 1904

NUMBER OF RECORDS ESTABLISHED: 68

NATIONAL & MAJOR LEAGUE RECORDS

Rookie Batting Records

1879	Highest Home Run Percentage	2.4	6

Season Batting Records

1881	Highest Home Run Percentage	3.0	3
1883	Most Hits	159	1
	Most Extra Base Hits	61	3
	Most Total Bases	243	1
1886	Most Extra Base Hits	66	1
	Most Total Bases	284	1
1887	Most Extra Base Hits	68	6

Batting Title Records

1881	Most Home Run Titles	1	5
	Most Slugging Titles	1	1
1882	Most Hits Titles	2	1
	Most Slugging Titles	2	1
1883	Most Hits Titles	2	9
	Most Triples Titles	1	3
	Most Batting Ave. Titles	2	5
	Most Slugging Titles	3	1
	Most Total Bases Titles	2	3
1884	Most Slugging Titles	4	1
1885	Most Slugging Titles	5	1
1886	Most Home Runs Titles	2	32
	Most Home Run Percentage Titles	2	28
	Most Total Bases Titles	3	6
	Most Slugging Titles	6	39
1888	Most Doubles Titles	3	13
	Most Runs Scored Titles	2	7
1889	Most Batting Ave. Titles	3	3
1891	Most Batting Ave. Titles	4	1
1892	Most Slugging Titles	7	26
	Most Batting Ave. Titles	5	16
	Most Total Bases Titles	4	17
	Most Hits Titles	3	17

Season Fielding Records—1B

Most Putouts	1,040	1
Most Total Chances	1,119	1

Career Batting Records

Highest Slugging Ave.	.519	31

SUMMARY

All of Dan Brouthers's major league records are the same as his National League records because none of the players in the other major leagues surpassed any of his achievements.

Dan Brouthers was one of the first power-hitting superstars. After a fabulous 19-year career, he had a solid .343 batting average, still the ninth best in baseball. His 206 triples are the eighth best.

First baseman Brouthers was a three-time most-hits king, a three-time doubles leader, and was the leader once in triples, twice in homers and home run percentage, twice in runs scored, and once in RBIs. He batted over .300 16 consecutive times and was a five-time batting average champion. He also won the slugging crown seven times.

Brouthers entered the Hall of Fame in 1945.

CAREER STATISTICS:

19 Years
Games 1,673
At Bats 6,716
Hits 2,304
Doubles 461
Triples 206 (8th)

Home Runs 106
Home Run Percentage 1.6
Runs Scored 1,523
RBIs 1,056
Bases on Balls 840
Stolen Bases 235

Strikeouts 238
Batting Ave. .343 (9th)
Slugging Ave. .520
Pinch Hit At Bats 1
Pinch Hits 0

Mordecai Peter Centennial Brown
(Three Finger, Miner)
B. Oct. 19, 1876, D. Feb. 14, 1948

StL–NL 1903, Chi–NL 1904–12, Cin–NL 1913,
StL–FL 1914, Bkn–FL 1914, Chi–FL 1915, Chi–NL 1916
Manager: StL–FL 1914

NUMBER OF RECORDS ESTABLISHED AS PLAYER: 55

NATIONAL LEAGUE RECORDS

Season Pitching Records

Year	Record			
1906	Lowest ERA	1.04		Never Broken
1908	Relief Wins & Saves	9	2	
1909	Saves	7	1	
1910	Saves	7	1	
1911	Saves	13	20	
	Relief Games	26	1	
	Relief Wins & Saves	18	20	

Season Pitching Title Records

Year	Record		
1911	Saves Titles	4	73

Career Pitching Records

	Lowest ERA	2.06		Never Broken
	Relief Games	130	2	
	Relief Losses	15	21	
	Saves	45	29	
	Wins & Saves	70	25	

MAJOR LEAGUE RECORDS

Season Pitching Records

1909	Saves	7	2
1910	Saves	7	1
1911	Relief Games	26	1
	Saves	13	13
	Wins & Saves	26	1

Season Pitching Title Records

1911	Saves Titles	4	21

Career Pitching Records

	Relief Games	130	2
	Relief Losses	19	7
	Saves	48	17
	Wins & Saves	77	10

Career Pitching Title Records

	Saves Titles	4	16

WORLD SERIES RECORDS

Game Pitching Records

1906	Innings	9	1	
	Innings	9	1	
	Fewest Earned Runs	0		Tied
	Most Earned Runs	6	2	
1907	Fewest Earned Runs	0		Tied
1908	Fewest Bases on Balls	0		Tied
	Fewest Earned Runs	0		Tied
1910	Most Earned Runs	7	18	
	Most Hits Allowed	13	14	

5-Game Series Pitching Records

1908	Relief Games	1	2
	Fewest Hits Allowed	6	41
	Fewest Bases on Balls	1	25

1910	Losses	2		Tied
	Highest ERA	5.0	3	
	Most Hits Allowed	23		Never Broken

6-Game Series Pitching Records

1906	Total Games	3	53	
	Starts	3		Never Broken
	Complete Games	2	5	
	Losses	2	11	
	Shutouts	1		Tied
	Highest ERA	3.66	11	
	Innings	19.2	5	
	Hits Allowed	14	5	

Career Pitching Records

	Total Games	9	3
	Wins	5	4
	Losses	4	3
	Shutouts	3	3
	Most Hits Allowed	50	3
	Most Series	4	3
	Scoreless Innings	29	8
	Games Started	7	3

SUMMARY

"Three Finger" Brown actually was missing only one finger—he had three fingers and a thumb on his pitching arm.

Brown won 239 games and lost only 129 in his career, and his 2.06 ERA is the lowest in National League history and the third best in the major leagues. His winning percentage of .649 and his 57 shutouts place him eighth on the all-time list.

One of the first outstanding relief pitchers in the game, many of his records were set in relief. Brown also excelled in World Series games, where he posted 31 of his 55 records. Eight of these are still unbroken.

Brown became a member of the Hall of Fame in 1949.

CAREER STATISTICS:

14 Years   Games Started 332   Shutouts 57 (8th)
Wins 239   Games Completed 272   Relief Appearances 149
Losses 129   Innings 3,172   Relief Wins 29
Winning Percentage .649   Hits 2,708   Relief Losses 19
ERA 2.06 (3rd)   Bases on Balls 673   Saves 48
Total Games 481   Strikeouts 1,375

CAREER STATISTICS AS MANAGER:

1 Year   Wins 50   Winning Percentage .442
Games 114   Losses 63   First-place Finishes 0

Jesse Cail Burkett

(The Crab)

B. Dec. 4, 1868, D. May 27, 1953

NY–NL 1890, Cle–NL 1891–98, StL–NL 1899–1901, StL–AL 1902–04, Bos–AL 1905

NUMBER OF RECORDS ESTABLISHED: 29

NATIONAL LEAGUE RECORDS

Season Batting Records

1896	Most Singles	191	1
	Most Hits	240	1

Season Batting Title Records

1893	Most Hits Titles	3	3
1901	Most Hits Titles	4	6

Season Fielding Records—LF

1893	Most Errors	46	2

Career Batting Records

	Highest Batting Ave.	.355	1

Career Fielding Records—LF

Most Games Played	1,360	12
Most Putouts	2,728	12
Most Assists	180	12
Most Double Plays	44	12
Most Total Chances	3,175	12

AMERICAN LEAGUE RECORDS

Season Fielding Records—LF

1902	Most Putouts	300	2
	Most Errors	26	27
	Most Total Chances	343	2

Career Fielding Records—LF

Most Games Played	565	5
Most Putouts	1,072	5
Most Assists	62	5
Most Double Plays	13	5
Most Total Chances	1,205	5
Most Errors	71	6
Highest Fielding Ave.	.934	5

MAJOR LEAGUE RECORDS

Season Batting Records

1896	Most Singles	191	1
	Most Hits	240	1

Season Fielding Records—LF

1893	Most Errors	46	2

Career Fielding Records—LF

Most Games Played	1,925	10
Most Putouts	3,800	10
Most Assists	242	10
Most Double Plays	57	8
Most Total Chances	4,390	10

SUMMARY

Leftfielder Jesse Burkett led the league in various batting departments eleven times, and three times he had season batting averages over .400. He batted .423 in 1895 and .410 in 1896 to accomplish a rare feat of having back-to-back .400 seasons. (Only Ty Cobb and Rogers Hornsby have duplicated this feat.) He batted .402 in 1899. Burkett also hit in the .300s in eight seasons.

He was traded to the St. Louis Browns after having batting averages of .403, .363, and .382.

Jesse twice led the league in at bats and four times in hits. He was a leader in runs scored and batting average three times.

Burkett was not the best-fielding outfielder, but his bat was so loud that it propelled him into the Hall of Fame in 1946.

CAREER STATISTICS:

16 Years
Games 2,072
At Bats 8,430
Hits 2,873
Doubles 320
Triples 185

Home Runs 75
Home Run Percentage 0.9
Runs Scored 1,713
RBIs 952
Bases on Balls 1,029
Stolen Bases 392

Strikeouts 230
Batting Ave. .341
Slugging Ave. .449
Pinch Hit At Bats 0
Pinch Hits 0

Roy Campanella
(Campy)

B. Nov. 19, 1921
Bkn–NL 1948–57

NUMBER OF RECORDS ESTABLISHED: 6

NATIONAL LEAGUE RECORDS

Season Fielding Records—C

1953	Most Putouts	807	6	
	Most Total Chances	891	6	

Career Batting Title Records

Most MVP Titles	3		Tied

Career Fielding Records—C

Most Putouts/Game	5.5	10

MAJOR LEAGUE RECORDS

Season Fielding Records—C

1953	Most Putouts	807	6

Career Batting Title Records

Most MVP Titles	3	Tied

SUMMARY

Roy Campanella is one of the great catchers of modern times. He starred for the Brooklyn Dodgers and is one of the few players to win three MVP titles. His lifetime batting average was .276, and he slugged an even .500. His 242 home runs place him third on the all-time catchers list.

Campy batted over .300 three times, with a high of .325 in 1951. His best season was in 1953, when he led the league in RBIs with 142. He also had 41 home runs, batted .312, and slugged .611.

Campanella was a fine defensive catcher, leading the league nineteen times in various fielding departments.

Campanella was inducted into the Hall of Fame in 1969.

POSTSEASON AWARDS

1951 MVP
1953 MVP
1955 MVP

CAREER STATISTICS:

10 Years	Home Runs 242	Strikeouts 501
Games 1,215	Home Run Percentage 5.8	Batting Ave. .276
At Bats 4,205	Runs Scored 627	Slugging Ave. .500
Hits 1,161	RBIs 856	Pinch Hit At Bats 45
Doubles 178	Bases on Balls 533	Pinch Hits 15
Triples 18	Stolen Bases 25	

Max George Carey
(Scoops)

B. Jan. 11, 1890, D. May 30, 1976

Pit–NL 1910–26, Bkn–NL 1926–29
Manager: Bkn–NL 1932–33

NUMBER OF RECORDS ESTABLISHED AS PLAYER: 30

NATIONAL LEAGUE RECORDS

Season Fielding Records

1912	Most Putouts—LF	369	9
1916	Most Putouts—CF	419	1
	Most Total Chances—CF	459	1
1917	Most Putouts—CF	440	5
	Most Total Chances—CF	478	5
1921	Most Chances per Game—CF	3.4	7
1922	Most Putouts—CF	449	1
	Most Total Chances—CF	486	1
1923	Most Putouts—CF	450	5
	Most Total Chances—CF	497	5

Season Base-Running Title Records

1920	Most Stolen Bases Titles	6	2	
1922	Most Stolen Bases Titles	7	1	
1923	Most Stolen Bases Titles	8	1	
1924	Most Stolen Bases Titles	9	1	
1925	Most Stolen Bases Titles	10		Never Broken

Career Batting Records

	Most Strikeouts	695	1

Career Base-Running Records

	Most Stolen Bases	738	50

MAJOR LEAGUE RECORDS

Season Fielding Records—CF

1917	Most Putouts	440	3
	Most Total Chances	478	3
1921	Most Chances per Game	3.4	7

Season Base-Running Title Records

1920	Most Stolen Bases Titles	6	2	
1922	Most Stolen Bases Titles	7	1	
1923	Most Stolen Bases Titles	8	1	
1924	Most Stolen Bases Titles	9	1	
1925	Most Stolen Bases Titles	10		Never Broken

Career Batting Records

	Most Strikeouts	695	1

WORLD SERIES RECORDS

Game Batting Records

1925	Most Runs Scored	3	1

7-Game Series Batting Records

1925	Most Doubles	4	9
	Highest Batting Ave.	.458	6

7-Game Series Fielding Records

1925	Most Errors	1	9

SUMMARY

Max Carey, whose real name was Maximilian Canarius, led the league in various batting categories 17 times during his illustrious 20-year career. He led the league ten times in stolen bases, and his career total of 738 is the fourth best in baseball history.

Carey led in at bats twice, triples twice, and bases on balls twice. He also led the league in runs scored in 1913. His lifetime batting average was .285, and he accumulated 2,665 hits.

His exceptional speed enabled him to reach balls other outfielders could not, and this ability resulted in his leading the league in various fielding categories an amazing total of twenty-six times!

Hall of Fame honors were bestowed on Carey in 1961.

CAREER STATISTICS:

20 Years	Home Runs 69	Strikeouts 695
Games 2,476	Home Run Percentage 0.7	Batting Ave. .285
At Bats 9,363	Runs Scored 1,545	Slugging Ave. .385
Hits 2,665	RBIs 800	Pinch Hit At Bats 42
Doubles 419	Bases on Balls 1,040	Pinch Hits 17
Triples 159	Stolen Bases 738 (4th)	

CAREER STATISTICS AS MANAGER:

2 Years	Wins 146	Winning Percentage .476
Games 311	Losses 161	First-place Finishes 0

Frank LeRoy Chance
(The Peerless Leader, Husk)

B. Sept. 9, 1877, D. Sept. 14, 1924

Chi–NL 1898–1912, NY–AL 1913–14
Manager: Chi–NL 1905–12, NY–AL 1913–14, Bos–AL 1923

NUMBER OF RECORDS ESTABLISHED AS PLAYER: 18

NUMBER OF RECORDS ESTABLISHED AS MANAGER: 15

TOTAL: 33

PLAYER RECORDS

WORLD SERIES RECORDS

Game Batting Records

1906	Most Stolen Bases	2	3
1907	Most Bases on Balls	2	2
1908	Most Stolen Bases	2	1

Game Fielding Records—1B

1907	Most Putouts	15	1	
1908	Most Putouts	17	4	

5-Game Series Batting Records

1908	Most Hits	8	2	
	Most Singles	8		Tied
	Most Stolen Bases	5		Never Broken

5-Game Series Fielding Records—1B

1908	Most Putouts	66	8

6-Game Series Batting Records

1906	Most Stolen Bases	2	11

Career Batting Records—1906–10

Most Games Played	21	5
Most Stolen Bases	10	9
Most Series	4	5

Career Fielding Records—1906–10

Most Putouts	223	8
Most Total Chances	230	8
Most Chances w/o Errors	105	11

MANAGER RECORDS

National League Season Records

1906	Wins	116	Never Broken

Major League Season Records

1906	Wins	116	Never Broken

National League World Series Career Records—1905–12

Series	4	20	
Games	21	20	
Series Won	2	20	
Games Won	11	20	
Games Lost	9	20	
Cons. Series Won	2	57	
Winning Percentage	.550		Never Broken

Major League World Series Career Records—1905–12

Series	4	9
Games	21	6
Series Won	2	5
Games Won	11	6
Cons. Series Won	2	5
Winning Percentage	.550	27

SUMMARY

Frank Chance was one of baseball's greatest player-managers. From 1905 to 1912 he managed the Cubs and played first base.

Chance had a fabulous 17-year career, with a lifetime batting average of .297. His greatest achievements were in World Series play, where he accumulated all 18 of his records.

Called the "Peerless Leader," Chance managed for 11 years, winning three consecutive pennants for the Cubs in 1906–08. He won again in 1910. In all, he won 932 games and lost 640, and his .593 winning percentage is the seventh best in the game.

In four World Series, Chance won 2 and lost 2, with a winning percentage of .550, which places him fifth on the all-time list.

Chance entered the Hall of Fame in 1946.

CAREER STATISTICS:

17 Years	Home Runs 20	Strikeouts 29
Games 1,286	Home Run Percentage 0.5	Batting Ave. .297
At Bats 4,295	Runs Scored 798	Slugging Ave. .394
Hits 1,274	RBIs 596	Pinch Hit At Bats 31
Doubles 199	Bases on Balls 554	Pinch Hits 8
Triples 80	Stolen Bases 405	

CAREER STATISTICS AS MANAGER:

11 Years	Wins 932	Winning Percentage .593 (7th)
Games 1,597	Losses 640	First-place Finishes 4

John Dwight Chesbro
(Happy Jack)
B. June 5, 1874, D. Nov. 6, 1931
Pit–NL 1899–1902, NY–AL 1903–09

NUMBER OF RECORDS ESTABLISHED: 17

NATIONAL LEAGUE TITLE RECORDS

Season Pitching Title Records

1902	Winning Percentage Titles	2	6

AMERICAN LEAGUE RECORDS

Season Pitching Records

1904	Total Games	55	3	
	Starts	51		Never Broken
	Complete Games	48		Never Broken
	Wins	41		Never Broken
	Innings	455	4	
	Relief Wins	3	1	

Season Pitching Title Records

1904	Winning Percentage Titles	1	7
	Total Games Titles	1	2
	Fewest Hits Titles	1	9
1906	Fewest Hits Titles	2	4
	Total Games Titles	2	1

Career Pitching Records

	Total Games	270	1
	Wins	129	1
	Strikeouts	916	1
	Relief Games	42	1
	Relief Wins	10	1

SUMMARY

Jack Chesbro was the first great pitcher for the New York Yankees. Prior to coming to New York, Chesbro enjoyed four outstanding seasons with the Pirates, twice winning over 20 games.

In 1901 and 1902 he led the Pirates to consecutive pennants, winning 21 and 28 games. He also led the league in winning percentage, and his 1902 28 and 6 record yielded his highest winning percentage, .824.

In 1903, he was traded to the Yankees and promptly won 21 games. His greatest season, however, was the following year, when he won 41 and lost only 12. It was a spectacular year in which he led the league in seven departments. Three of his leading marks are American League records and still stand.

Chesbro was elected to the Hall of Fame in 1946.

CAREER STATISTICS:

11 Years	Games Started 332	Shutouts 35
Wins 198	Games Completed 261	Relief Appearances 60
Losses 132	Innings 2,897	Relief Wins 14
Winning Percentage .600	Hits 2,642	Relief Losses 4
ERA 2.68	Bases on Balls 690	Saves 4
Total Games 392	Strikeouts 1,265	

Fred Clifford Clarke

(Cap)

B. Oct. 3, 1872, D. Aug. 14, 1960

Lou–NL 1894–99, Pit–NL 1900–15
Manager: Lou–NL 1897–99, Pit–NL 1900–15

NUMBER OF RECORDS ESTABLISHED AS PLAYER: 38

NUMBER OF RECORDS ESTABLISHED AS MANAGER: 15

TOTAL: 53

PLAYER RECORDS

NATIONAL LEAGUE RECORDS

Season Fielding Records—LF

1895	Most Putouts	344	4	
	Most Errors	49		Never Broken
	Most Total Chances	413	31	
1898	Most Putouts	344	1	
1907	Highest Fielding Ave.	.987	12	

| 1909 | Most Putouts | 362 | 3 | |
| | Highest Fielding Ave. | .987 | 10 | |

Career Fielding Records—LF

	Most Games Played	2,191	11	
	Most Putouts	4,788	11	
	Most Putouts per Game	2.2	26	
	Most Total Chances	5,301		Never Broken

MAJOR LEAGUE RECORDS

Season Fielding Records—LF

1895	Most Putouts	344	4	
	Most Errors	49		Never Broken
	Most Total Chances	413	26	
1898	Most Putouts	344	1	
1907	Highest Fielding Ave.	.987	5	
1909	Highest Fielding Ave.	.987	3	
	Most Putouts	362	3	

Career Fielding Records—LF

	Most Games Played	2,191	11	
	Most Putouts	4,788	11	
	Most Total Chances	5,301		Never Broken

WORLD SERIES RECORDS

Game Batting Records

| 1903 | Most At Bats | 5 | | 1 Game Before Broken |
| | Most Singles | 2 | | 1 Game Before Broken |

Game Fielding Records—LF

1903	Most Putouts	4	6	
	Most Putouts	4	6	
	Most Errors	1		Tied
1909	Most Putouts	5	6	
	Most Errors	1		Tied

7-Game Series Batting Records

1909	Most Home Runs	2	15	
	Most RBIs	7	22	
	Most Bases on Balls	5	3	

7-Game Series Fielding Records—LF

1909	Most Putouts	19	17	
	Most Errors	1	11	

8-Game Series Fielding Records—LF

1903	Most Putouts	18		Never Broken
	Most Errors	1		Never Broken

Career Fielding Records—LF—1903, 09

	Most Putouts	37	19
	Most Errors	2	26
	Most Total Chances	39	19
	Chances w/o Errors	12	2

MANAGER RECORDS

National League Season Records

1902	Most Wins	103	2	
	Most Games Won Pennant By	27½		Never Broken

National League Career Records—1897–1915

	Most Games	2,822	17
	Most Wins	1,602	17
	Most Losses	1,179	17

Major League Season Records

1902	Most Wins	103	2

Major League Career Records—1897–1915

	Most Games	2,822	5
	Most Wins	1,602	17
	Most Losses	1,179	5

Major League World Series Career Records—1903, 09

	Most Series	2	5
	Most Games	15	5
	Games Won	7	8
	Games Lost	8	5
1909	Most Series Won	1	8

SUMMARY

Fred Clarke not only had a 21-year career, he managed for 19 of those years. His lifetime batting average was a solid .315. He hit .406 in 1897 and had 11 seasons with averages well over .300.

Clarke was one of the most active leftfielders the game has ever seen. To this day, he holds the record for most total chances.

Clarke was welcomed into the Hall of Fame in 1945.

CAREER STATISTICS:

21 Years
Games 2,245
At Bats 8,588
Hits 2,708
Doubles 359
Triples 223 (6th)

Home Runs 67
Home Run Percentage 0.8
Runs Scored 1,626
RBIs 1,015
Bases on Balls 870
Stolen Bases 506

Strikeouts 135
Batting Ave. .315
Slugging Ave. .432
Pinch Hit At Bats 41
Pinch Hits 16

CAREER STATISTICS AS MANAGER:

19 Years
Games 2,822

Wins 1,602
Losses 1,179

Winning Percentage .576
First-place Finishes 4

John Gibson Clarkson
B. July 1, 1861, D. Feb. 4, 1909
Wor–NL 1882, Chi–NL 1884–87, Bos–NL 1888–92, Cle–NL 1892–94

NUMBER OF RECORDS ESTABLISHED: 26

NATIONAL LEAGUE RECORDS

Season Pitching Title Records

1886	Strikeout Titles	2	1
1887	Wins Titles	2	2
	Strikeout Titles	3	2
	Innings Titles	2	1
	Total Games Titles	2	2
1888	Innings Titles	3	1
1889	Wins Titles	3	15
	Strikeout Titles	4	6
	Complete Games Titles	3	27
	Innings Titles	4	27
	Total Games Titles	3	15

Career Pitching Records

	Wins	326	12
	Strikeouts	2,015	22

MAJOR LEAGUE RECORDS

Season Pitching Title Records

1882	Wins Titles	2	2
	Innings Titles	2	1
	Strikeout Titles	3	2
	Total Games Titles	2	2
1886	Strikeout Titles	2	1
1888	Innings Titles	3	1
1889	Wins Titles	3	14
	Strikeout Titles	4	6
	Complete Games Titles	3	25
	Innings Titles	4	15
	Total Games Titles	3	15

Career Pitching Records

	Wins	326	12
	Strikeouts	2,015	22

SUMMARY

John Clarkson was the second pitcher in baseball to win over 300 games. His best season was in 1885, when he won 53 and lost 16. He was 50 percent of the pitching staff that year. Jim McCormick was the other half.

During this season, Clarkson started 70 games, completed 68 of them, worked in 623 innings, tossed 10 shutouts, and had an ERA of 1.85. He led the league in seven departments.

His next best season was in 1889, when he won 49 and lost 19. He started 72 games, completed 68, and spun 8 shutouts. He led the league in 11 categories. In his 12-year career, Clarkson won 30 or more games six times and was a league leader 29 times.

Clarkson was inducted into the Hall of Fame in 1963.

CAREER STATISTICS:

12 Years
Wins 326 (10th)
Losses 177
Winning Percentage .648
ERA 2.81
Total Games 531

Games Started 518
Games Completed 485 (8th)
Innings 4,536
Hits 4,295
Bases on Balls 1,191
Strikeouts 2,015

Shutouts 37
Relief Appearances 13
Relief Wins 1
Relief Losses 4
Saves 5

Roberto Walker Clemente
(Bob)
B. Aug. 18, 1934, D. Dec. 31, 1972
Pit–NL 1955–72

NUMBER OF RECORDS ESTABLISHED: 2

NATIONAL LEAGUE RECORDS

Fielding Records—RF

Most Games Played	2,370	Never Broken

MAJOR LEAGUE RECORDS

Fielding Records—RF

Most Games Played	2,370	2

SUMMARY

Modern players have a difficult time establishing records because they have to do better than such greats as Babe Ruth and Ty Cobb.

Roberto Clemente will, however, go down in baseball history as one of its greatest rightfielders. No other National League rightfielder has played as many games, and only Al Kaline in the American League has played more games.

In a fabulous 18-year career, Clemente batted over .300 13 times; twice he batted over .350, and four times he had more than 200 hits in a season. In all, he led the league in various batting categories seven times and was a four-time batting champion.

Defensively, he was one of the very best and nine times led the league in a variety of fielding departments.

In two World Series appearances, Roberto had a composite batting average of .362, which ranks sixth on the all-time list.

Clemente won the MVP Award in 1966 and was inducted into the Hall of Fame in 1973, the year after his death in an airplane accident.

POSTSEASON AWARDS

1966 MVP

CAREER STATISTICS:

18 Years
Games 2,433
At Bats 9,454
Hits 3,000
Doubles 440
Triples 166

Home Runs 240
Home Run Percentage 2.5
Runs Scored 1,416
RBIs 1,305
Bases on Balls 621
Stolen Bases 83

Strikeouts 1,230
Batting Ave. .317
Slugging Ave. .475
Pinch Hit At Bats 73
Pinch Hits 19

Tyrus Raymond Cobb
(Ty, The Georgia Peach)
B. Dec. 18, 1886, D. July 17, 1961
Det–AL 1905–26, Phi–AL 1927–28
Manager: Det–AL 1921–26

NUMBER OF RECORDS ESTABLISHED AS PLAYER: 123

AMERICAN LEAGUE RECORDS

Season Batting Records

1909	Most Stolen Bases	76	1
1911	Most Hits	248	9
	Most Singles	169	9
	Most RBIs	144	10
	Most RBIs per Game	0.98	10
	Most Stolen Bases	83	1
1915	Most Stolen Bases	96	65

Season Batting Title Records

1908	Most Total Bases Titles	2	1
	Most Hits Titles	2	1
	Most RBI Titles	2	1

1909	Most Triple Crowns	1	38	
	Most Batting Ave. Titles	3	1	
	Most Slugging Ave. Titles	3	1	
	Most RBI Titles	3	2	
	Most Hits Titles	3	2	
	Most Stolen Bases Titles	2	2	
1910	Most Batting Ave. Titles	4	1	
	Most Slugging Ave. Titles	4	1	
	Most Runs Scored Titles	2	1	
1911	Most MVP Awards	1	13	
	Most Batting Ave. Titles	5	1	
	Most Slugging Ave. Titles	5	1	
	Most Total Bases Titles	4	4	
	Most RBI Titles	4	24	
	Most Hits Titles	4	1	
	Most Stolen Bases Titles	3	4	
	Most Runs Scored Titles	3	4	
1912	Most Batting Ave. Titles	6	1	
	Most Slugging Ave. Titles	6	2	
	Most Hits Titles	5	3	
1913	Most Batting Ave. Titles	7	1	
1914	Most Batting Ave. Titles	8	1	
	Most Slugging Ave. Titles	7	3	
1915	Most Batting Ave. Titles	9	2	
	Most Total Bases Titles	5	2	
	Most Hits Titles	6	2	
	Most Stolen Bases Titles	4	1	
	Most Runs Scored Titles	4	1	
1916	Most Stolen Bases Titles	5	1	
	Most Runs Scored Titles	5	8	
1917	Most Batting Ave. Titles	10	1	
	Most Slugging Ave. Titles	8	10	
	Most Total Bases Titles	6		Tied
	Most Hits Titles	7	2	
	Most Stolen Bases Titles	6	45	
1918	Most Batting Ave. Titles	11	1	
1919	Most Batting Ave. Titles	12		Never Broken
	Most Hits Titles	8		Never Broken

Season Fielding Records—CF

| 1911 | Most Putouts | 376 | 1 |
| | Most Total Chances | 418 | 1 |

Career Batting Records

| | Most Games Played | 3,034 | 55 |
| | Most At Bats | 11,429 | 55 |

Most Hits	4,191		Never Broken
Most Singles	3,052		Never Broken
Most Triples	297		Never Broken
Most Home Runs	118	1	
Most Extra Base Hits	1,139	6	
Most Total Bases	5,863		Never Broken
Most Runs Scored	2,245		Never Broken
Highest Batting Ave.	.367		Never Broken
Most Stolen Bases	892		Never Broken

Career Fielding Records—CF—1905–26

Most Games Played	2,666	3
Most Putouts	5,207	3
Most Assists	293	3
Most Double Plays	80	3
Most Errors	214	3
Most Total Chances	5,714	3

MAJOR LEAGUE RECORDS

Season Batting Records

1911	Most Hits	248	9
	Most Stolen Bases	83	1
1915	Most Stolen Bases	96	47

Season Batting Title Records

1909	Most Triple Crowns	1	16	
1911	Most MVP Titles	1	13	
	Most Hits Titles	4	1	
	Most RBI Titles	4	15	
1912	Most Hits Titles	5	3	
1914	Most Batting Ave. Titles	8	1	
	Most Slugging Ave. Titles	7	3	
1915	Most Batting Ave. Titles	9	2	
	Most Hits Titles	6	2	
	Most Total Bases Titles	5	2	
	Most Runs Scored Titles	4	1	
1916	Most Runs Scored Titles	5	8	
1917	Most Batting Ave. Titles	10	1	
	Most Slugging Ave. Titles	8	10	
	Most Hits Titles	7	2	
	Most Total Bases Titles	6	8	
1918	Most Batting Ave. Titles	11	1	
1919	Most Batting Ave. Titles	12		Never Broken
	Most Hits Titles	8		Never Broken

Career Batting Records

Most Games Played	3,034	48
Most At Bats	11,429	48
Most Hits	4,191	56
Most Singles	3,052	Never Broken
Most Extra Base Hits	1,139	7
Most Total Bases	5,863	35
Most Runs Scored	2,245	Never Broken
Most RBIs	1,961	7
Highest Batting Ave.	.367	Never Broken
Most Stolen Bases	892	50

Career Fielding Records—CF—1905–26

Most Games Played	2,666	3
Most Putouts	5,207	3
Most Assists	293	3
Most Errors	214	3
Most Double Plays	80	3
Most Total Chances	5,714	3

WORLD SERIES RECORDS

Game Batting Records

1908	Most Stolen Bases	2	1
	Most Hits	4	74

Game Fielding Records—RF

1907	Most Putouts	5	5
1908	Most Errors	1	9
1909	Most Errors	1	8

5-Game Series Batting Records

1907	Most Triples	1	6

5-Game Series Fielding Records

1907	Most Putouts	10	6
	Most Errors	1	14

7-Game Series Fielding Records—RF

1909	Most Putouts	8	11
	Most Errors	1	55

Career Batting Records—1907–09

Most Games Played	17	1

Most Hits	17	1
Most Singles	12	1
Most Series Played	3	1

Career Fielding Records—RF—1907–09

Most Putouts	21	9
Most Errors	2	15
Most Total Chances	23	4

SUMMARY

Ty Cobb hated to lose and would do whatever it took to win. Prior to Babe Ruth, the "Georgia Peach" was the greatest offensive player the game had ever seen. Many still think he is. When all the tabulations are done, they show Cobb created 123 records, 15 of which remain unbroken. He was a league leader an amazing 52 times, and it is doubtful that anyone will ever better his .367 lifetime batting average.

Cobb was an all-around player, as can be seen by his remarkable records. He had seven seasons with more than 200 hits, won three doubles titles, four triples titles, four runs scored titles, four RBI titles, six stolen base crowns, and seven slugging honors, and was a 12-time batting average champion. He also was an excellent defensive player, with eight league-leading statistics.

Cobb put on his spikes for 24 years and batted well over .300 23 years in a row! This feat has never been approached by any player in baseball history.

Cobb won the Triple Crown in 1909 and the MVP Award in 1911.

Cobb became a Hall of Famer in 1936.

POSTSEASON AWARDS

1911 MVP

CAREER STATISTICS:

24 Years	Home Runs 118	Strikeouts 357
Games 3,034 (4th)	Home Run Percentage 1.0	Batting Ave. .367 (1st)
At Bats 11,429 (4th)	Runs 2,245 (1st)	Slugging Ave. .513
Hits 4,191 (2nd)	RBIs 1,961 (4th)	Pinch Hit At Bats 69
Doubles 724 (4th)	Bases on Balls 1,249	Pinch Hits 15
Triples 297 (2nd)	Stolen Bases 892 (2nd)	

CAREER STATISTICS AS MANAGER:

6 Years	Wins 479	Winning Percentage .519
Games 933	Losses 444	First-place Finishes 0

Gordon Stanley Cochrane
(Black Mike, Mickey)
B. Apr. 6, 1903, D. June 28, 1962
Phi–AL 1925–33, Det–AL 1934–37
Manager: Det–AL 1934–38

NUMBER OF RECORDS ESTABLISHED AS PLAYER: 5

AMERICAN LEAGUE RECORDS

Season Fielding Records—C

1930	Highest Fielding Ave.	.993	1

Career Fielding Records—C

	Highest Fielding Ave.	.985	1

MAJOR LEAGUE RECORDS

Season Fielding Records—C

1930	Highest Fielding Ave.	.993	1

Career Fielding Records—C

	Highest Fielding Ave.	.985	1

WORLD SERIES RECORDS

5-Game Series Batting Records

1921	Most Bases on Balls	7	Tied

SUMMARY

Mickey Cochrane was one of the game's best catchers. In his 13-year career, he had a batting average of .320. He participated in five World Series, in which he slammed 27 hits and received 25 bases on balls.

In addition to his outstanding hitting, Cochrane was sensational behind the plate. He won 20 fielding crowns in 13 years. His best season was in 1930, when he led his team to the pennant by batting a whopping .357 and led all catchers in putouts, assists, double plays, total chances per game, and fielding average (.993). He made only 5 errors all year.

Cochrane was the first catcher to win the MVP title, in 1928. He won again in 1934.

Cochrane was named to the Hall of Fame in 1947.

POSTSEASON AWARDS

1928 MVP
1934 MVP

CAREER STATISTICS:

13 Years	Home Runs 119	Strikeouts 217
Games 1,482	Home Run Percentage 2.3	Batting Ave. .320
At Bats 5,169	Runs Scored 1,041	Slugging Ave. .478
Hits 1,652	RBIs 832	Pinch Hit At Bats 27
Doubles 333	Bases on Balls 857	Pinch Hits 4
Triples 64	Stolen Bases 64	

CAREER STATISTICS AS MANAGER:

5 Years	Wins 413	Winning Percentage .582
Games 712	Losses 297	First-place Finishes 2

Edward Trowbridge Collins, Sr.

(Eddie, Cocky)

B. May 2, 1887, D. Mar. 25, 1951

Phi–AL 1906–14, Chi–AL 1915–26, Phi–AL 1927–30
Manager: Chi–AL 1925–26

NUMBER OF RECORDS ESTABLISHED AS PLAYER: 48

AMERICAN LEAGUE RECORDS

Season Batting Title Records

1914	Most MVP Titles	1	10

Season Base-Running Records

1910	Most Stolen Bases	81	1

Career Batting Records

	Most Bases on Balls	1,503	4

Career Fielding Records—2B

Most Games Played	2,650	Never Broken
Most Putouts	6,526	Never Broken

Most Assists	7,630		Never Broken
Most Errors	435		Never Broken
Most Double Plays	1,215	12	
Highest Fielding Ave.	.969	12	
Most Total Chances	14,591		Never Broken

MAJOR LEAGUE RECORDS

Season Batting Titles Records

1914	Most MVP Titles	1	10	

Season Base-Running Records

1910	Most Stolen Bases	81	1	

Career Batting Records

	Most Bases on Balls	1,503	5	

Career Fielding Records—2B

Most Games Played	2,650		Never Broken
Most Putouts	6,526		Never Broken
Most Assists	7,630		Never Broken
Most Double Plays	1,215	12	
Most Total Chances	14,591		Never Broken
Highest Fielding Ave.	.969	5	

WORLD SERIES RECORDS

Game Fielding Records—2B

1917	Most Assists	8		Tied

4-Game Series Fielding Records—2B

1914	Most Putouts	9	13	
	Most Errors	1	14	

5-Game Series Batting Records

1910	Most Extra Base Hits	4		Tied
	Most Hits	9		Tied
	Most Doubles	4		Tied
	Most Total Bases	13	7	
1913	Most Triples	2		Tied

5-Game Series Fielding Records—2B

1910	Most Putouts	17	6	

6-Game Series Batting Records

1911	Most Stolen Bases	2	6
1917	Most Stolen Bases	3	64

6-Game Series Fielding Records—2B

1911	Most Putouts	13	7
	Most Assists	22	6
1917	Most Assists	23	6

8-Game Series Fielding Records—2B

1919	Most Assists	31	2

Career Batting Records—1910–19

Most Games Played	34	13	
Most At Bats	128	13	
Most Hits	42	15	
Most Singles	33	15	
Most Runs Scored	20	13	
Most RBIs	11	3	
Most Total Bases	53	13	
Most Extra Base Hits	9	3	
Most Stolen Bases	14		Tied
Most Series Played	6	13	

Career Fielding Records—2B—1910–19

Most Putouts	87	15	
Most Assists	127	15	
Most Errors	9		Tied
Most Total Chances	223	15	

SUMMARY

Eddie Collins will go down in baseball history as one of the greatest second basemen of all time.

He terrorized enemy pitchers for 25 years during one of the game's longest playing careers. Collins established a bushel of records and starred in World Series play, where he posted 29 of his 48 records. Even more impressive are his 16 records, which have remained unbroken for more than a half century.

Collins batted over .300 17 times (full seasons), with a high of .369 in 1920. During the 1920 season, he slammed 222 hits. He led the league in runs scored for three consecutive years and was a four-time stolen bases champion. His 743 stolen bases rank him third on the all-time list.

Only nine others have played in more games than Collins, and only seven have accumulated more base hits. Collins won the MVP title in 1914.

Collins's lifetime batting average of .333 and his outstanding fielding talents earned him Hall of Fame honors in 1939.

POSTSEASON AWARDS

1914 MVP

CAREER STATISTICS:

25 Years	Home Runs 47	Strikeouts 286
Games 2,826 (10th)	Home Run Percentage 0.5	Batting Ave. .333
At Bats 9,949	Runs Scored 1,818	Slugging Ave. .428
Hits 3,311 (8th)	RBIs 1,299	Pinch Hit At Bats 104
Doubles 437	Bases on Balls 1,503	Pinch Hits 27
Triples 187	Stolen Bases 743 (5th)	

CAREER STATISTICS AS MANAGER:

2 Years	Wins 160	Winning Percentage .521
Games 309	Losses 147	First-place Finishes 0

James Joseph Collins

B. Jan. 16, 1870, D. Mar 6, 1943

Bos–NL 1895, Lou–NL 1895, Bos–NL 1896–1900, Bos–AL 1901–07, Phi–AL 1907–08
Manager: Bos–AL 1901–06

NUMBER OF RECORDS ESTABLISHED AS PLAYER: 33

NUMBER OF RECORDS ESTABLISHED AS MANAGER: 19

TOTAL: 52

PLAYER RECORDS ESTABLISHED

NATIONAL LEAGUE RECORDS

Season Fielding Records—3B

1899	Most Putouts	243	1	
1900	Most Putouts	251		Tied

AMERICAN LEAGUE RECORDS

Season Fielding Records—3B

1901	Most Assists	328	1

	Most Total Chances	581	10
1902	Fewest Errors	19	7
	Highest Fielding Ave.	.954	2

Career Fielding Records—3B

Most Assists	1,832	2
Most Double Plays	109	2

MAJOR LEAGUE RECORDS

Career Fielding Records

Most Games Played	1,658	29
Most Putouts	2,372	69
Most Total Chances	6,539	59
Most Double Plays	243	14

WORLD SERIES RECORDS

Game Batting Records

1903	Most At Bats	6	70
	Most Runs Scored	2	2
1913	Most Runs Scored	3	13

Game Base-Running Records

1903	Most Stolen Bases	2	6

Game Fielding Records—3B

1903	Most Putouts	2		1 Game Before Broken
	Most Putouts	3	2	
	Most Assists	3		1 Game Before Broken
	Most Assists	6	20	

8-Game Series Batting Records

1903	Most At Bats	36	Never Broken

8-Game Series Base-Running Records

1903	Most Stolen Bases	3	Tied

8-Game Series Fielding Records—3B

1903	Most Putouts	8	9
	Most Assists	18	18

Career Batting Records—1903–13

Most Games Played	8	3
Most At Bats	36	3
Most Series Played	1	3
Longest Hitting Streak	7	5

Career Base-Running Records

Most Stolen Bases	3	6

Career Fielding Records—3B—1903–13

Most Putouts	8	5
Most Assists	18	7
Most Total Chances	27	7
Chances w/o Errors	22	10

MANAGER RECORDS

American League Season Records

1903	Wins	91	1
	Winning Percentage	.659	7
	Won Pennant By	14½	20
1904	Wins	95	5

American League Career Records

Years	6	5
Games	864	5
Games Won	464	5
Games Lost	389	5
Winning Percentage	.544	3
Pennants Won	2	14
Cons. Pennants Won	2	5

American League World Series Career Records—1901–06

Series	1	14
Games	8	14
Series Won	1	23
Games Won	5	23
Games Lost	3	14

Major League World Series Career Records—1901–06

Series Won	1	17
Games Won	5	11
Games Lost	3	11

SUMMARY

Jimmy Collins, only 5'7½" tall and 160 pounds, is an example of a little man making it big in the big leagues. He starred for 14 years with four different teams and compiled a lifetime batting average of .294. He accumulated 52 records, most of them in World Series play.

Collins batted over .300 five times; his best average was .346 in 1897. Despite his small stature, Collins became a home run champion in 1898, when he slammed 15 round-trippers and led the league in home run percentage with 2.5.

Collins was more than just a solid hitter. He was a fine third baseman as well and led all keystone sackers in various fielding departments 17 times. When he retired in 1908, he had played more games at third base, made more putouts, total chances, and double plays than any previous player.

As a manager, he put in six years with the Boston Red Sox and won back-to-back pennants in 1903 and 1904.

Collins won the first World Series played in 1903.

Collins became a Hall of Famer in 1945.

CAREER STATISTICS:

14 Years	Home Runs 64	Strikeouts 32
Games 1,728	Home Run Percentage 0.9	Batting Ave. .294
At Bats 6,796	Runs Scored 1,055	Slugging Ave. .408
Hits 1,997	RBIs 982	Pinch Hit At Bats 7
Doubles 352	Bases on Balls 426	Pinch Hits 1
Triples 116	Stolen Bases 194	

CAREER STATISTICS AS MANAGER:

6 Years	Wins 464	Winning Percentage .544
Games 864	Losses 389	First-place Finishes 2

Earle Bryan Combs
(The Kentucky Colonel)
B. May 14, 1899, D. July 21, 1976
NY–AL 1924–35

NUMBER OF RECORDS ESTABLISHED: 7

AMERICAN LEAGUE RECORDS

Rookie Fielding Records—CF

1925	Most Putouts	401	5
	Most Total Chances	422	2
	Highest Fielding Ave.	.979	5

WORLD SERIES RECORDS

Game Batting Records

1932	Most Runs Scored	4		Tied

4-Game Series Batting Records

1926	Most Runs Scored	6	2

4-Game Series Fielding Records—CF

1927	Most Putouts	16		Never Broken

Career Fielding Records—CF—1926–32

	Chances w/o Errors	43	19

SUMMARY

Earle Combs was a charter member of the Yankees' Murderers' Row.

An exciting player, Combs led the league in hits, at bats, and triples in 1927. He was a 3-time triples king. His lifetime batting average was .325.

Combs was elected to the Hall of Fame in 1970.

CAREER STATISTICS:

12 Years	Home Runs 58	Strikeouts 278
Games 1,454	Home Run Percentage 1.0	Batting Ave. .325
At Bats 5,748	Runs Scored 1,186	Slugging Ave. 462
Hits 1,866	RBIs 629	Pinch Hit At Bats 56
Doubles 309	Bases on Balls 670	Pinch Hits 17
Triples 154	Stolen Bases 96	

Charles Albert Comiskey
(Commy, The Old Roman)
B. Aug. 15, 1859, D. Oct. 26, 1931
StL–AA 1882–89, Chi–PL 1890, StL–AA 1891, Cin–NL 1892–94
Manager: StL–AA 1883–89, Chi–PL 1890, StL–AA 1891, Cin–NL 1892–94

NUMBER OF RECORDS ESTABLISHED AS PLAYER: 27

NUMBER OF RECORDS ESTABLISHED AS MANAGER: 15
TOTAL: 42

PLAYER RECORDS

AMERICAN ASSOCIATION RECORDS

Rookie Fielding Records—1B

1882	Putouts	860	2	
	Total Chances	904	2	
	Total Chances per Game	11.7		Tied

Season Fielding Records—1B

1882	Putouts	860	1
	Total Chances	904	1
	Total Chances per Game	11.7	1
1883	Putouts	1,085	1
	Total Chances	1,148	1
	Total Chances per Game	12.0	5
1884	Putouts	1,193	2
	Total Chances	1,271	2

Career Fielding Records—1B—1882–91

Games	1,036	Never Broken
Putouts	10,259	Never Broken
Assists	349	Never Broken
Total Chances	10,922	Never Broken
Errors	314	Never Broken
Double Plays	492	Never Broken

NATIONAL LEAGUE RECORDS

Season Fielding Records—1B

1892	Double Plays	103	6

MAJOR LEAGUE RECORDS

Rookie Fielding Records—1B

1882	Putouts	860	1

Season Fielding Records—1B

1883	Putouts	1,085	1
	Total Chances	1,148	1
1892	Double Plays	103	6

Career Fielding Records—1B—1882–94

Games	1,275	3
Assists	367	3
Errors	370	3
Double Plays	688	3
Total Chances	13,776	3

MANAGER RECORDS

American Association Season Records

1885	Wins	79	1

	Winning Percentage	.705		Never Broken
	Games Won Pennant By	16		Never Broken
1886	Wins	93	1	
1887	Wins	95		Never Broken

American Association Career Records—1883–91

Years	7		Never Broken
Games	826		Never Broken
Wins	547		Never Broken
Losses	265		Never Broken
Winning Percentage	.662		Never Broken
Pennants Won	4		Never Broken
Cons. Pennants Won	4		Never Broken

Major League Season Records

1887	Wins	95	5

Major League Career Records

Pennants Won	4	4
Cons. Pennants Won	4	65

SUMMARY

As a player, Charlie Comiskey starred as a fine defensive first baseman. As a manager, he won 824 and lost 533 for a winning percentage of .607, which places him third on the all-time list. From 1885 to 1888, he won four consecutive pennants. Many of Comiskey's achievements still stand in American Association records—and will continue to go unchallenged forever, presumably. Comiskey had the Chicago White Sox Stadium named after him.

Comiskey was elected to the Hall of Fame in 1939.

CAREER STATISTICS:

13 Years	Home Runs 29	Strikeouts 84
Games 1,390	Home Run Percentage 0.5	Batting Ave. .264
At Bats 5,796	Runs Scored 994	Slugging Ave. .338
Hits 1,531	RBIs 466	Pinch Hit At Bats 0
Doubles 206	Bases on Balls 197	Pinch Hits 0
Triples 68	Stolen Bases 378	

CAREER STATISTICS AS MANAGER:

11 Years	Wins 824	Winning Percentage .607 (3rd)
Games 1,382	Losses 533	First-place Finishes 4

Roger Connor

B. July 1, 1857, D. Jan. 4, 1931

Tro–NL 1880–82, NY–NL 1883–89, NY–PL 1890,
NY–NL 1891, Phi–NL 1892, NY–NL 1893–94,
StL–NL 1894–97
Manager: StL–NL 1896

NUMBER OF RECORDS ESTABLISHED AS PLAYER: 27

NATIONAL LEAGUE RECORDS

Season Batting Records

1882	Most Extra Base Hits	44	1
	Most Triples	18	2
1884	Most Singles	115	1
1885	Most Singles	130	1
	Most Hits	169	1
1886	Most Triples	20	1

Season Batting Title Records

1882	Most Triples Titles	1	4
1886	Most Triples Titles	2	22

Season Fielding Records–1B

1887	Most Putouts	1,325	1
	Highest Fielding Ave.	.993	10

Career Batting Records

	Most Triples	218	10
	Highest Home Run Percentage	1.7	1
	Most Home Runs	123	1
	Highest Slugging Ave.	.487	7
	Most Extra Base Hits	758	10

Career Fielding Records—1B

	Highest Fielding Ave.	.977	1

MAJOR LEAGUE RECORDS

Season Batting Records

1882	Most Extra Base Hits	44	1
1885	Most Singles	130	1
	Most Hits	169	1

Season Batting Title Records

1882	Most Triples Titles	1	4
1886	Most Triples Titles	2	22

Season Fielding Records–1B

1887	Highest Fielding Ave.	.993	10

Career Batting Records

	Most Extra Base Hits	811	19
	Most Triples	233	10
	Most Home Runs	136	38
	Most Bases on Balls	1,002	4

Career Fielding Records—1B

	Highest Fielding Ave.	.977	2

SUMMARY

Of the early pioneer players, Roger Connor was one of the most outstanding long-ball hitters. When he retired in 1897, he had hit the most triples, home runs, and extra base hits of any player in the game.

Connor was a fine defensive first baseman as well and led the league 18 times in various fielding categories.

Connor enjoyed an 18-year career during which he led the league 11 times in various batting areas. He batted over .300 11 times, with a high of .371 in 1885. He led the league in slugging and triples twice and once in hits, doubles, home runs, home run percentage, RBIs, bases on balls, and batting average.

Connor was inducted into the Hall of Fame in 1976 with a lifetime batting average of .318.

CAREER STATISTICS:

18 Years	Home Runs 136	Strikeouts 449
Games 1,998	Home Run Percentage 1.7	Batting Ave. .318
At Bats 7,798	Runs Scored 1,621	Slugging Ave. .487
Hits, 2,480	RBIs 1,077	Pinch Hit At Bats 0
Doubles 442	Bases on Balls 1,002	Pinch Hits 0
Triples 233 (5th)	Stolen Bases 227	

CAREER STATISTICS AS MANAGER:

1 Year	Wins 9	Winning Percentage .196
Games 46	Losses 37	First-place Finishes 0

☆

Stanley Anthony Coveleski
(Stan)

B. July 13, 1889, D. Mar. 20, 1984

Phi–AL 1912, Cle–AL 1916–24, Was–AL 1925–27, NY–AL 1928

NUMBER OF RECORDS ESTABLISHED: 6

WORLD SERIES RECORDS

7-Game Series Pitching Records

1920	Starts	3	42	
	Innings	27	38	
	Complete Games	3		Tied
	Wins	3		Tied
	Shutouts	1	37	
1925	Losses	2		Tied

SUMMARY

Stan Coveleski spent his entire 14-year career in the American League, mostly with the Cleveland Indians. He won over 20 games four years in a row (1918–1921). He was a two-time ERA king and a two-time shutout leader, and when he was traded to Washington, he responded by winning 20 and only losing 5 to lead the league in winning percentage (.800) and ERA (2.84).

Stan won a total of 215 games and lost 142. All his records were set during World Series play. During the 1920 series, Coveleski pitched three complete games, and allowed only two runs for an ERA of 0.67. Coveleski was inducted into the Hall of Fame in 1969.

CAREER STATISTICS:

14 Years

Wins 215

Losses 142

Winning Percentage .602

ERA 2.88

Total Games 450

Games Started 384

Games Completed 225

Innings 3,093

Hits 3,055

Bases on Balls 802

Strikeouts 981

Shutouts 38

Relief Appearances 66

Relief Wins 9

Relief Losses 12

Saves 21

Samuel Earl Crawford
(Wahoo Sam)

B. Apr. 18, 1880, D. June 15, 1968
Cin–NL 1899–1902, Det–AL 1903–17

NUMBER OF RECORDS ESTABLISHED: 50

AMERICAN LEAGUE RECORDS

Season Batting Records

| 1903 | Most Triples | 25 | 9 | |
| 1914 | Most Triples | 26 | | Tied |

Season Batting Title Records

1913	Most Triples Titles	3	1	
1914	Most Triples Titles	4	1	
1915	Most Triples Titles	5		Never Broken

Season Fielding Records—RF

| 1904 | Most Double Plays | 8 | 3 | |
| 1905 | Highest Fielding Ave. | .988 | 2 | |

Career Batting Records—1903–17

Most Games Played	2,114	11
Most At Bats	7,994	11
Most Triples	250	11
Most Home Runs	70	5
Most Runs Scored	1,115	11
Most RBIs	1,264	11
Most Extra Base Hits	723	11
Most Total Bases	3,579	11
Most Strikeouts	104	3
Most Stolen Bases	317	5
Highest Slugging Ave.	.448	3

Career Fielding Records–RF—1903–17

Most Games Played	1,489	8
Most Putouts	2,049	8
Most Assists	159	8
Most Double Plays	38	8
Most Total Chances	2,268	8
Highest Fielding Ave.	.975	31

MAJOR LEAGUE RECORDS

Season Batting Title Records

1914	Most Triples Titles	4	1	
1915	Most Triples Titles	5		Tied

Season Fielding Records—RF

1905	Highest Fielding Ave.	.988	2

Career Batting Records–1899–1917

	Most Triples	312	Never Broken

Career Fielding Records—RF

Most Games Played	1,786	8
Most Putouts	2,522	8

WORLD SERIES RECORDS

Game Fielding Records–CF

1907	Most Assists	1	11
1909	Most Errors	1	25

5-Game Series Fielding Records–CF

1907	Most Assists	2		Tied
1908	Most Putouts	16	2	

7-Game Series Batting Records

1909	Most Total Bases	13	3

7-Game Series Fielding Records

1909	Most Assists	2	11	
	Most Errors	2		Tied

Career Batting Records—1907–09

	Most Games Played	17	1
	Most At Bats	70	1
	Most Hits	17	1
	Most Doubles	5	1
	Most Series Played	3	1

Career Fielding Records—CF

	Most Putouts	39	9	
	Most Assists	2	21	
	Most Errors	2		Tied
	Total Chances	43	8	
	Chances w/o Errors	22	1	

SUMMARY

"Wahoo Sam" Crawford was one of the early premier rightfielders in the American League. He got his nickname from his birthplace: Wahoo, Nebraska. Crawford is best known for having hit the most triples of any player in baseball history. His 312 three-base hits is a record that has never been seriously challenged. Crawford is a five-time triples leader, and his lifetime batting average is .309.

Crawford was inducted into the Hall of Fame in 1957.

CAREER STATISTICS:

19 Years
Games 2,517
At Bats 9,580
Hits 2,964
Doubles 457
Triples 312 (1st)

Home Runs 97
Home Run Percentage 1.0
Runs Scored 1,393
RBIs 1,525
Bases on Balls 760
Stolen Bases 366

Strikeouts 104
Batting Ave. .309
Slugging Ave. .453
Pinch Hit At Bats 64
Pinch Hits 18

Joseph Edward Cronin

(Joe)

B. Oct. 12, 1906, D. Sept. 7, 1984

Pit–NL 1926–27, Was–AL 1928–34, Bos–AL 1935–45
Manager: Was–AL 1933–34, Bos–AL 1935–47

NUMBER OF RECORDS ESTABLISHED AS PLAYER: 14

ALL-STAR GAME RECORDS

Game Batting Records

1933	Most Games Played	1	1	
	Most Runs Scored	1	1	
1934	Most Games Played	2	1	
1935	Most Games Played	3	1	
1936	Most Games Played	4	1	
1937	Most Games Played	5	1	
1939	Most Games Played	6	1	

Game Fielding Records—SS

| 1933 | Most Assists | 4 | 1 | |
| 1934 | Most Assists | 8 | | Never Broken |

Career Batting Records—1933–39

Most Games Played	6	1	
Most Doubles	3		Tied
Most Extra Base Hits	3	21	

Career Fielding Records—SS—1933–39

Most Assists	25		Never Broken
Most Errors	1	23	

SUMMARY

Joe Cronin was a good-hitting shortstop with a lifetime batting average of .302, which covers a 20-year career. His best season was in 1930 when he batted .346 and got 203 hits. He was a two-time doubles champion and smacked 515 in all.

Cronin was an exceptional fielder who led the American League in various fielding departments 16 times.

He was a player-manager with the Red Sox from 1935 to 1945, and with the Senators in 1933 and 1934.

Cronin was the first player to rise through the ranks to become president of either league. He was voted the outstanding shortstop by the *Sporting News* from 1930 to 1934 and in 1938 and 1939. In 1943, he set an American League record by hitting 5 pinch-hit home runs. Connie Mack was quoted as saying, "Joe Cronin was the best clutch hitter I ever saw."

From 1948 to 1959, Cronin served the Boston Red Sox as treasurer, vice president, and general manager. He became American League president in 1959 and held that position until 1973. He was the chairman of the American League board from 1973 to 1984 and was director of the National Baseball Hall of Fame. In 1970 he became chairman of its Veterans Committee and in 1977 became president of the Baseball Players Association. He helped incorporate the Reorganization Agreement into the American League constitution and was instrumental in adding new teams to the league.

Cronin became a Hall of Famer in 1956.

CAREER STATISTICS:

20 Years	Home Runs 170	Strikeouts 700
Games 2,124	Home Run Percentage 2.2	Batting Ave. .302
At Bats 7,579	Runs Scored 1,233	Slugging Ave. .468
Hits 2,285	RBIs 1,424	Pinch Hit At Bats 104
Doubles 515	Bases on Balls 1,059	Pinch Hits 30
Triples 118	Stolen Bases 87	

CAREER STATISTICS AS MANAGER:

15 Years	Wins 1,236	Winning Percentage .540
Games 2,315	Losses 1,055	First-place Finishes 2

William Arthur Cummings
(Candy)
B. Oct. 18, 1848, D. May 16, 1924
Har–NL 1876, Cin–NL 1877

NUMBER OF RECORDS ESTABLISHED: 0

SUMMARY

"Candy" Cummings stood 5′9″ tall, weighed 120 pounds, and gave baseball the curve ball. He played most of his career in the amateur and professional leagues before the formation of the National League in 1876.

From 1872 to 1875, Cummings played in the old National Association, averaging 31 wins per season. When he first realized he could make the ball curve, he tried to keep it a secret, always blaming the effect on the wind current. But it was not long before every player was trying to figure out how to hit the curve, and batters spent many a day and night arguing about how to hit it. Sometimes players fell to the ground to try to avoid being hit, only to see the ball break over the plate for a strike.

For his baffling new pitch, Cummings was inducted into the Hall of Fame in 1939.

CAREER STATISTICS:

2 Years
Wins 21
Losses 22
Winning Percentage .488
ERA 2.78
Total Games 43

Games Started 43
Games Completed 40
Innings 372
Hits 434
Bases on Balls 27
Strikeouts 37

Shutouts 5
Relief Appearances 0
Relief Wins 0
Relief Losses 0
Saves 0

Hazen Shirley Cuyler
(Kiki)

B. Aug. 30, 1899, D. Feb. 11, 1950

Pit–NL 1921–27, Chi–NL 1928–35, Cin–NL 1935–37, Bkn–NL 1938

NUMBER OF RECORDS ESTABLISHED: 6

NATIONAL LEAGUE RECORDS 1921–38

Career Batting Records

	Most Strikeouts	752	8

Season Fielding Records—RF

1925	Most Total Chances	396	3
	Most Putouts	362	3
1930	Most Putouts	377	2

Career Fielding Records—RF—1925–38

	Highest Fielding Ave.	.974	13

WORLD SERIES RECORDS

7-Game Series Fielding Records—RF

1925	Most Errors	1	39

SUMMARY

"Kiki" Cuyler terrorized opposing pitchers with a lifetime batting average of .321. He was a back-to-back run-scoring champion in 1925 and 1926 and for three consecutive years led the National League in stolen bases (1928–30). He also led the league in doubles in 1934 and in triples in 1925.

During his 18-year career, he batted over .300 ten times, with a high of .360 in 1929. Cuyler received Hall of Fame honors in 1968.

CAREER STATISTICS:

18 Years
Games 1,879
At Bats 7,161
Hits 2,299
Doubles 394
Triples 157

Home Runs 127
Home Run Percentage 1.8
Runs Scored 1,305
RBIs 1,065
Bases on Balls 676
Stolen Bases 328

Strikeouts 752
Batting Ave. .321
Slugging Ave. .473
Pinch Hit At Bats 62
Pinch Hits 14

Jay Hanna Dean
(Dizzy)
B. Jan. 16, 1911, D. July 17, 1974
StL–NL 1930–37, Chi–NL 1938–41, StL–AL 1947

NUMBER OF RECORDS ESTABLISHED: 5

ALL-STAR GAME RECORDS

Game Pitching Records

1936	Fewest Hits Allowed/3 Inn.	0		Tied

Career Pitching Records—1933–37

	Most Hits Allowed	10	1
	Most Strikeouts	10	3

WORLD SERIES RECORDS

7-Game Series Pitching Records

1934	Most Games Started	3	28
	Most Shutouts	1	23

SUMMARY

In a brilliant career shortened by injuries, "Dizzy" Dean proved he was one of baseball's most exciting pitchers. In all, he won 150 games and lost only 83, which represents an excellent winning percentage of .644. He was a central figure in St. Louis's "Gashouse Gang."

Dean's greatest year was 1934, when he won 30 and lost 7. In 1935 he had 28 wins and in 1936, 24. He led the league in strikeouts four consecutive years (1932–35) and in complete games (1933–36). In all, he led the league in 18 various pitching departments.

After he retired, Dean became a broadcaster for his St. Louis Cardinals and maintained the reputation of his nickname by regularly mangling the English language.

Dean was voted into the Hall of Fame in 1953.

CAREER STATISTICS:

12 Years	Games Started 230	Shutouts 26
Wins 150	Games Completed 154	Relief Appearances 87
Losses 83	Innings 1,966	Relief Wins 11
Winning Percentage .644	Hits 1,927	Relief Losses 16
ERA 3.03	Bases on Balls 458	Saves 30
Total Games 317	Strikeouts 1,155	

Edward James Delahanty
(Big Ed)
B. Oct. 30, 1867, D. July 2, 1903

Phi–NL 1888–89, Cle–PL 1890, Phi–NL 1891–1901, Was–AL 1902–03

NUMBER OF RECORDS ESTABLISHED: 22

NATIONAL LEAGUE RECORDS

Season Batting Records

1893	Most Total Bases	347	1
	Most Extra Base Hits	72	1
1895	Most Doubles	49	4
1899	Most Doubles	56	31

Season Batting Title Records

1899	Most Doubles Titles	3	2
1901	Most Doubles Titles	4	6

Season Fielding Records—LF

1893	Most Putouts	318	2
	Most Assists	31	10

Most Double Plays	8	1	
Most Total Chances	368	2	

Career Fielding Records—LF

Most Assists per Game	0.17		Tied
Most Total Chances per Game	2.6		Tied
Highest Fielding Ave.	.952	1	

MAJOR LEAGUE RECORDS

Season Batting Records

1899	Most Doubles	56	24

Season Batting Title Records

1899	Most Doubles Titles	3	2
1901	Most Doubles Titles	4	1
1902	Most Doubles Titles	5	5

Season Fielding Records—LF

1893	Most Putouts	318	2
	Most Total Chances	368	2

Career Fielding Records—LF

Most Assists per Game	0.17		Tied
Total Chances per Game	2.6		Tied
Highest Fielding Ave.	.952	1	

SUMMARY

"Big Ed" Delahanty was one of the greatest righthanded hitters in baseball history. His lifetime batting average of .345 is the fourth best on the all-time list.

Delahanty enjoyed a fine 16-year career during which he batted over .300 12 times consecutively. His greatest years produced batting averages of .408, .400, .399, and .397. He was a 5-time doubles champion, a 2-time batting average leader, and a 5-time slugging champion.

Delahanty was voted into the Hall of Fame in 1945.

CAREER STATISTICS:

16 Years	Home Runs 100	Strikeouts 244
Games 1,834	Home Run Percentage 1.3	Batting Ave. .345 (4th)
At Bats 7,502	Runs Scored 1,599	Slugging Ave. .504
Hits 2,591	RBIs 1,464	Pinch Hit At Bats 6
Doubles 521	Bases on Balls 741	Pinch Hits 3
Triples 183	Stolen Bases 456	

William Malcolm Dickey
(Bill)

B. June 6, 1907
NY–AL 1928–46
Manager: NY–AL 1946

NUMBER OF RECORDS ESTABLISHED AS PLAYER: 14

AMERICAN LEAGUE RECORDS

Season Fielding Records—C

1931	Highest Fielding Ave.	.996	15

Career Fielding Records—C

Most Putouts	7,965	19
Highest Fielding Ave.	.988	5

MAJOR LEAGUE RECORDS

Season Fielding Records—C

1931	Highest Fielding Ave.	.966	1

Career Fielding Records—C

Most Putouts	7,965	19
Highest Fielding Ave.	.988	5

WORLD SERIES RECORDS

Game Batting Records

1932	Most At Bats	6	42
1936	Most RBIs	5	22
1938	Most Hits	4	44
	Most Singles	4	44

4-Game Series Fielding Records—C

1938	Most Assists	5	Tied

Career Fielding Records—1932–43—C

Most Putouts	224	17
Most Total Chances	245	17
Chances w/o Errors	140	17

SUMMARY

Bill Dickey was one of baseball's finest all-around catchers. A lifetime batting average of .313 proved he could hit, and his 21 times leading the league in fielding departments for catchers showed he was one of the best defensive men behind the plate.

In 1938, he belted 4 hits in one World Series game, a mark that lasted 44 years.

When he retired, he had the most putouts and total chances in World Series play of any catcher in baseball history.

Dickey batted over .300 11 times, with a high of .362 in 1936.

Dickey was inducted into the Hall of Fame in 1954.

CAREER STATISTICS:

17 Years	Home Runs 202	Strikeouts 289
Games 1,789	Home Run Percentage 3.2	Batting Ave. .313
At Bats 6,300	Runs Scored 930	Slugging Ave. .486
Hits 1,969	RBIs 1,209	Pinch Hit At Bats 67
Doubles 343	Bases on Balls 678	Pinch Hits 18
Triples 72	Stolen Bases 36	

CAREER STATISTICS AS MANAGER:

1 Year	Wins 57	Winning Percentage .543
Games 105	Losses 48	First-place Finishes 0

Joseph Paul DiMaggio
(The Yankee Clipper, Joltin' Joe)
B. Nov. 25, 1914
NY–AL 1936–51

NUMBER OF RECORDS ESTABLISHED: 26

AMERICAN LEAGUE RECORDS

Rookie Batting Records

1936	Most Runs Scored	132		Never Broken

Rookie Fielding Records—LF

1936	Highest Fielding Ave.	.978	43	

Season Batting Records

1941	Longest Hitting Streak	56		Never Broken

Season Fielding Records—CF

1947	Highest Fielding Ave.	.997	21	

111

Career Batting Title Records

| | Most MVP Titles | 3 | | Tied |

MAJOR LEAGUE RECORDS

Season Batting Records

| 1941 | Longest Hitting Streak | 56 | | Never Broken |

Season Fielding Records—CF

| 1947 | Highest Fielding Ave. | .997 | 5 | |

Career Batting Title Records

| | Most MVP Titles | 3 | | Tied |

ALL-STAR GAME RECORDS

Game Batting Records

1939	Most Home Runs	1	2
1941	Most Runs Scored	3	5
1950	Most Games Played	11	13

Career Batting Records

	Most Games Played	11	13
	Most At Bats	40	13
	Most Runs Scored	7	10
	Most RBIs	6	10

WORLD SERIES RECORDS

Game Batting Records

| 1936 | Most At Bats | 6 | 37 |

5-Game Series Fielding Records—CF

| 1937 | Most Putouts | 18 | 5 | |
| 1942 | Most Putouts | 20 | | Never Broken |

6-Game Series Fielding Records—CF

| 1936 | Most Putouts | 18 | 8 | |
| | Most Errors | 1 | | Tied |

Career Batting Records—1936–51

Most Games Played	51	4
Most At Bats	199	13
Most Series Played	10	13

Career Fielding Records—1936–51

Most Putouts	150	Never Broken
Most Total Chances	151	Never Broken
Chances w/o Errors	132	Never Broken

SUMMARY

"Joltin' Joe's" 56-game hitting streak remains one of baseball's greatest treasures. Since 1941 only Pete Rose has made a serious attempt at it, but he came up short with 44.

The "Yankee Clippper" racked up 26 outstanding records, 12 of which still stand. He was a league leader in various batting categories 11 times, and his lifetime slugging average of .579 is the sixth best in baseball. This is a tremendous accomplishment because he played in Yankee Stadium, where "death valley" took away many extra base hits that would be home runs in most other stadiums.

DiMaggio batted over .300 11 of the 13 years he wore the Yankee pinstripes. He probably would have added another three if he had not been interrupted by World War II.

During World Series play, "Joltin' Joe" compiled 11 records. His 199 at bats is the third best; he ranks fourth in hits, fifth in runs scored and RBIs, and seventh in games and home runs.

Joe was also a super player in All-Star Games, where he picked up another seven records. When he retired, he had played in more All-Star games, had more at bats, scored more runs, and had more RBIs than any player in history. Despite the fact that most of DiMaggio's 400-foot-plus fly ball outs would have been home runs in most other parks, the Yankee Clipper has the best home run–strikeout ratio of any player in baseball history.

No player has ever had as many home runs as strikeouts, but Joe D. came the closest with 361 home runs and 369 strikeouts.

DiMaggio was inducted into the Hall of Fame in 1955.

CAREER STATISTICS:

13 Years	Home Runs 361	Strikeouts 369
Games 1,736	Home Run Percentage 5.3	Batting Ave. .325
At Bats 6,821	Runs Scored 1,390	Slugging Ave. .579 (6th)
Hits 2,214	RBIs 1,537	Pinch Hit At Bats 12
Doubles 389	Bases on Balls 790	Pinch Hits 6
Triples 131	Stolen Bases 30	

Robert Pershing Doerr

B. Aug. 7, 1918
Bos–AL 1937–51

NUMBER OF RECORDS ESTABLISHED: 8

AMERICAN LEAGUE RECORDS

Season Fielding Records—2B

| 1948 | Highest Fielding Ave. | .993 | 16 |

Career Fielding Records—2B—1937–51

| | Most Double Plays | 1,478 | 16 |
| | Highest Fielding Ave. | .980 | 14 |

MAJOR LEAGUE RECORDS

Season Fielding Records—2B

| 1948 | Highest Fielding Ave. | .993 | 16 |

Career Fielding Records—2B—1937–51

| 1937–51 | Most Double Plays | 1,478 | 14 |
| | Highest Fielding Ave. | .980 | 14 |

114

WORLD SERIES RECORDS

Game Fielding Records—2B

1946	Most Assists	8	Tied

7-Game Series Fielding Records—2B

1946	Most Assists	31	36

SUMMARY

Bobby Doerr was the greatest second baseman in the history of the Boston Red Sox. He was a gentleman of the game and was said to have never made an enemy in the 14 years he played. He batted over .300 three times and ended his career with a .288 batting average.

Doerr was a power-hitting second baseman who belted 223 home runs and had a lifetime slugging average of .461.

In 1950, the penultimate year of his career, he led the American League in triples with 11, even though he didn't have great speed. In his entire career, he stole only 54 bases. His greatest season was 1944, when he batted .325 and led the league in slugging with a .528 average. An outstanding clutch hitter, Doerr drove in more than 100 runs six times.

His fielding records show that Doerr was an exceptional defensive second baseman. He led the league 20 times in various fielding categories and never once was a league leader in the negative category of most errors. He produced 24 Red Sox club records.

He only appeared in one World Series, and had a batting average of .409 on 9 hits in 22 at bats.

Doerr was inducted into the Hall of Fame in 1986.

CAREER STATISTICS:

14 Years	Home Runs 223	Strikeouts 608
Games 1,865	Home Run Percentage 3.1	Batting Ave. .288
At Bats 7,093	Runs Scored 1,094	Slugging Ave. .461
Hits 2,042	RBIs 1,247	Pinch Hit At Bats 4
Doubles 381	Bases on Balls 809	Pinch Hits 0
Triples 89	Stolen Bases 54	

Donald Scott Drysdale
(Don)
B. July 23, 1936
LA–NL 1956–69

NUMBER OF RECORDS ESTABLISHED: 11

NATIONAL LEAGUE RECORDS

Season Pitching Records

1965	Cons. Scoreless Innings	57	23

Season Pitching Title Records

1962	Most Cy Young Titles	1	3

ALL-STAR GAME RECORDS

Game Pitching Records

1959	Fewest Hits Allowed/3 Inn.	0		Tied

Career Pitching Records—1959–68

Most Games	8		Tied
Most Strikeouts	19		Never Broken

116

WORLD SERIES RECORDS

4-Game Series Pitching Records

1966	Most Starts	2		Tied
	Most Losses	2		Tied
1963	Most Shutouts	1		Tied
	Lowest ERA	0.00		Tied
	Fewest Bases on Balls	1		Tied

MAJOR LEAGUE RECORDS

Season Pitching Records

| 1965 | Cons. Scoreless Innings | 57 | 23 |

SUMMARY

Don Drysdale did all pitching work for the Dodgers and finished a fine 14-year career with 209 victories and 166 defeats. He led the league in various pitching departments 12 times. He was a league leader four consecutive years in games started and was a three-time strikeout champion. In all, he whiffed 2,486 batters while tossing 49 shutouts. Don's best season was 1962, when he won 25 games and lost only 9, and won the Cy Young Award. "Big Don" was magnificent in 1965, when he tossed six consecutive shutouts and did not yield a run in 57 innings.

Drysdale was voted into the Hall of Fame in 1984.

POSTSEASON AWARDS

| 1962 | Cy Young Award |

CAREER STATISTICS:

14 Years	Games Started 465	Shutouts 49
Wins 209	Games Completed 167	Relief Appearances 53
Losses 166	Innings 3,432	Relief Wins 6
Winning Percentage .557	Hits 3,084	Relief Losses 6
ERA 2.95	Bases on Balls 855	Saves 6
Total Games 518	Strikeouts 2,486	

Hugh Duffy

B. Nov. 26, 1866, D. Oct. 19, 1954

Chi–NL 1888–89, Chi–PL 1890, Bos–AA 1891, Bos–NL 1892–1900, Mil–AL 1901, Phi–NL 1904–06
Manager: Mil–AL 1901, Phi–NL 1904–06, Chi–AL 1910–11, Bos–AL 1921–22

NUMBER OF RECORDS ESTABLISHED AS PLAYER: 16

NUMBER OF RECORDS ESTABLISHED AS MANAGER: 1

TOTAL: 17

PLAYER RECORDS

NATIONAL LEAGUE RECORDS

Season Batting Records

1890	Most At Bats	596	1	
1893	Most Singles	167	1	
1894	Most Hits	236	2	
	Highest Batting Ave.	.438		Never Broken
	Highest Slugging Ave.	.688	28	
	Most Total Bases	366	27	
	Most Extra Base Hits	81	1	

Season Batting Title Records

1894	Most Triple Crowns	1	31	
1897	Most Home Runs Titles	2	20	

Season Fielding Records—LF

1897	Highest Fielding Ave.	.975	2	

MAJOR LEAGUE RECORDS

Season Batting Records

1893	Most Singles	167	1	
1894	Most Hits	236	2	
	Highest Batting Ave.	.438		Never Broken
	Most Total Bases	366	26	

Season Batting Title Records

1894	Most Triple Crowns	1	31	

MANAGER RECORDS

American League Season Records

1901	Losses	89	2	

SUMMARY

Hugh Duffy's .438 batting average in 1894 helped win him the Triple Crown. In that fantastic season, he had 236 hits, 50 doubles, 18 home runs, 145 RBIs, and a whopping .679 slugging average. During his 17-year career he averaged a smart .328. He batted over .300 13 times, ten times in a row from 1889 to 1898. Duffy led the league in various batting departments ten times.

He managed four different teams intermittently from 1901 through 1922 but was unsuccessful in winning any pennants.

Duffy was inducted into the Hall of Fame in 1945.

CAREER STATISTICS:

17 Years	Home Runs 103	Stolen Bases 599
Games 1,736	Home Run Percentage 1.5	Batting Ave. .328
At Bats 7,062	Runs Scored 1,553	Slugging Ave. .450
Hits 2,314	RBIs 1,299	Pinch Hit At Bats 18
Doubles 324	Bases on Balls 662	Pinch Hits 5
Triples 116	Strikeouts 211	

CAREER STATISTICS AS MANAGER:

8 Years	Wins 535	Winning Percentage .444
Games 1,221	Losses 671	First-place Finishes 0

John Joseph Evers
(Johnny, The Trojan, The Crab)

B. July 21, 1881, D. May 28, 1947

Chi–NL 1902–13, Bos–NL 1914–17, Phi–NL 1917, Chi–AL 1922, Bos–NL 1929
Manager: Chi–NL 1913, 1921, Chi–AL 1924

NUMBER OF RECORDS ESTABLISHED: 11

NATIONAL LEAGUE RECORDS

Career Fielding Records—2B

	Most Games	1,735	8
	Most Assists	4,998	2

WORLD SERIES RECORDS

4-Game Series Batting Records

1914	Most Hits	7	13
	Most Singles	7	8

5-Game Series Batting Records

1908	Most Runs Scored	5	2

6-Game Series Batting Records

1906	Most Stolen Bases	2	11

Career Batting Records—1906–14

Most Singles	20	5
Most Runs	11	5
Most Series	4	1

Career Fielding Records—2B—1906–14

Most Assists	67	5
Most Total Chances	110	5

SUMMARY

Grantland Rice immortalized the double-play combination of Tinker to Evers to Chance. The middle man, Johnny Evers, rang up nine World Series records and his 8 stolen bases are the eighth best in baseball. He was a fine fielder and led the league seven times in various fielding departments. When he retired in 1929, he had played more games and had scooped up more ground balls than any second baseman in National League history.

Evers was voted into the Hall of Fame in 1946.

CAREER STATISTICS:

18 Years	Home Runs 12	Strikeouts 142
Games 1,783	Home Run Percentage 0.2	Batting Ave. .270
At Bats 6,134	Runs Scored 919	Slugging Ave. .334
Hits 1,658	RBIs 538	Pinch Hit At Bats 4
Doubles 216	Bases on Balls 778	Pinch Hits 1
Triples 70	Stolen Bases 324	

CAREER STATISTICS AS MANAGER:

3 Years	Wins 196	Winning Percentage .485
Games 406	Losses 208	First-place Finishes 0

William Ewing

(Buck)

B. Oct. 17, 1859, D. Oct. 20, 1906

Tro–NL 1880–82, NY–NL 1883–89, NY–PL 1890, NY–NL 1891–92,
Cle–NL 1893–94, Cin–NL 1895–97
Manager: NY–PL 1890, Cin–NL 1895–99, NY–NL 1900

NUMBER OF RECORDS ESTABLISHED AS PLAYER: 10

NATIONAL LEAGUE RECORDS

Rookie Fielding Records—C

1881	Most Double Plays	9	6
	Highest Fielding Ave.	.915	6

Season Batting Records

1883	Most Home Runs	10	1
1884	Most Triples	20	3

Season Batting Title Records

1883	Most Home Runs Titles	1	3
1884	Most Triples Titles	1	2

MAJOR LEAGUE RECORDS

Rookie Fielding Records—C

1881	Most Double Plays	9	2
	Highest Fielding Ave.	.915	1

Season Batting Title Records

1883	Most Home Runs Titles	1	3
1884	Most Triples Titles	1	2

SUMMARY

Buck Ewing played catcher, first, second, third, and the outfield during his 18-year career. He hit over .300 11 times, ten times in succession. He led the league in homers and home run percentage in 1883 and in triples in 1884.

During his catching days, Ewing was the best as a league leader nine times in various fielding categories.

Ewing was recognized by the Hall of Fame in 1939.

CAREER STATISTICS:

18 Years
Games 1,315
At Bats 5,363
Hits 1,625
Doubles 250
Triples 178

Home Runs 70
Home Run Percentage 1.3
Runs Scored 1,129
RBIs 732
Stolen Bases 336
Bases on Balls 392

Strikeouts 294
Batting Ave. .303
Slugging Ave. .455
Pinch Hit At Bats 0
Pinch Hits 0

CAREER STATISTICS AS MANAGER:

7 Years
Games 903

Wins 489
Losses 395

Winning Percentage .553
First-place Finishes 0

Urban Clarence Faber

(Red)

B. Sept. 6, 1888, D. Sept. 25, 1976

Chi–AL 1914–33

NUMBER OF RECORDS ESTABLISHED: 3

WORLD SERIES RECORDS

6-Game Series Pitching Records

1917	Most Games	3	
	Most Wins	3	
	Most Innings	27	Tied

SUMMARY

Red Faber won 254 games for the White Sox, tossed 30 shutouts, and won back-to-back ERA crowns in 1921 and 1922. In the same two years he completed more games than any American League pitcher, and in 1922 led the league by working 353 innings.

Faber is a four-time 20-game winner. His best season was 1921, when he won 25 and had a league-leading ERA of 2.48.

Faber was welcomed into the Hall of Fame in 1964.

CAREER STATISTICS:

20 Years

Wins 254

Losses 212

Winning Percentage .545

ERA 3.15

Total Games 669

Games Started 484

Games Completed 274

Innings 4,088

Hits 4,106

Bases on Balls 1,213

Strikeouts 1,471

Shutouts 30

Relief Appearances 185

Relief Wins 27

Relief Losses 27

Saves 28

Robert William Andrew Feller
(Rapid Robert)
B. Nov. 3, 1918
Cle–AL 1936–56

NUMBER OF RECORDS ESTABLISHED: 8

AMERICAN LEAGUE RECORDS

Season Pitching Records

1938	Most Bases on Balls	208		Never Broken

Season Pitching Title Records

1946	No-Hit Titles	2	5	
1947	Innings Titles	5		Tied
1951	Wins Titles	6		Tied

Career Pitching Title Records

	Wins Titles	6		Tied
	Innings Titles	5		Tied

MAJOR LEAGUE RECORDS

Season Pitching Title Records

1951   Wins Titles   6   9

ALL-STAR GAME RECORDS

Career Pitching Records—1939–50

      Total Games   5   1

SUMMARY

Bob Feller had one of the very best fastballs the game has ever seen, and he led the American League in strikeouts seven times in eight years.

    Feller was a league leader a remarkable 37 times in his sensational 18-year career. For five consecutive years he led the league in wins, and he won 20 or more games 6 times. In 1946, Feller won 26 games, tossed 10 shutouts, and led the league in nine categories. He won 266 games and lost 162 and spun 3 no-hitters and 10 one-hitters in his career. Feller was inducted into the Hall of Fame in 1962.

CAREER STATISTICS:

18 Years	Games Started 484	Shutouts 46
Wins 266	Games Completed 279	Relief Appearances 86
Losses 162	Innings 3,827	Relief Wins 6
Winning Percentage .621	Hits 3,271	Relief Losses 8
ERA 3.25	Bases on Balls 1,764 (3rd)	Saves 21
Total Games 570	Strikeouts 2,581	

Richard Benjamin Ferrell
(Rick)

B. Oct. 12, 1905

StL–AL 1929–33, Bos–AL 1933–37, Was–AL 1938–41, StL–AL 1941–43, Was–AL 1944–47

NUMBER OF RECORDS ESTABLISHED: 1

AMERICAN LEAGUE RECORDS

Career Fielding Records—1929–47

Most Games Played	1,805	Never Broken

SUMMARY

Rick Ferrell caught more games than any other catcher in American League history. He led the league in various fielding departments 11 times, and hit over .300 five times, with a high of .315 in 1932. His lifetime batting average was .281.

Ferrell was inducted into the Hall of Fame in 1984.

CAREER STATISTICS:

18 Years	Home Runs 28	Strikeouts 277
Games 1,884	Home Run Percentage 0.5	Batting Ave. .281
At Bats 6,028	Runs Scored 687	Slugging Ave. .361
Hits 1,692	RBIs 734	Pinch Hit At Bats 73
Doubles 324	Bases on Balls 931	Pinch Hits 11
Triples 45	Stolen Bases 29	

Elmer Harrison Flick

B. Jan. 11, 1876, D. Jan. 9, 1971
Phi–NL 1898–1901, Phi–AL 1902, Cle–AL 1903–10

NUMBER OF RECORDS ESTABLISHED: 9

NATIONAL LEAGUE RECORDS

Rookie Batting Records

1898	Most Stolen Bases	23	1

AMERICAN LEAGUE RECORDS

Season Batting Title Records

1906	Most Triples Titles	2	1
	Most Stolen Bases Titles	2	5
1907	Most Triples Titles	3	7

Career Batting Records—1902–10

	Most Triples	109	7
	Highest Batting Ave.	318	6

Career Fielding Records—1902–10

Most Assists	91	7
Most Errors	64	15

MAJOR LEAGUE RECORDS

Rookie Batting Records

1898	Most Stolen Bases	23	1

SUMMARY

Elmer Flick was a fleet-footed outfielder who could hit, run, and throw. In three consecutive years (1905–07), he led the league in triples.

Flick played the first four years of his career in the National League, where he had a composite batting average of .342. He batted over .300 four consecutive years (1904–07) in the American League and ended up with a lifetime batting average of .315.

Flick's entrance into the Hall of Fame came in 1963.

CAREER STATISTICS:

13 Years	Home Runs 47	Strikeouts No Stats Recorded
Games 1,484	Home Run Percentage 0.8	Batting Ave. .315
At Bats 5,603	Runs Scored 950	Slugging Ave. .449
Hits 1,767	RBIs 756	Pinch Hit At Bats 12
Doubles 268	Bases on Balls 597	Pinch Hits 3
Triples 170	Stolen Bases 334	

Edward Charles Ford
(Whitey, Chairman of the Board)
B. Oct. 21, 1928
NY–AL 1950–67

NUMBER OF RECORDS ESTABLISHED: 21

AMERICAN LEAGUE RECORDS

Season Pitching Title Records

1961	Most Cy Young Awards	1	8

MAJOR LEAGUE RECORDS

Career Pitching Title Records

1961	Most Cy Young Awards	1	1

ALL-STAR GAME RECORDS

Game Pitching Records

1955	Most Hits/1 Inn.	5	Tied

131

Career Pitching Records—1954–61

Losses	2	Tied
Hits Allowed	19	Never Broken
Runs Allowed	13	Never Broken

WORLD SERIES RECORDS

4-Game Series Pitching Records

1963	Starts	2		Tied
	Losses	2		Tied

7-Game Series Pitching Records

1958	Starts	3	4	
1960	Lowest ERA	0.00		Tied
	Shutouts	2		Tied

Career Pitching Records—1950–64

Series Played	11	Never Broken
Games	22	Never Broken
Starts	22	Never Broken
Wins	10	Never Broken
Losses	8	Never Broken
Innings	146	Never Broken
Cons. Scoreless Innings	33	Never Broken
Most Bases on Balls Allowed	34	Never Broken
Strikeouts	94	Never Broken
Hits Allowed	132	Never Broken

SUMMARY

"Whitey" Ford created 15 World Series records, and 14 of them remain unbroken after 24 years. He has the most unbroken records of any pitcher in World Series history.

Ford is the greatest lefty pitcher in New York Yankee history. At 236–106, he compiled a winning percentage of .690, which ranks him third on the all-time major league list. He was a league leader 15 times in various pitching departments while leading the Yankees to 11 pennants.

"Whitey" is a three-time wins and winning percentage leader, a two-time ERA, innings, shutouts, and games started leader, and has won a single crown in complete games.

Ford enjoyed his greatest season in 1961, when he won 25 games, lost only 4, and captured the Cy Young Award.

Ford entered the Hall of Fame in 1974.

POSTSEASON AWARDS

1961 Cy Young Award

CAREER STATISTICS:

16 Years
Wins 236
Losses 106
Winning Percentage .690
(3rd)
ERA 2.75
Total Games 498

Games Started 438
Games Completed 156
Innings 3,170
Hits 2,766
Bases on Balls 1,086
Strikeouts 1,956

Shutouts 45
Relief Appearances 60
Relief Wins 9
Relief Losses 7
Saves 10

James Emory Foxx
(Jimmie, Double X, The Beast)
B. Oct. 22, 1907, D. July 21, 1967
Phi–AL 1925–35, Bos–AL 1936–42, Chi–NL 1942–44, Phi–NL 1945

NUMBER OF RECORDS ESTABLISHED: 7

ALL-STAR GAME RECORDS

1935	Most Home Runs	1	6
	Most Total Bases	5	2
	Most RBIs	3	2

Career Batting Records—1934–41

| | Most Games | 7 | 2 |
| | Most Strikeouts | 7 | 19 |

WORLD SERIES RECORDS

5-Game Series Batting Records

| 1929 | Most Home Runs | 2 | 40 |
| | Most Total Bases | 14 | 40 |

SUMMARY

Jimmie Foxx, sometimes known as "Double X" and "The Beast," was a frightening sight to enemy pitchers. He led the league in home runs four times, and four times was the home run percentage leader. He was a three-time RBI champion, twice a batting average king, and a five-time slugging average leader. He led the league in various batting departments 26 times. He was the first American Leaguer to win consecutive MVP honors (1932–33) and then become the first to win three MVPs in 1938.

Foxx's lifetime slugging average of .609 is the fourth-best in baseball. His lifetime batting average was .325, and his 534 home runs rank him number 7. Only five others have driven in more runs.

Foxx entered the Hall of Fame in 1951.

POSTSEASON AWARDS

1932 MVP
1933 MVP
1938 MVP

CAREER STATISTICS:

20 Years
Games 2,317
At Bats 8,134
Hits 2,646
Doubles 458
Triples 125

Home Runs 534 (7th)
Home Run Percentage 6.6 (8th)
Runs Scored 1,751
RBIs 1,921 (6th)
Bases on Balls 1,452
Stolen Bases 88

Strikeouts 1,311
Batting Ave. .325
Slugging Ave. .609 (4th)
Pinch Hit At Bats 112
Pinch Hits 30

Frank Francis Frisch
(Frankie, The Fordham Flash)

B. Sept. 9, 1898, D. Mar. 12, 1973
NY–NL 1919–26, StL–NL 1927–1937
Manager: StL–NL 1933–38, Pit–NL 1940–46, Chi–NL 1949–51

NUMBER OF RECORDS ESTABLISHED AS PLAYER: 47

NATIONAL LEAGUE RECORDS

Season Fielding Records—2B

1927	Most Assists	641		Never Broken
	Most Total Chances	1,059		Never Broken

Career Fielding Records—2B

	Most Games Played	1,775	10
	Most Putouts	4,348	10
	Most Assists	6,026	35
	Most Total Chances	10,654	10
	Most Double Plays	1,060	10
	Highest Fielding Ave.	.972	26

MAJOR LEAGUE RECORDS

Season Fielding Records—2B

1927	Most Assists	641		Never Broken
	Most Total Chances	1,059		Never Broken

Career Fielding Records—2B

	Highest Fielding Ave.	.972	6

ALL-STAR GAME RECORDS

Game Batting Records

1933	Most Hits	2	1
	Most Games Played	1	1
	Most Home Runs	1	8
	Most Total Bases	5	4
	Most Extra Base Hits	1	1
	Most Runs Scored	1	1
1934	Most Games Played	2	1
	Most Runs Scored	3	12

Career Batting Records—1933–34

	Most Games Played	2	1
	Most At Bats	8	1
	Most Hits	4	1
	Most Runs Scored	4	8
	Most RBIs	2	4
	Most Singles	2	1
	Most Home Runs	2	26
	Most Total Bases	10	4
	Most Extra Base Hits	2	1

Career Fielding Records—2B—1933–34

	Most Putouts	5	1
	Most Assists	4	4

WORLD SERIES RECORDS

Game Batting Records

1921	Most Hits	4	61
	Most Runs Scored	3	5

Game Fielding Records—3B

1921	Most Assists	6	2

5-Game Series Fielding Records—2B

1922	Most Assists	20	21

6-Game Series Fielding Records—2B

1923	Most Putouts	17	36

7-Game Series Batting Records

1924	Most Doubles	4	10
	Most Extra Base Hits	5	10

8-Game Series Base-Running Records

1921	Most Stolen Bases	3	Tied

Career Batting Records

Most Games Played	50	16	
Most At Bats	197	16	
Most Hits	58	29	
Most Singles	45	29	
Most Doubles	10		Tied

Career Fielding Records—2B

Most Putouts	105	Never Broken
Most Assists	137	Never Broken
Most Total Chances	249	Never Broken

SUMMARY

Of "The Fordham Flash's" 47 records, 34 were set in All-Star and World Series play. No player has surpassed Frisch's career totals of putouts, assists, and total chances at second base. He won nine fielding crowns, and his major league totals in assists and total chances still stand as major league unbroken marks.

But Frankie Frisch could do more than just handle the leather. He was an outstanding stick man who turned in a career batting average of .316. He hit .300 or over thirteen times, doing it 11 times in a row from 1921 to 1931.

Among his other talents, Frisch could steal bases with the best of them. He won three stolen bases titles and swiped 419 in all.

Frisch was named to the Hall of Fame in 1947.

POSTSEASON AWARDS

1931 MVP

CAREER STATISTICS:

19 Years
Games 2,311
At Bats 9,112
Hits 2,880
Doubles 466
Triples 138

Home Runs 105
Home Run Percentage 1.2
Runs Scored 1,532
RBIs 1,244
Bases on Balls 728
Stolen Bases 419

Strikeouts 272
Batting Ave. .316
Slugging Ave. .432
Pinch Hit At Bats 47
Pinch Hits 12

CAREER STATISTICS AS MANAGER:

16 Years
Games 2,245

Wins 1,137
Losses 1,078

Winning Percentage .513
First-place Finishes 1

James Francis Galvin
(Gentle Jeems, Pud, The Little Steam Engine)

B. Dec. 25, 1855, D. May 7, 1902

Buf–NL 1879–85, Pit–AA 1885–86, Pit–NL 1887–89, Pit–PL 1890, Pit–NL 1891–92, StL–NL 1892
Manager: Buf–NL 1885

NUMBER OF RECORDS ESTABLISHED AS PLAYER: 28

NATIONAL LEAGUE RECORDS

Season Batting Records

1879	Strikeouts	56	1
1880	Strikeouts	57	1
1881	Strikeouts	70	2
1883	Strikeouts	79	1

Season Pitching Records

1883	Total Games	76	82
	Saves	5	22

Career Pitching Records

	Wins	317	2
	Losses	269	Never Broken
	Total Games	610	14
	Starts	596	73
	Complete Games	556	Never Broken

Innings	5,188	38
Shutouts	54	24
Hits Allowed	5,544	Never Broken

MAJOR LEAGUE RECORDS

Season Batting Records

1879	Most Strikeouts	56	1
1880	Most Strikeouts	57	1
1881	Strikeouts	70	2
1883	Strikeouts	79	1

Season Pitching Records

1883	Total Games	76	82
	Saves	5	22

Career Pitching Records

Wins	361	19
Losses	310	19
Total Games	697	19
Starts	682	19
Complete Games	639	19
Innings	5,941	19
Shutouts	57	19
Hits Allowed	6,352	19

SUMMARY

"Pud" Galvin was one of the most active of the early pioneer pitchers. His 556 complete games is the most of any National League pitcher. He was the second pitcher to retire with more than 300 wins. His 361 wins place him sixth on the all-time list. "The Little Steam Engine's" two most productive seasons were 1883 and 1884. He won 46 games each year! Galvin won 37 games as a rookie; in other fine seasons he won 29 games twice, 28 twice, and 23 twice. Pud spun 57 shutouts during his 14-year career, which places him eighth on the all-time list.

Galvin made the Hall of Fame in 1965.

CAREER STATISTICS:

14 Years	Games Started 682	Shutouts 57 (8th)
Wins 361 (6th)	Games Completed 639 (2nd)	Relief Appearances 15
Losses 310 (2nd)	Innings 5,941 (2nd)	Relief Wins 3
Winning Percentage .538	Hits 6,352	Relief Losses 2
ERA 2.87	Bases on Balls 744	Saves 1
Total Games 697	Strikeouts 1,799	

CAREER STATISTICS AS MANAGER:

1 Year	Wins 8	Winning Percentage .267
Games 30	Losses 22	First-place Finishes 0

☆

Henry Louis Gehrig
(The Iron Horse, The Pride of the Yankees, Lou, Twinkle Toes, Columbia Lou)

B. June 19, 1903, D. June 6, 1941

NY–AL 1923–39

NUMBER OF RECORDS ESTABLISHED: 51

AMERICAN LEAGUE RECORDS

Rookie Batting Records

1925	Most Home Runs	20	4	

Season Batting Records

1927	Most RBIs	175	4	
1931	Most RBIs	184		Never Broken

Season Batting Title Records

1934	Most Triple Crowns	1	13
1936	Most MVP Titles	2	2

Season Fielding Records—1B

1938	Most Double Plays	157	6

Career Batting Records

Cons. Games Played	2,130		Never Broken

Career Fielding Records—1B

Most Games Played	2,136	19	
Cons. Games Played	2,130		Never Broken
Most Putouts	19,510	19	
Most Double Plays	1,574	8	
Most Total Chances	20,790	19	

MAJOR LEAGUE RECORDS

Season Batting Records

1927	Most RBIs	175	3

Season Batting Title Records

1936	Most MVP Titles	2	2

Season Fielding Records—1B

1938	Most Double Plays	157	6

Career Batting Records

Cons. Games Played	2,130		Never Broken

Career Fielding Records—1B

Cons. Games Played	2,130		Never Broken

ALL-STAR GAME RECORDS

Game Batting Records

1933	Most Games Played	1	1	
	Most Bases on Balls	2	1	
1934	Most Games Played	2	1	
1935	Most Games Played	3	1	
1936	Most Games Played	4	1	
	Most Home Runs	1	5	
1937	Most Games Played	5	1	
	Most Home Runs	1	4	
	Most Total Bases	6	4	
	Most Extra Base Hits	2		Tied
	Most RBIs	4	9	
1938	Most Games Played	6	4	

Game Fielding Records—1B

1933	Most Putouts	12	15	
1935	Most Putouts	12	13	

Career Batting Records—1933–38

	Most Games Played	6	4	
	Most Runs Scored	4	4	
	Most RBIs	5	12	
	Most Home Runs	2	22	
	Most Extra Base Hits	3	22	
	Most Strikeouts	6	3	

Career Fielding Records—1B—1933–38

	Most Errors	2	24	
	Most Putouts	54		Never Broken

WORLD SERIES RECORDS

4-Game Series Batting Records

1927	Most Triples	2		Tied
1928	Most Bases on Balls	6	26	
	Most Home Runs	4		Never Broken
	Most RBIs	9		Never Broken
	Highest Slugging Ave.	.727	11	
1932	Most Runs Scored	9		Tied

4-Game Series Fielding Records—1B

1927	Most Assists	3	26	
1932	Most Errors	1		Tied
1938	Most Assists	3	16	

Career Batting Records—1926–38

	Most RBIs	35	25	

Career Fielding Records—1B—1926–38

	Most Putouts	309	21
	Most Total Chances	321	21

SUMMARY

"The Iron Horse's" 2,130 consecutive games played is one of baseball's best known records. In his 17-year career "The Pride of the Yankees" batted .300 or over 14 times; his best season was in 1930 when he hit .379.

Gehrig's lifetime batting average of .340 is the fifteenth best, and his .632 slugging average is third behind Babe Ruth and Ted Williams. He broke more of Babe Ruth's records than any player in baseball history.

Gehrig won the MVP Award in 1927, when he batted .373 with 52 doubles, 47 homers, and 175 RBIs. He won the Triple Crown in 1934, with 49 homers, 165 RBIs, and a .363 batting average. In 1936 he won his second MVP title by smashing 205 hits, 49 homers, and 152 RBIs and slugging a smart .696 while batting .354. Only two players in baseball history have driven in more runs than Gehrig (Ruth and Aaron). From 1925 to 1934 the Babe hit 424 home runs and 1,609 hits while Gehrig watched from the on-deck circle. How many more RBIs would Gehrig have if he batted before the Babe?

Gehrig was voted into the Hall of Fame in 1939.

POSTSEASON AWARDS

1927 MVP
1936 MVP

CAREER STATISTICS:

17 Years	Home Runs 493	Strikeouts 789
Games 2,164	Home Run Percentage 6.2	Batting Ave. .340
At Bats 8,001	Runs Scored 1,888 (7th)	Slugging Ave. .632 (3rd)
Hits 2,721	RBIs 1,990 (3rd)	Pinch Hit At Bats 16
Doubles 535	Bases on Balls 1,508 (10th)	Pinch Hits 4
Triples 162	Stolen Bases 102	

Charles Leonard Gehringer
(Charlie)
B. May 11, 1903
Det–AL 1924–42

NUMBER OF RECORDS ESTABLISHED: 23

AMERICAN LEAGUE RECORDS

Career Fielding Records—2B

Most Double Plays	1,444	9
Highest Fielding Ave.	.976	9

MAJOR LEAGUE RECORDS

Career Fielding Records—2B

Most Double Plays	1,444	9
Highest Fielding Ave.	.976	9

ALL-STAR GAME RECORDS

Game Batting Records

1933	Most Games Played	1	1
	Most Runs Scored	1	1

1934	Most Games Played	2	1	
	Most Singles	2	3	
	Most Bases on Balls	3		Tied
1935	Most Games Played	3	1	
1936	Most Games Played	4	1	
1937	Most Games Played	5	1	
	Most Singles	3		Tied
1938	Most Games Played	6	4	

Career Batting Records

Most Games Played	6	3	
Most At Bats	29	12	
Most Hits	10	5	
Most Singles	8	5	
Most Total Bases	12	4	
Most Bases on Balls	9	22	
Most Stolen Bases	2	35	
Highest Batting Ave.	.500		Tied

Career Fielding Records—2B

Most Assists	15	1

SUMMARY

Charlie Gehringer was one of baseball's most outstanding second basemen. During his 19-year career he participated in more double plays and had the highest fielding average of any second baseman in the game's history. He led all second basemen in fielding departments 25 times.

Gehringer was an exceptional batter as well. He retired with a .320 batting average and led the league in various batting categories 9 times. His 574 doubles place him tenth on the all-time list.

In three World Series, he belted 26 hits and batted a solid .321.

Gehringer had his best year in 1937, when he won the MVP Award. He hit safely 209 times while batting .371.

Gehringer was elected to the Hall of Fame in 1949.

POSTSEASON AWARDS

1937 MVP

CAREER STATISTICS:

19 Years	Home Runs 184	Strikeouts 372
Games 2,323	Home Run Percentage 2.1	Batting Ave. .320
At Bats 8,860	Runs Scored 1,774	Slugging Ave. .480
Hits 2,839	RBIs 1,427	Pinch Hit At Bats 91
Doubles 574 (10th)	Bases on Balls 1,185	Pinch Hits 23
Triples 146	Stolen Bases 182	

☆

Robert Gibson

(Bob)

B. Nov. 9, 1935
StL–NL 1959–75

NUMBER OF RECORDS ESTABLISHED: 6

NATIONAL LEAGUE RECORDS

Career Pitching Records

Strikeouts	3,117	11	

WORLD SERIES RECORDS

Game Pitching Records

1968	Strikeouts	17	Never Broken

7-Game Series Pitching Records

1964	Strikeouts	31	4	
1967	Most Wins	3		Tied
1968	Strikeouts	35		Never Broken

Career Pitching Records—1964–68

Strikeouts per 9 Inn.	10.2	Never Broken

SUMMARY

Bob Gibson was one of the great strikeout pitchers. In a sensational 17-year career, the man with the blazing fastball whiffed 3,117 batters, the most of any National League pitcher up to that time.

Gibson won 20 or more games five times and won 251 games in all. He was a seven-time league leader.

Gibson had spectacular years in 1968 and 1970 when he won the Cy Young and MVP awards. In 1968 he won 22, lost 9, tossed 13 shutouts, and spun an incredible 1.12 ERA, which was the lowest in over 50 years.

Gibson excelled in World Series play and struck out more batters in one game and in a seven-game series than any pitcher in baseball history.

Bob Gibson was welcomed into the Hall of Fame in 1981.

POSTSEASON AWARDS

1968 MVP, Cy Young
1970 MVP, Cy Young

CAREER STATISTICS:

17 Years	Games Started 482	Shutouts 56
Wins 251	Games Completed 255	Relief Appearances 46
Losses 174	Innings 3,885	Relief Wins 6
Winning Percentage .591	Hits 3,279	Relief Losses 4
ERA 2.91	Bases on Balls 1,336	Saves 6
Total Games 528	Strikeouts 3,117 (8th)	

Vernon Louis Gomez
(Lefty, Goofy, The Gay Castillion)
B. Nov. 26, 1909, D. June 10, 1989
NY–AL 1930–42, Was–AL 1943

NUMBER OF RECORDS ESTABLISHED: 9

ALL-STAR GAME RECORDS

Game Pitching Records

1935	Most Innings	6		Never Broken

Career Pitching Records—1933–38

Wins	3		Never Broken
Games	5	13	
Innings	18	28	
Hits Allowed	11	2	

WORLD SERIES RECORDS

4-Game Series Pitching Records

1932	Fewest Bases on Balls	1		Tied

6-Game Series Pitching Records

1936	Most Bases on Balls	11		Tied

Career Pitching Records—1932–39

	Wins	6	3	
	Highest Winning Percentage	1.000		Tied

SUMMARY

Known as "Goofy" because of his sense of humor, Lefty Gomez led the league in strikeouts three times and won more than 20 games four times. His best year was in 1934, when he was 26–5. He was a 14-time league leader.

Not only did Gomez have a 6–0 record in World Series play, he also won more All-Star Games than any other pitcher.

Gomez was elected into the Hall of Fame in 1972.

CAREER STATISTICS:

14 Years	Games Started 320	Shutouts 28
Wins 189	Games Completed 173	Relief Appearances 48
Losses 102	Innings 2,503	Relief Wins 5
Winning Percentage .649	Hits 2,290	Relief Losses 12
ERA 3.34	Bases on Balls 1,095	Saves 9
Total Games 368	Strikeouts 1,468	

Leon Allen Goslin
(Goose)
B. Oct. 16, 1900, D. May 15, 1971
Was–AL 1921–30, StL–AL 1930–32, Was–AL 1933, Det–AL 1934–37, Was–AL 1938

NUMBER OF RECORDS ESTABLISHED: 23

AMERICAN LEAGUE RECORDS

Season Fielding Records—LF

1925	Most Putouts	385	7
	Most Total Chances	421	7

Career Fielding Records—LF

	Most Games Played	2,007	Never Broken
	Most Putouts	4,395	Never Broken
	Most Errors	195	Never Broken
	Most Total Chances	4,791	Never Broken

MAJOR LEAGUE RECORDS

Season Fielding Records—LF

1925	Most Putouts	385	1
	Most Total Chances	421	1

WORLD SERIES RECORDS

Game Batting Records

1924	Most At Bats	6	49	
	Most Hits	4	58	
1934	Most At Bats	6	39	

Game Fielding Records—LF

1934	Most Errors	1	Tied
	Most Errors	1	Tied
1935	Most Errors	1	Tied

7-Game Series Batting Records

1924	Most Hits	11	1
	Most Home Runs	3	2
	Most RBIs	7	7
	Most Total Bases	21	1
1925	Most Home Runs	3	1

Career Fielding Records—LF—1924–35

Most Putouts	62	Never Broken
Most Errors	3	Tied
Most Total Chances	65	Never Broken
Chances w/o Errors	45	Never Broken

SUMMARY

"Goose" Goslin was one of the game's most successful leftfielders. When he retired in 1938 he had played the most games and had the most putouts and total chances of any leftfielder in American League history. Goslin was a five-time league leader in fielding.

His lifetime batting average is a strong .316, and he slugged an even .500. He batted .300 or over 11 times, with a high of .379 in 1928.

Goslin was inducted into the Hall of Fame in 1968.

CAREER STATISTICS:

18 Years
Games 2,287
At Bats 8,655
Hits 2,735
Doubles 500
Triples 173

Home Runs 248
Home Run Percentage 2.9
Runs Scored 1,483
RBIs 1,609
Bases on Balls 949
Stolen Bases 175

Strikeouts 585
Batting Ave. .316
Slugging Ave. .500
Pinch Hit At Bats 75
Pinch Hits 22

Henry Benjamin Greenberg
(Hammerin' Hank)
B. Jan. 1, 1911
Det–AL 1930–46, Pit–NL 1947

NUMBER OF RECORDS ESTABLISHED: 2

WORLD SERIES RECORDS

Game Batting Records

1934	Most Hits	4	48

7-Game Series Batting Records

1934	Most Strikeouts	9	24

SUMMARY

Hank Greenberg established only two records during his career, yet he was a genuine super-star. He led the league in various batting departments 18 times!

Greenberg was a four-time home run champion and a four-time RBI leader. He twice led the league in doubles and bases on balls. He scored more runs in 1938 than any other American League player and three times had the highest home run percentage.

In 1940, Hank led the league in slugging, RBIs, home runs, home run percentage, and doubles while batting .340 and winning his second MVP title. He ended his career with a .313 batting average, and his .605 slugging average is the fifth best in the game.

During his 13 years of play, he batted over .300 nine times, eight of them in a row. And as a defensive first baseman, he won five fielding crowns.

Greenberg entered the Hall of Fame in 1956.

POSTSEASON AWARDS

1935 MVP
1940 MVP

CAREER STATISTICS:

13 Years	Home Runs 331	Strikeouts 844
Games 1,394	Home Run Percentage 6.4 (9th)	Batting Ave. .313
At Bats 5,193	Runs Scored 1,051	Slugging Ave. .605 (5th)
Hits 1,628	RBIs 1,276	Pinch Hit At Bats 16
Doubles 379	Bases on Balls 852	Pinch Hits 3
Triples 71	Stolen Bases 58	

Clark Calvin Griffith
(The Old Fox)
B. Nov. 20, 1869, D. Oct. 27, 1955

StL–AA 1891, Bos–AA 1891, Chi–NL 1893–1900, Chi–AL 1901–02, NY–AL 1903–07,
Cin–NL 1909–11, Was–AL 1912–20
Manager: Chi–AL 1901–02, NY–AL 1903–08, Cin–NL 1909–11, Was–AL 1912–20

NUMBER OF RECORDS ESTABLISHED AS PLAYER: 18

NUMBER OF RECORDS ESTABLISHED AS MANAGER: 10

TOTAL: 28

PLAYER RECORDS

AMERICAN ASSOCIATION RECORDS

Rookie Pitching Records

1891	Wins in Relief	7	Never Broken
	Cons. Wins in Relief	7	Never Broken
	Highest Winning Percentage	1.000	Tied
	Wins & Saves	7	Never Broken

Season Pitching Records

1891	Wins in Relief	7		Never Broken
	Cons. Wins in Relief	7		Never Broken
	Highest Winning Percentage	1.000		Tied
	Wins & Saves	7		Never Broken

AMERICAN LEAGUE RECORDS

Season Pitching Records

1901	Highest Winning Percentage	.774	1
	Shutouts	5	2
	Relief Wins	3	4
	Wins & Saves	4	1
1905	Relief Games	18	3

Season Pitching Title Records

1901	Winning Percentage Titles (Starting Pitchers)	1	10
	Shutout Titles	1	1

MAJOR LEAGUE RECORDS

Season Pitching Records

1891	Relief Wins	7	3	
	Cons. Relief Wins	7	3	
	Winning Percentage	1.000		Tied

MANAGER RECORDS

American League Season Records

1901	Wins	83	2
	Winning Percentage	.610	2
	Games Won Pennant By	4	1

American League Career Records

	Years	17	30
	Games	2,444	30
	Wins	1,269	30
	Losses	1,129	30

Major League Career Records

	Years	20	12
	Games	2,916	12
	Losses	1,367	12

SUMMARY

In his rookie season, Clark Griffith was a fine pitcher. He starred in relief at a time when relief pitching was not a big part of the game. Later, as a starter, he won over 20 games seven times. In all, he won 240 and lost 141 for a fabulous .630 winning percentage.

Clark Griffith's White Sox won the pennant in 1901, the very first year he managed them. Unfortunately, there was no World Series that year because the American and National Leagues were at war.

Griffith put in 20 years as a manager but he never won another pennant. He finished second four times and third twice. When he retired from managing he had won 1,491 games and had a winning percentage of .522.

Griffith became a Hall of Famer in 1946.

CAREER STATISTICS:

21 Years
Wins 240
Losses 141
Winning Percentage .630
ERA 3.31
Total Games 453

Games Started 372
Games Completed 337
Innings 3,386
Hits 3,670
Bases on Balls 774
Strikeouts 955

Shutouts 23
Relief Appearances 181
Relief Wins 26
Relief Losses 9
Saves 6

CAREER STATISTICS AS MANAGER:

20 Years
Games 2,916

Wins 1,491
Losses 1,367

Winning Percentage .522
First-place Finishes 1

Burleigh Arland Grimes
(Ol' Stubblebeard)

B. Aug. 18, 1893, D. Dec. 6, 1985

Pit–NL 1916–17, Bkn–NL 1918–26, NY–NL 1927, Pit–NL 1928–29, Bos–NL 1930, StL–NL 1930–31,
Chi–NL 1932–33, StL–NL 1933–34, Pit–NL 1934, NY–AL 1934
Manager: Bkn–NL 1937–38

NUMBER OF RECORDS ESTABLISHED AS PLAYER: 9

WORLD SERIES RECORDS

Game Pitching Records

1920	Most Earned Runs Allowed	7	8

4-Game Series Pitching Records

1932	Total Games	2	6
	Relief Games	2	22

6-Game Series Pitching Records

1930	Losses	2	51

7-Game Series Pitching Records

1920	Starts	3	42	
	Losses	2		Tied
	Shutouts	1	37	
	Most Bases on Balls	9	4	
	Hits Allowed	23	4	

SUMMARY

Burleigh Grimes appeared in 617 games during a hard-traveled 19-year career. Winning 270 games and dropping 212, he won over 20 games five times and was a 21-time league leader.

Grimes played with nine teams, but did his best work with the Brooklyn Dodgers from 1918 through 1926. During that time he won 20 or more games four times. He also had a brilliant season with Pittsburgh in 1928, when he won 25 and lost 14. In that year he led the league in six categories.

Grimes was a famous spitball pitcher, who in the early days did not have to conceal the fact. The rules committee passed a rule in 1920 permitting all spitball pitchers to continue until the end of their careers.

Grimes was accepted by the Hall of Fame in 1964.

CAREER STATISTICS:

19 Years	Games Started 495	Shutouts 35
Wins 270	Games Completed 314	Relief Appearances 122
Losses 212	Innings 4,180	Relief Wins 21
Winning Percentage .560	Hits 4,412	Relief Losses 19
ERA 3.53	Bases on Balls 1,295	Saves 18
Total Games 617	Strikeouts 1,512	

CAREER STATISTICS AS MANAGER:

2 Years	Wins 130	Winning Percentage .432
Games 305	Losses 171	First-place Finishes 0

Robert Moses Grove
(Mose, Lefty)
B. Mar. 6, 1900, D. May 23, 1975
Phi–AL 1925–33, Bos–AL 1934–41

NUMBER OF RECORDS ESTABLISHED: 24

AMERICAN LEAGUE RECORDS

Season Pitching Records

1931	Highest Winning Percentage	.886	5

Season Pitching Title Records

1931	Winning Percentage Titles	3	2
1932	ERA Titles	5	3
1933	Winning Percentage Titles	4	6
1935	ERA Titles	6	1
1936	ERA Titles	7	2
1938	ERA Titles	8	1
1939	ERA Titles	9	Never Broken
	Winning Percentage Titles	5	Never Broken

Career Pitching Records

	Highest Winning Percentage	.680	6

MAJOR LEAGUE RECORDS

Season Pitching Records

1931	Highest Winning Percentage	.886	5

Season Pitching Title Records

1931	Winning Percentage Titles	3	2	
1932	ERA Titles	5	3	
1933	Winning Percentage Titles	4	6	
1935	ERA Titles	6	1	
1936	ERA Titles	7	2	
1938	ERA Titles	8	1	
1939	ERA Titles	9		Never Broken
	Winning Percentage Titles	5		Never Broken

ALL-STAR GAME RECORDS

Game Pitching Records

1933	Strikeouts	3	1
	Saves	1	4

Career Pitching Records—1933

	Saves	1	4

WORLD SERIES RECORDS

5-Game Series Pitching Records

1929	Saves	2	Tied

7-Game Series Pitching Records

1931	Starts	3	31

SUMMARY

In a 17-year career, Lefty Grove won 300 games and lost 141. This winning percentage of .680 is the fifth best in baseball. In 1931 he compiled an amazing 31–4 record.

Grove led the league in various pitching categories 35 times. He was an eight-time 20-game winner (four titles), he had eight seasons with a winning percentage of over .700 (five titles), he was a nine-time ERA champion (a major league record), a three-time consecutive complete games leader (1931–33), a seven-time consecutive strikeouts king, and a three-time shutouts king, and he won single crowns in total games, starts, bases on balls, and saves.

Grove became a member of the Hall of Fame in 1947.

CAREER STATISTICS:

17 Years

Wins 300

Losses 141

Winning Percentage .680 (5th)

ERA 3.06

Total Games 616

Games Started 456

Games Completed 300

Innings 3,941

Hits 3,849

Bases on Balls 1,187

Strikeouts 2,266

Shutouts 35

Relief Appearances 160

Relief Wins 33

Relief Losses 22

Saves 55

Charles James Hafey
(Chick)
B. Feb 12, 1903, D. July 2, 1973
StL–NL 1924–31, Cin–NL 1932–37

NUMBER OF RECORDS ESTABLISHED: 13

NATIONAL LEAGUE RECORDS

Career Fielding Records—LF

Highest Fielding Ave.	.973	1	

MAJOR LEAGUE RECORDS

Career Fielding Records—LF

Highest Fielding Ave.	.973	1	

WORLD SERIES RECORDS

Game Fielding Records—LF

1926	Most Putouts	6	47	
1928	Most Errors	1		Tied
1931	Most Errors	1		Tied

4-Game Fielding Records—LF

1928	Most Putouts	8	11	
	Most Errors	1		Tied

6-Game Batting Records

1930	Most Doubles	5	47
	Most Extra Base Hits	5	47

7-Game Fielding Records—LF

1926	Most Putouts	21		Tied
	Most Assists	1	29	

Career Fielding Records—LF—1926–31

Most Putouts	46	4
Most Errors	2	4

SUMMARY

Chick Hafey batted over .300 nine times with a league-leading high of .349 in 1931. He also led the National League in slugging in 1927 with a .590 average.

Hafey participated in four World Series with the Cardinals and rousted opposing pitchers for 18 hits, 7 of which were doubles. He ranks eighth on the all-time doubles list.

Hafey was voted into the Hall of Fame in 1971.

CAREER STATISTICS:

13 Years
Games 1,283
At Bats 4,625
Hits 1,466
Doubles 341
Triples 67

Home Runs 164
Home Run Percentage 3.5
Runs Scored 777
RBIs 833
Bases on Balls 372
Stolen Bases 70

Strikeouts 477
Batting Ave. .317
Slugging Ave. .526
Pinch Hit At Bats 88
Pinch Hits 22

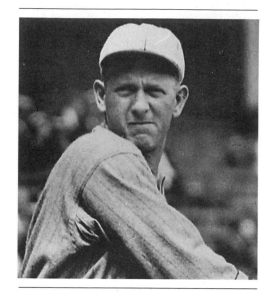

Jesse Joseph Haines
(Pop)
B. July 22, 1893, D. Aug. 5, 1978
Cin–NL 1918, StL–NL 1920–37

NUMBER OF RECORDS ESTABLISHED: 1

WORLD SERIES RECORDS

7-Game Series Pitching Records

1926	Shutouts	1	31

SUMMARY

Jesse Haines had a 19-year career, winning 210 games and losing 158. He had three seasons of winning 20 or more games, and he was a four-time league leader in various pitching departments. In 1920 he appeared in the most games, tossed the most shutouts in 1921, and in 1927 was the leader in complete games and shutouts.

His most successful season was 1927, when he won 24 and lost 10. In 1928 his record was 20–8.

Haines was elected to the Hall of Fame in 1970.

CAREER STATISTICS:

19 Years

Wins 210

Losses 158

Winning Percentage .571

ERA 3.64

Total Games 555

Games Started 388

Games Completed 209

Innings 3,209

Hits 3,460

Bases on Balls 871

Strikeouts 981

Shutouts 24

Relief Appearances 167

Relief Wins 25

Relief Losses 14

Saves 10

William Robert Hamilton
(Sliding Billy)
B. Feb. 16, 1866, D. Dec. 15, 1940
KC–AA 1888–89, Phi–NL 1890–95, Bos–NL 1896–1901

NUMBER OF RECORDS ESTABLISHED: 41

NATIONAL LEAGUE RECORDS

Season Batting Records

1891	Most Stolen Bases (Old Rule—1876–97)	115		Never Broken
1894	Most Singles	176	1	
	Most Runs Scored	196		Never Broken
1898	Most Stolen Bases (New Rule—1898–Present)	59	1	

Season Batting Title Records

1895	Most Bases on Balls Titles	3	1
	Most Runs Scored Titles	3	2
1896	Most Bases on Balls Titles	4	1
1897	Most Bases on Balls Titles	5	9
	Most Runs Scored Titles	4	23

Season Fielding Records—LF

1891	Most Putouts	287	1
	Most Total Chances	335	1
1892	Most Putouts	291	1
	Most Total Chances	345	1

Season Base-Running Title Records

1890	Most Stolen Bases Titles	1	1
1891	Most Stolen Bases Titles	2	3
1894	Most Stolen Bases Titles	3	1
1895	Most Stolen Bases Titles	4	1
1896	Most Stolen Bases Titles	5	2
1898	Most Stolen Bases Titles	6	24

Career Batting Records

	Most Runs Scored per Game	1.06		Never Broken
	Most Bases on Balls	1,096	12	
	Highest Bases on Balls Ave.	159	52	
	Stolen Bases (Old Rule)	811		Never Broken
	Stolen Bases (New Rule)	126	16	

MAJOR LEAGUE RECORDS

Season Base-Running Title Records

1890	Most Stolen Bases Titles	1	1
1891	Most Stolen Bases Titles	2	3
1894	Most Stolen Bases Titles	3	1
1895	Most Stolen Bases Titles	4	1
1896	Most Stolen Bases Titles	5	2
1898	Most Stolen Bases Titles	6	24

Season Batting Records

| 1894 | Most Singles | 176 | 1 | |
| | Most Runs Scored | 196 | | Never Broken |

Season Base-Running Records

| 1891 | Most Stolen Bases (Old Rule) | 115 | | Never Broken |
| 1898 | Most Stolen Bases (New Rule) | 59 | 1 | |

Season Fielding Records—LF

| 1891 | Most Putouts | 287 | 1 |
| 1892 | Most Putouts | 291 | 1 |

Career Batting Records

Most Runs Scored per Game	1.06		Never Broken
Most Bases on Balls	1,187	27	
Most Stolen Bases (Old Rule)	811		Never Broken
Most Stolen Bases (New Rule)	126	16	
Highest Bases on Balls Ave.	159	52	

SUMMARY

Billy Hamilton was the first great base stealer in baseball. Under the old rules, from 1876 to 1897, a runner was given credit for a stolen base if he advanced from first to third on a single or advanced a base on a fly or ground ball. In 1898, the rule was changed so that a stolen base was granted only when a runner advanced a base on the throw from the pitcher to the catcher. Under the old rule Hamilton set a record by stealing 115 bases. Under the new rule, he set a record by stealing 59.

Hamilton led the league four times in getting walks. He was also an outstanding hitter, with a lifetime batting average of .344, eighth on the all-time list. His best seasons were in 1893, 1894, and 1895, when he batted .380, .399, and .389. He had 12 consecutive years of batting over .300.

In 1894 Hamilton scored 196 runs, which averaged out to slightly more than 1½ per game, one of the least likely records to be broken.

Hamilton was elected to the Hall of Fame in 1961.

CAREER STATISTICS:

14 Years
Games 1,593
At Bats 6,284
Hits 2,163
Doubles 242
Triples 94

Home Runs 40
Home Run Percentage 0.6
Runs Scored 1,692
RBIs 736
Bases on Balls 1,187
Stolen Bases 937 (2nd)

Strikeouts 218
Batting Ave. .344 (8th)
Slugging Ave. .432
Pinch Hit At Bats 5
Pinch Hits 2

Stanley Raymond Harris
(Bucky)

B. Nov. 8, 1896, D. Nov. 8, 1977

Was–AL 1919–28, Det–AL 1929, 1931
Manager: Was–AL 1924–28, Det–AL 1929–33, Bos–AL 1934, Was–AL 1935–42, Phi–NL 1943,
NY–AL 1947–48, Was–AL 1950–54, Det–AL 1955–56

NUMBER OF RECORDS ESTABLISHED AS PLAYER: 16

AMERICAN LEAGUE RECORDS

Season Fielding Records—2B

1921	Most Double Plays	91	1
1922	Most Double Plays	116	1
	Most Putouts	479	52
1923	Most Double Plays	120	12

MAJOR LEAGUE RECORDS

Season Fielding Records—2B

| 1922 | Most Double Plays | 116 | 1 |
| 1923 | Most Double Plays | 120 | 12 |

WORLD SERIES RECORDS

Game Batting Records

1924	Most At Bats	6	49

Game Fielding Records—2B

1924	Most Putouts	8	9	
	Most Assists	8		Tied

7-Game Series Records

1924	Most At Bats	33		Tied
	Most Hits	11	1	
	Most Singles	9	1	
	Most RBIs	7	7	
	Most Putouts	26		Never Broken
	Most Assists	28	22	
	Most Errors	2	10	

SUMMARY

As a rookie in 1920, Bucky Harris played a steady second base and batted an even .300. He remained a consistent if nonstellar hitter throughout his 12-year career and ended with a .274 average.

Harris was a player-manager from 1924 to 1931. In his first two seasons as manager he won two pennants and one World Series. Harris did not win another pennant until 1947, when he managed the New York Yankees. He then won his second World Series.

In three stints Bucky Harris managed the Washington Senators for 15 years during his 29-year career. In World Series play, he managed in 21 games, won 11 (9th), lost 10, and had a winning percentage of .524 (7th).

Harris entered the Hall of Fame in 1975.

CAREER STATISTICS:

12 Years	Home Run Percentage 0.2	Slugging Ave. .354
Games 1,264	Runs Scored 722	Pinch Hit At Bats 1
At Bats 4,736	RBIs 506	Pinch Hits 1
Hits 1,297	Bases on Balls 472	
Doubles 224	Stolen Bases 166	
Triples 64	Strikeouts 310	
Home Runs 9	Batting Ave. .274	

CAREER STATISTICS AS MANAGER:

29 Years	Wins 2,159 (3rd)	Winning Percentage .493
Games 4,410 (3rd)	Losses 2,219 (3rd)	First-place Finishes 3

Charles Leo Hartnett

(Gabby)

B. Dec. 20, 1900, D. Dec. 20, 1972

Chi–NL 1922–40, NY–NL 1941
Manager: Chi–NL 1938–40

NUMBER OF RECORDS ESTABLISHED AS PLAYER: 13

NATIONAL LEAGUE RECORDS

Career Fielding Records—C

Most Games Played	1,790	2	
Most Putouts	7,292	24	
Most Double Plays	173		Never Broken
Most Total Chances	8,685	33	

MAJOR LEAGUE RECORDS

Career Fielding Records—C

Most Games Played	1,790	5
Most Putouts	7,292	5

ALL-STAR GAME RECORDS

Game Batting Records

1933	Most Games Played	1	1
1934	Most Games Played	2	1
1935	Most Games Played	3	1
1936	Most Games Played	4	1
	Most Triples	1	42
1937	Most Games Played	5	1

Career Batting Records—1933–37

	Most Games Played	5	1
	Most Triples	1	36

WORLD SERIES RECORDS

4-Game Series Fielding Records—C

1932	Most Assists	5	Never Broken

SUMMARY

Gabby Hartnett was a fine hitting catcher with a lifetime batting average of .297. His most productive season was 1937, when he batted at a .354 clip. In 1935 he smoked enemy pitchers for a .344 average.

Gabby was a superior catcher on defense and led the National League a record-setting 30 times! From 1934 to 1937 he led the league in fielding average. He made only two errors in 1937 for a .996 average. When he retired in 1941 he had played more games behind the plate, made more putouts and double plays, and had more total chances than any catcher in National League history.

Hartnett was welcomed into the Hall of Fame in 1955.

CAREER STATISTICS:

20 Years	Home Runs 236	Strikeouts 697
Games 1,990	Home Run Percentage 3.7	Batting Ave. .297
At Bats 6,432	Runs Scored 867	Slugging Ave. .489
Hits 1,912	RBIs 1,179	Pinch Hit At Bats 144
Doubles 396	Bases on Balls 703	Pinch Hits 39
Triples 64	Stolen Bases 28	

CAREER STATISTICS AS MANAGER:

3 Years	Wins 203	Winning Percentage .536
Games 383	Losses 176	First-place Finishes 0

Harry Edwin Heilmann
(Slug)

B. Aug. 3, 1894, D. July 9, 1951
Det–AL 1914–29, Cin–NL 1930–32

NUMBER OF RECORDS ESTABLISHED: 0

SUMMARY

Harry Heilmann enjoyed a fabulous 17-year career with a lifetime batting average of .342, but he did not create a single record.

Harry was a four-time batting champion, with averages of .403, .398, .394, and .393. Heilmann played for the Detroit Tigers with other Hall of Famers and batting champions Ty Cobb and Heinie Manush, yet during this time they never won a pennant.

Heilmann entered the Hall of Fame in 1952.

CAREER STATISTICS:

17 Years	Home Runs 183	Strikeouts 550
Games 2,146	Home Run Percentage 2.4	Batting Ave. .342
At Bats 7,787	Runs Scored 1,291	Slugging Ave. .520
Hits 2,660	RBIs 1,551	Pinch Hit At Bats 75
Doubles 542	Stolen Bases 112	Pinch Hits 23
Triples 151	Bases on Balls 856	

William Jennings Bryan Herman
(Billy)
B. July 7, 1909
Chi–NL 1931–41, Bkn–NL 1941–46, Bos–NL 1946, Pit–NL 1947
Manager: Pit–NL 1947, Bos–AL 1964–66

NUMBER OF RECORDS ESTABLISHED AS PLAYER: 15

NATIONAL LEAGUE RECORDS

Rookie Fielding Records—2B

1932	Most Assists	527	12	

Season Fielding Records—2B

1933	Most Putouts	466		Never Broken

Career Fielding Records—2B

Most Games Played	1,829	16
Most Putouts	4,780	25
Most Total Chances	10,815	25
Most Double Plays	1,183	16

MAJOR LEAGUE RECORDS

Rookie Fielding Records—2B

| 1932 | Most Assists | 527 | 12 | |

ALL-STAR GAME RECORDS

Game Batting Records

1936	Most Singles	2	1	
1940	Most Singles	3		Never Broken
1943	Most Games Played	9	1	

Career Batting Records—1934–43

	Most Games Played	9	1
	Most Hits	11	17
	Most Singles	9	20

Career Fielding Records—2B

| | Most Errors | 2 | 19 |

WORLD SERIES RECORDS

4-Game Series Fielding Records—2B

| 1938 | Most Errors | 2 | Tied |

SUMMARY

Billy Herman had a lifetime batting average of .304 and won batting crowns in most hits, doubles, and triples. He had eight seasons of batting over .300, with a high of .341 in 1935, when he led the league in hits with 227 and doubles with 57.

Herman also was an outstanding glove man, as he led all second basemen in various fielding categories 26 times.

Herman was named to the Hall of Fame in 1975.

CAREER STATISTICS:

15 Years	Home Runs 47	Strikeouts 428
Games 1,922	Home Run Percentage 0.6	Batting Ave. .304
At Bats 7,707	Runs Scored 1,163	Slugging Ave. .407
Hits 2,345	RBIs 839	Pinch Hit At Bats 8
Doubles 486	Bases on Balls 737	Pinch Hits 1
Triples 82	Stolen Bases 67	

CAREER STATISTICS AS MANAGER:

| 4 Years | Wins 189 | Winning Percentage .408 |
| Games 465 | Losses 274 | First-place Finishes 0 |

Harry Bartholomew Hooper

B. Aug. 24, 1887, D. Dec. 18, 1974
Bos–AL 1909–20, Chi–AL 1921–25

NUMBER OF RECORDS ESTABLISHED: 19

AMERICAN LEAGUE RECORDS

Career Fielding Records—RF

Most Games Played	2,153	49	
Most Putouts	3,718	49	
Most Assists	322		Never Broken
Most Errors	140		Never Broken
Most Double Plays	79		Never Broken
Most Total Chances	4,180	49	

MAJOR LEAGUE RECORDS

Career Fielding Records—RF

Most Games Played	2,153	20	
Most Putouts	3,718	20	
Most Double Plays	79		Never Broken
Most Total Chances	4,180	20	

WORLD SERIES RECORDS

Game Fielding Records—RF

1912	Most Assists	2		Tied
1915	Most Errors	1	2	

5-Game Series Batting Records

1915	Most Home Runs	2	54	
	Most Total Bases	13	2	
	Most Runs Scored	6		Tied

5-Game Series Fielding Records—RF

1915	Most Errors	1	7	
1916	Most Assists	2		Tied

8-Game Series Fielding Records—RF

1912	Most Assists	2		Tied

Career Batting Records—1912–18

	Longest Hitting Streak	13	39

SUMMARY

When Harry Hooper retired in 1925, he had made the most assists, errors, putouts, double plays, and total chances, and played in more games in right field than any player in American League history. He also established four major league marks, and his 79 double plays is a major league record that still stands.

Hooper batted over .300 five times and had a lifetime batting average of .281, but he really sparkled with the glove. He had a tremendous throwing arm, and his 322 assists are still an American League record. In his 17-year career, Hooper led the league in various fielding departments five times.

Hooper was inducted into the Hall of Fame in 1971.

CAREER STATISTICS:

17 Years	Home Runs 75	Strikeouts 412
Games 2,308	Home Run Percentage 0.9	Batting Ave. .281
At Bats 8,785	Runs Scored, 1,429	Slugging Ave. .387
Hits 2,466	RBIs 817	Pinch Hit At Bats 18
Doubles 389	Bases on Balls 1,136	Pinch Hits 5
Triples 160	Stolen Bases 375	

Rogers Hornsby
(The Rajah)

B. Apr. 27, 1896, D. Jan. 5, 1963

StL–NL 1915–26, NY–NL 1927, Bos–NL 1928, Chi–NL 1929–32, StL–NL 1933, StL–AL 1933–37
Manager: StL–NL 1925–26, Bos–NL 1928, Chi–NL 1930–32, StL–AL 1933–37, 1952,
Cin–NL 1952–53

NUMBER OF RECORDS ESTABLISHED AS PLAYER: 33

NATIONAL LEAGUE RECORDS

Season Batting Records

1921	Most Total Bases	378	1	
1922	Most Total Bases	450		Never Broken
	Most Hits	250	7	
	Most Home Runs	42	7	
	Highest Home Run Percentage	6.7	1	
	Most Extra Base Hits	102	8	
	Highest Slugging Ave.	.722	3	
1925	Highest Home Run Percentage	7.7	3	
	Highest Slugging Ave.	.756		Never Broken

Season Batting Title Records

1922	Most Triple Crown Titles	1	3	
1924	Most Hits Titles	4	25	
	Most Total Bases Titles	5	1	
	Most Slugging Titles	6	1	
1925	Most MVP Titles	1	4	
	Most Triple Crown Titles	2		Tied
	Most Total Bases Titles	6	4	
	Most RBI Titles	4		Tied
	Most Slugging Titles	7	3	
1928	Most Slugging Titles	8	1	
1929	Most MVP Titles	2	1	
	Most Total Bases Titles	7	40	
	Most Runs Scored Titles	5	57	
	Most Slugging Titles	9		Never Broken

Career Batting Records

	Most Home Runs	297	10	
	Highest Home Run Percentage	3.7	10	
	Highest Slugging Ave.	.577		Never Broken

MAJOR LEAGUE RECORDS

Season Batting Title Records

1922	Most Triple Crown Titles	1	3	
1925	Most Triple Crown Titles	2		Tied
	Most Total Bases Titles	6	4	
	Most RBI Titles	4	1	
1929	Most MVP Titles	2	9	
	Most Total Bases Titles	7	40	

WORLD SERIES RECORDS

5-Game Series Batting Records

1929	Most Strikeouts	8	Tied

SUMMARY

One of the greatest National League players and right-hand hitters of all time is Rogers Hornsby. The "Rajah" was a league leader in various batting categories a fantastic 43 times! He won the Triple Crown in 1922 and 1925 and was awarded the MVP in 1925. In 1929, Hornsby won his second MVP honor. He also won nine titles in various fielding departments at second base.

Hornsby's achievements include seven seasons of more than 200 hits (four titles), seven seasons of more than 40 doubles (four titles), three seasons of 17 or more triples (two titles), five seasons of more than 25 homers (two titles), three home run percentage titles, six seasons of scoring more than 100 runs (five titles), five seasons of more than 100 RBIs (four titles), three bases on balls crowns, no strikeout titles, 19 seasons of batting well over .300, including four seasons of batting over .400 (seven titles), and 12 seasons of slugging over .500 (9 titles). Hornsby is the only player in baseball history who had a 5-year batting average of over .400. From 1921 to 1925 he averaged .402.

Hornsby became a Hall of Famer in 1942.

POSTSEASON AWARDS

1922 MVP
1929 MVP

CAREER STATISTICS:

23 Years	Home Runs 301	Strikeouts 679
Games 2,259	Home Run Percentage 3.7	Batting Ave. .358 (2nd)
At Bats 8,173	Runs Scored 1,579	Slugging Ave. .577 (7th)
Hits 2,930	RBIs 1,584	Pinch Hit At Bats 86
Doubles 541	Bases on Balls 1,038	Pinch Hits 26
Triples 169	Stolen Bases 135	

CAREER STATISTICS AS MANAGER:

13 Years	Wins 680	Winning Percentage .460
Games 1,494	Losses 798	First-place Finishes 1

Waite Charles Hoyt
(Schoolboy)

B. Sept. 9, 1899, D. Aug. 25, 1984

NY–NL 1918, Bos–AL 1919–20, NY–AL 1921–30, Det–AL 1930–31,
Phi–AL 1931, Bkn–NL 1932, NY–NL 1932, Pit–NL 1933–37, Bkn–NL 1937–38

NUMBER OF RECORDS ESTABLISHED: 13

WORLD SERIES RECORDS

4-Game Series Pitching Records

1922	Games	2	16	
1928	Games	2	10	
	Starts	2		Tied
	Complete Games	2		Tied
	Wins	2		Tied
	Innings	18		Tied
	Most Bases on Balls	6	26	

7-Game Series Pitching Records

1926	Fewest Bases on Balls (Min. 10 Inn.)	1	8

8-Game Series Pitching Records

1921	Lowest ERA	0.00	Never Broken

Career Pitching Records—1921–31

Wins	6	11
Games	12	22
Series Played	7	11
Starts	11	33

SUMMARY

Waite Hoyt is one of the few pitchers who have had careers of 20 years or more. He played on seven different teams, including the New York Yankees, Boston, Detroit, Philadelphia, Brooklyn, Pittsburgh, and the New York Giants.

The 1927 and 1928 Yankees were helped by his 22–7 and 23–7 records. Hoyt played for the Yankees from 1921 to 1930.

Hoyt established 13 records, all in World Series play. He appeared in six World Series with the Yankees and one with the Athletics. The highlight of his Series career came in 1928, when he set six records, four of which remain unbroken.

Hoyt's oldest unbroken record, however, was set in the 1921 Series, where he was unscored upon in 27 innings and posted a perfect 0.00 ERA.

When Hoyt retired in 1938, he had participated in the most World Series, won the most Series games, and had the most appearances and games started. Overall he won 237 games and lost 182.

Hoyt was elected to the Hall of Fame in 1969.

CAREER STATISTICS:

21 Years	Games Started 434	Shutouts 26
Wins 237	Games Completed 224	Relief Appearances 240
Losses 182	Innings 3,763	Relief Wins 39
Winning Percentage .566	Hits 4,037	Relief Losses 26
ERA 3.59	Bases on Balls 1,003	Saves 52
Total Games 674	Strikeouts 1,206	

Carl Owen Hubbell
(The King, The Meal Ticket)
B. June 22, 1903, D. Nov. 21, 1988
NY–NL 1928–43

NUMBER OF RECORDS ESTABLISHED: 7

NATIONAL LEAGUE RECORDS

Season Pitching Title Records

1936	MVP Titles	2	2

MAJOR LEAGUE RECORDS

Season Pitching Title Records

1936	MVP Titles	2	2

ALL-STAR GAME RECORDS

Game Pitching Records

1934	Strikeouts	6	Tied
	Cons. Strikeouts	5	Tied

Career Pitching Records—1933–40

Total Games	5	11
Strikeouts	11	11

WORLD SERIES RECORDS

Game Pitching Records

1933	Fewest Earned Runs (11 Inn.)	0	Never Broken

SUMMARY

Carl Hubbell used his unusual screwball pitch to win over 20 games five times in a row. In a 17-year career he was a twelve-time league leader. In 1933 he won 23 games, with a 1.66 ERA, 308.2 innings, and 10 shutouts! In 1936 he won 26 while only losing 6, which represents a .813 winning percentage and a cool 2.31 ERA. In 1933 and 1936, "King Carl" won the MVP awards.

Hubbell was a three-time wins and ERA champion. He is perhaps most famous for striking out Hall of Famers Babe Ruth, Lou Gehrig, Jimmie Foxx, Al Simmons, and Joe Cronin consecutively in the 1934 All-Star game.

A less well-known record is his 11 innings of shutout ball in one game in the 1933 World Series—a record that still stands.

Hubbell became a Hall of Famer in 1947.

POSTSEASON AWARDS

1933 MVP
1936 MVP

CAREER STATISTICS:

16 Years	Games Started 432	Shutouts 36
Wins 253	Games Completed 258	Relief Appearances 103
Losses 154	Innings 3,589	Relief Wins 20
Winning Percentage .622	Hits 3,463	Relief Losses 8
ERA 2.97	Bases on Balls 724	Saves 33
Total Games 535	Strikeouts 1,678	

Miller James Huggins
(Hug, The Mighty Mite)

B. Mar. 27, 1879, D. Sept. 25, 1929

Cin–NL 1904–09, StL–NL 1910–16
Manager: StL–NL 1913–17, NY–AL 1918–29

NUMBER OF RECORDS ESTABLISHED AS PLAYER: 6

NUMBER OF RECORDS ESTABLISHED AS MANAGER: 19

TOTAL: 25

PLAYER RECORDS

NATIONAL LEAGUE RECORDS

Rookie Fielding Records—2B

1904	Putouts	337	19
	Assists	448	19
	Total Chances	831	19
	Fielding Ave.	.945	2

Career Fielding Records—2B

Games	1,531	4
Assists	4,683	13

MANAGER RECORDS

American League Season Records

1927	Wins	110	27	
	Winning Percentage	.714	27	
	Games Pennant Won By	23		Never Broken

American League Career Records

Winning Percentage	.595	21
Pennants Won	6	21
Cons. Pennants Won (1921–23)	3	16
Cons. Pennants Won (1926–28)	3	3

Major League Career Records

Pennants Won	6	3

American League World Series Career Records

Most Series	6	21
Games	34	21
Series Won	3	21
Games Won	18	21
Games Lost	15	21
Cons. Series Won	2	22
Winning Percentage (Min. 3 Series)	.545	21

Major League World Series Career Records—1921–28

Games	34	3
Games Won	18	3
Games Lost	15	3
Series Won	3	21

SUMMARY

Little Miller Huggins stood 5'6½" and weighed 140 pounds. His small strike zone enabled him to win four bases on balls titles, and his fleet feet took him to 324 stolen bases. He belted 1,474 hits in a 13-year career, but his .265 batting average was not his calling card into the Hall of Fame. Rather, Huggins ensured his fame as the manager of the New York Yankees "Murderers' Row." His great Yankee team of 1927 won the pennant by 23 games, the most of any team in the American League's history.

When Huggins retired in 1929, he had won more World Series than any manager in baseball history.

Huggins became a Hall of Famer in 1964.

CAREER STATISTICS:

13 Years

Games 1,585

At Bats 5,557

Hits 1,474

Doubles 146

Triples 50

Home Runs 9

Home Run Percentage 0.2

Runs Scored 947

RBIs 318

Bases on Balls 1,002

Stolen Bases 324

Strikeouts 312

Batting Ave. .265

Slugging Ave. .314

Pinch Hit At Bats 30

Pinch Hits 6

CAREER STATISTICS AS MANAGER:

17 Years

Games 2,569

Wins 1,413

Losses 1,134

Winning Percentage .555

First-place Finishes 6

James Augustus Hunter
(Catfish)
B. Apr. 18, 1946
KC–AL 1965–67, Oak–AL, 1968–74, NY–AL 1975–79

NUMBER OF RECORDS ESTABLISHED: 5

AMERICAN LEAGUE RECORDS

Season Pitching Records

1968	Most Perfect Games	1	Tied

Career Pitching Records

	Most Perfect Games	1	Tied

MAJOR LEAGUE RECORDS

	Most Perfect Games	1	Tied

ALL-STAR GAME RECORDS

Career Pitching Records—1967–76

	Losses	2	Tied

SUMMARY

In a 15-year career, "Catfish" Hunter won 224 games and lost 166. He won over 20 games per season for five consecutive years and was an eight-time league leader. Twice he led in wins and winning percentage, and he had single crowns in ERA, starts, complete games, and innings.

Hunter was an excellent control pitcher who never walked more than 85 batters in a season. He struck out more than 100 batters in 11 consecutive seasons. In 1974, he won the Cy Young Award with a 25–12 record.

The "Catfish" appeared in six World Series and is ranked sixth in starts, seventh in games, eighth in wins, and tenth in innings.

Hunter became a Hall of Famer in 1987.

POSTSEASON AWARDS

1974 Cy Young Award

CAREER STATISTICS:

15 Years	Games Started 476	Shutouts 42
Wins 224	Games Completed 181	Relief Appearances 24
Losses 166	Innings 3,448	Relief Wins 2
Winning Percentage .574	Hits 2,958	Relief Losses 0
ERA 3.26	Bases on Balls 954	Saves 1
Total Games 500	Strikeouts 2,012	

Monford Merrill Irvin
(Monte)
B. Feb. 25, 1919
NY–NL 1949–55, Chi–NL 1956

NUMBER OF RECORDS ESTABLISHED: 2

WORLD SERIES RECORDS

Game Batting Records

1951	Most Hits	4	31

6-Game Series Batting Records

1951	Most Singles	10	Tied

SUMMARY

Before coming to the major leagues, Monte Irvin played from 1938 to 1948 in the Negro Leagues. What records we have from those times show that Irvin had 440 at bats with 164 hits for a .373 batting average.

Negro Leagues star "Cool Papa" Bell said, "Most of the black players thought Monte Irvin should have been the first black player in the major leagues. Monte was our best young player at the time. But after Monte went to the Army and came back sick, they passed him up and looked for somebody else."

In his prime, many thought Irvin could throw like Willie Mays, Joe DiMaggio, and Carl Furillo. Irvin was a consistent and fabulous hitter in the clutch. Josh Gibson, the great Negro Leagues catcher, told Monte that when he (Gibson) retired, Irvin would take over as the next "King of Swat."

History was made on July 8, 1949, at Ebbets Field. Monte Irvin and black third baseman Hank Thompson were added to the New York Giants' line-up for the first time. The pitcher for the Dodgers was Don Newcombe. It was the first time a black pitcher faced a black hitter in the major leagues. Thompson went hitless and Irvin, who was used as a pinch hitter, walked.

Monte batted .299 in his first full season and then had three consecutive seasons in which he batted over .300. His best season was in 1953, when he batted .329.

Irvin played in two World Series and entered the record book in 1951, when he got 4 hits in one game and 10 singles in a six-game series.

Irvin was welcomed into the Hall of Fame in 1973.

CAREER STATISTICS:

8 Years	Home Runs 99	Strikeouts 220
Games 764	Home Run Percentage 4.0	Batting Ave. .293
At Bats 2,499	Runs Scored 366	Slugging Ave. .475
Hits 731	RBIs 443	Pinch Hit At Bats 73
Doubles 97	Bases on Balls 351	Pinch Hits 17
Triples 31	Stolen Bases 28	

Travis Calvin Jackson

(Stonewall)

B. Nov. 2, 1903
NY–NL 1922–36

NUMBER OF RECORDS ESTABLISHED: 1

WORLD SERIES RECORDS

Game Batting Records

1924	Most At Bats	6	49

SUMMARY

Travis Jackson was an excellent all-around shortstop. He batted over .300 six times; his best season came in 1930, when he smacked 146 hits and batted .339. Jackson also had power. In 1929, he belted 21 home runs. His lifetime batting average was .291.

Jackson was a marvelous glove man. He led the league in fielding statistics 14 times.

Jackson was elected to the Hall of Fame in 1982.

CAREER STATISTICS:

15 Years	Home Runs 135	Strikeouts 565
Games 1,656	Home Run Percentage 2.2	Batting Ave. .291
At Bats 6,086	Runs Scored 833	Slugging Ave. .433
Hits 1,768	RBIs 929	Pinch Hit At Bats 23
Doubles 291	Bases on Balls 412	Pinch Hits 5
Triples 86	Stolen Bases 71	

Hugh Ambrose Jennings

(Ee-Yah)

B. Apr. 2, 1869, D. Feb. 1, 1928

Lou–AA 1891, Lou–NL 1892–93, Bal–NL 1893–99, Bkn–NL 1899–1900, Phi–NL 1901–02,
Bkn–NL 1903, Det–AL 1907–18
Manager: Det–AL 1907–20

NUMBER OF RECORDS ESTABLISHED AS PLAYER: 11

NUMBER OF RECORDS ESTABLISHED AS MANAGER: 10

TOTAL: 21

PLAYER RECORDS

NATIONAL LEAGUE RECORDS

Season Fielding Records—SS

1892	Most Total Chances	970	6	
1894	Total Chances per Game	6.8	1	
1895	Most Putouts	425		Never Broken
	Total Chances per Game	7.2		Never Broken

Career Fielding Records—SS

Most Putouts per Game	2.5		Tied
Total Chances per Game	6.7		Tied
Highest Fielding Ave.	.927	1	

MAJOR LEAGUE RECORDS

Season Fielding Records—SS

1892	Most Total Chances	970	6	
1895	Most Putouts	425		Tied

Career Fielding Records—SS

Most Putouts per Game	2.4	9	
Total Chances per Game	6.4		Never Broken

MANAGER RECORDS

American League Season Records

1909	Wins	98	1

American League Career Records

Pennants Won	3	9
Cons. Pennants Won	3	30

American League World Series Career Records—1907–09

Series	3	9
Games	16	9
Games Lost	12	9
Winning Percentage	.250	9

Major League World Series Career Records—1907–09

Series	3	3
Games	16	3
Games Lost	12	9

SUMMARY

Hugh Jennings is one of the few shortstops who had a lifetime batting average over .300. In a well-traveled 17-year career, "Ee-Yah" batted a solid .312. He had a five-year hot streak, batting .398, .386, .355, .335, and .328.

One of his greatest fielding records occurred in 1895, when he had 425 putouts, a major league record that still stands. He led the league 13 times in various fielding departments.

Jennings put in 14 years as manager, winning 1,131 and losing 972. He won three consecutive pennants in his first three years but never won again. He had two second- and third-place finishes. His final winning percentage was .538.

Jennings was named to the Hall of Fame in 1945.

CAREER STATISTICS:

17 Years
Games 1,285
At Bats 4,905
Hits 1,531
Doubles 235
Triples 87

Home Runs 18
Home Run Percentage 0.4
Runs Scored 993
RBIs 840
Bases on Balls 347
Stolen Bases 359

Strikeouts 117
Batting Ave. .312
Slugging Ave. .407
Pinch Hit At Bats 6
Pinch Hits 2

CAREER STATISTICS AS MANAGER:

14 Years
Games 2,125

Wins 1,131
Losses 972

Winning Percentage .538
First-place Finishes 3

Walter Perry Johnson
(Big Train, Barney)
B. Nov. 6, 1887, D. Dec. 10, 1946
Was–AL 1907–27
Manager: Was–AL 1929–32, Cle–AL 1933–35

NUMBER OF RECORDS ESTABLISHED AS PLAYER: 76

AMERICAN LEAGUE RECORDS

Season Pitching Records

1913	Lowest ERA	1.09	1

Season Pitching Title Records

1911	Complete Games Titles	2	2
1912	Fewest Hits Titles	1	1
1913	Most MVP Titles	1	11
	Fewest Hits Titles	2	1
	ERA Titles	2	5
	Complete Games Titles	3	1
1914	Complete Games Titles	4	1
	Shutout Titles	3	3
1915	Wins Titles	3	3

	Innings Titles	4	1	
	Complete Games Titles	5	1	
	Shutout Titles	4	1	
1916	Strikeout Titles	6	1	
	Wins Titles	4	2	
	Innings Titles	5		Tied
	Complete Games Titles	6		Tied
1917	Strikeout Titles	7	1	
1918	Strikeout Titles	8	1	
	Wins Titles	5	6	
	ERA Titles	3	1	
	Shutout Titles	5	1	
1919	Strikeout Titles	9	2	
	Fewest Hits Titles	3	5	
	ERA Titles	4	5	
	Shutout Titles	6	5	
1921	Strikeout Titles	10	2	
1923	Strikeout Titles	11	1	
1924	Most MVP Titles	2	14	
	Strikeout Titles	12		Never Broken
	Wins Titles	6	27	
	Fewest Hits Titles	4	1	
	ERA Titles	5	11	
	Shutout Titles	7		Never Broken
1925	Fewest Hits Titles	6		Tied

Career Pitching Records

Most 20-Win Seasons	12		Never Broken
Most Games Pitched	802	54	
Most Games Started	666		Never Broken
Most Games Completed	531		Never Broken
Most Wins	416		Never Broken
Most Losses	279		Never Broken
Most Innings Pitched	5,924		Never Broken
Most Bases on Balls	1,405	20	
Most Shutouts	110		Never Broken
Most Relief Wins	40	5	
Most Relief Losses	30	2	

MAJOR LEAGUE RECORDS

Season Pitching Title Records

1913	Most MVP Titles	1	11
	Complete Games Titles	3	1
1914	Complete Games Titles	4	1
1915	Complete Games Titles	5	1

1916	Complete Games Titles	6	45	
	Strikeout Titles	6	1	
	Most Innings Titles	5	1	
1917	Most Strikeout Titles	7	1	
1918	Most Strikeout Titles	8	1	
1919	Most Strikeout Titles	9	1	
1921	Most Strikeout Titles	10	2	
1923	Most Strikeout Titles	11	1	
1924	Most Strikeout Titles	12		Never Broken
	Most MVP Titles	2	14	
	Most ERA Titles	5	8	
1925	Most Fewest Hits Titles	5	40	

Career Pitching Records

	Most Shutouts	110		Never Broken
	Most Strikeouts	3,508	55	
	Most Relief Wins	40	5	
	Most Relief Losses	30	2	

WORLD SERIES RECORDS

Game Pitching Records

1924	Most Hits per 9 Inn.	14	1	
	Most Strikeouts	12	5	
1925	Most Hits per 9 Inn.	15		Never Broken

7-Game Series Pitching Records

1924	Most Losses	2		Never Broken
	Most Hits	30		Never Broken
	Most Bases on Balls	11		Never Broken
	Most Strikeouts	20	21	
1925	Most Starts	3	37	
	Most Shutouts	1	32	
	Most Complete Games	3		Never Broken

SUMMARY

Walter "Big Train" Johnson was the greatest pitcher in American League history. This 6'1", 200-pounder established a bushel of records, all while pitching for the usually hapless Washington Senators.

Nineteen of Johnson's records remain unbroken after more than a half century. This places him number one on the American League composite all-time unbroken records list.

Johnson is also number one on the major league leaders list. "The Big Train" led the league in various pitching departments 53 times, far more than any other pitcher in baseball. He is also number one in the shutout department, with 110 whitewashes. He is second in wins and third in innings pitched.

Johnson was a tremendous strikeout pitcher. He led the league in strikeouts 12 times. From 1912 on he led the league in strikeouts for eight consecutive years. In his 21-year career, he won 20 or more games 12 times.

Johnson won the MVP title in 1913, when he astounded the baseball world by winning 36 and losing only 7, including 11 shutouts. In 1924 he won the MVP again, this time with a 23–7 mark.

"The Big Train" chugged into the Hall of Fame in 1936.

POSTSEASON AWARDS

1913 MVP
1924 MVP

CAREER STATISTICS:

21 Years	Games Started 666	Shutouts 110 (1st)
Wins 416 (2nd)	Games Completed 531 (5th)	Relief Appearances 136
Losses 279 (3rd)	Innings 5,924 (3rd)	Relief Wins 40
Winning Percentage .599	Hits 4,925	Relief Losses 30
ERA 2.17 (7th)	Bases on Balls 1,405	Saves 34
Total Games 802 (10th)	Strikeouts 3,508 (4th)	

CAREER STATISTICS AS MANAGER:

7 Years	Wins 530	Winning Percentage .551
Games 967	Losses 432	First-place Finishes 0

Adrian Joss
(Addie)
B. Apr. 12, 1880, D. Apr. 14, 1911
Cle–AL 1902–10

NUMBER OF RECORDS ESTABLISHED: 11

AMERICAN LEAGUE RECORDS

Rookie Pitching Records

1902	Shutouts	5	2

Season Pitching Records

1902	Shutouts	5	1
1904	Lowest ERA	1.59	1
1908	Lowest ERA	1.16	5

Season Pitching Title Records

1902	Shutout Titles	1	1
1904	ERA Titles	1	4
1908	ERA Titles	2	10
	Fewest Hits Titles	1	5

Career Pitching Records

Complete Games	234	1
Winning Percentage	.623	4
Lowest ERA	1.88	6

SUMMARY

During the first ten years of American League history, Addie Joss was one of the premier pitchers. He had four consecutive years of 20 or more wins. Joss's lifetime ERA of 1.88 is second best. In 1908, he won 24 and had a remarkable ERA of 1.16. He completed 234 of 286 games.

Joss died at the age of 31.

Joss's induction to the Hall of Fame came in 1978.

CAREER STATISTICS:

9 Years

Wins 160

Losses 97

Winning Percentage .623

ERA 1.88 (2nd)

Total Games 286

Games Started 260

Games Completed 234

Innings 2,336

Hits 1,895

Bases on Balls 370

Strikeouts 926

Shutouts 46

Relief Appearances 26

Relief Wins 5

Relief Losses 4

Saves 5

Albert William Kaline

(Al)

B. Dec. 19, 1934

Det–AL 1953–74

NUMBER OF RECORDS ESTABLISHED: 11

AMERICAN LEAGUE RECORDS

Season Fielding Records—RF

1961	Most Putouts	378	10	
1971	Highest Fielding Ave.	1.000		Tied

Career Fielding Records—RF

	Most Games Played	2,488	Never Broken
	Most Putouts	5,035	Never Broken
	Most Total Chances	5,278	Never Broken
	Highest Fielding Ave.	.985	Never Broken

MAJOR LEAGUE RECORDS

Career Fielding Records—RF

	Most Games Played	2,488	Never Broken

204

Most Putouts	5,035	Never Broken
Most Total Chances	5,278	Never Broken

WORLD SERIES RECORDS

Game Fielding Records—RF

1968	Most Putouts	7	Tied

SUMMARY

When Al Kaline retired in 1974, he had played the most games in right field, made the most putouts, and had the most total chances of any rightfielder in baseball history.

Kaline started his 22-year career at the age of 19. His lifetime batting average was .297, and he batted over .300 nine times. In 1955 he led the American League with a .340 batting average, and he won the slugging crown in 1959. In 1955 he led the league in hits and in 1961 was the doubles champion.

On defense, Al Kaline was sensational. His .985 fielding average is the best of any right-fielder in American League history; he was a league leader four times and in 1971 went through the season without making an error.

Kaline was inducted into the Hall of Fame in 1980.

CAREER STATISTICS:

22 Years
Games 2,834 (9th)
At Bats 10,116
Hits 3,007
Doubles 498
Triples 75

Home Runs 399
Home Run Percentage 3.9
Runs Scored 1,622
RBIs 1,583
Bases on Balls 1,277
Stolen Bases 137

Strikeouts 1,020
Batting Ave. .297
Slugging Ave. .480
Pinch Hit At Bats 115
Pinch Hits 37

Timothy John Keefe
(Tim, Smiling Timothy)
B. Jan. 1, 1857, D. Apr. 23, 1933
Tro–NL 1880–82, NY–AA 1883–84, NY–NL 1885–89, NY–PL 1890, NY–NL 1891, Phi–NL 1891–93

NUMBER OF RECORDS ESTABLISHED: 25

AMERICAN ASSOCIATION RECORDS

Season Pitching Records

1883	Strikeouts	361	1
	Strikeouts/9 Inn.	5.25	1
	Starts	68	1
	Complete Games	68	1
	Innings	619	1
	Total Games	68	1

NATIONAL LEAGUE RECORDS

Rookie Pitching Records

1880	Lowest ERA	0.86	Never Broken

Season Pitching Title Records

1880	Fewest Hits Titles	1	5
1885	ERA Titles	2	3
	Fewest Hits Titles	2	3
1888	Wins Titles	2	1
	ERA Titles	3	23
	Fewest Hits Titles	3	1
1889	Fewest Hits Titles	4	75

MAJOR LEAGUE RECORDS

Rookie Pitching Records

1880	Lowest ERA	0.86		Never Broken

Season Pitching Records

1883	Strikeouts	361	1

Season Pitching Title Records

1880	Fewest Hits Titles	1	5
1885	ERA Titles	2	3
	Fewest Hits Titles	2	3
1886	Total Games Titles	2	3
1888	Wins Titles	2	1
	ERA Titles	3	23
	Fewest Hits Titles	3	1
1889	Fewest Hits Titles	4	36

Career Pitching Records

	Strikeouts	2,533	18

SUMMARY

In an exceptional 14-year career during the early years of the game, Tim Keefe was a dominating pitcher.

In 1883 he completed all 68 of his starts and won 41 of them. In his rookie season his ERA was an astonishing 0.86. In 1886 he won 42 games, started 64, and completed 62. He also had six seasons with 32 or more wins. He was a league leader 17 times.

Keefe was named to the Hall of Fame in 1964.

CAREER STATISTICS:

14 Years	Games Started 595	Shutouts 40
Wins 344 (8th)	Games Completed 558 (3rd)	Relief Appearances 37
Losses 225	Innings 5,072 (8th)	Relief Wins 2
Winning Percentage .605	Hits 4,452	Relief Losses 0
ERA 2.62	Bases on Balls 1,231	Saves 2
Total Games 601	Strikeouts 2,533	

William Henry Keeler

(Willie, Wee Willie, Hit 'Em Where They Ain't)

B. Mar. 3, 1872, D. Jan. 1, 1923

NY–NL 1892–93, Bkn–NL 1893, Bal–NL 1894–98,
Bkn–NL 1899–1902, NY–AL 1903–09,
NY–NL 1910

NUMBER OF RECORDS ESTABLISHED: 20

NATIONAL LEAGUE RECORDS

Season Batting Records

1895	Most Singles	178	1	
1897	Most Singles	196	1	
	Most Hits	243	25	
1898	Most Singles	201		Never Broken
1899	Longest Hitting Streak	44		Tied

Season Fielding Records—RF

1901	Highest Fielding Ave.	.985	4	

Career Batting Records

Highest Batting Ave.	.372		Never Broken
Longest Hitting Streak	44		Tied

Career Fielding Records—RF

Highest Fielding Ave.   .961   4

AMERICAN LEAGUE RECORDS

Season Batting Records

1904	Most Singles	162	2
1906	Most Singles	167	5

SUMMARY

"Wee Willie" Keeler was famous for his ability to "hit 'em where they ain't." Keeler was one of the game's greatest contact hitters, and only a handful of players have bettered his lifetime batting average of .345.

No player in National League history, however, has ever matched Keeler's batting average of .372.

Willie belted more than 200 hits in one season eight consecutive times, and he stands alone in this accomplishment.

He batted over .300 in 14 consecutive seasons.

His highest batting average was .432 in 1897, and he had seasons of .392, .391, .379, .377, .368, and .355.

Keeler won Hall of Fame honors in 1939.

CAREER STATISTICS:

19 Years	Home Runs 34	Strikeouts 36
Games 2,124	Home Run Percentage 0.4	Batting Ave. .345 (5th)
At Bats 8,591	Runs Scored 1,722	Slugging Ave. .420
Hits 2,962	RBIs 810	Pinch Hit At Bats 17
Doubles 239	Bases on Balls 524	Pinch Hits 3
Triples 153	Stolen Bases 495	

George Clyde Kell

B. Aug. 23, 1922

Phi–AL 1943–46, Det–AL 1946–52, Bos–AL 1952–54, Chi–AL 1954–56, Bal–AL 1956–57

NUMBER OF RECORDS ESTABLISHED: 4

AMERICAN LEAGUE RECORDS

Season Fielding Records—3B

1946	Highest Fielding Ave.	.984	1

Career Fielding Records—3B

	Highest Fielding Ave.	.969	20

MAJOR LEAGUE RECORDS

Season Fielding Records—3B

1946	Highest Fielding Ave.	.984	1

Career Fielding Records—3B

	Highest Fielding Ave.	.969	20

SUMMARY

In 1950, George Kell led the league in hits, doubles, and fielding average, batted .340, and was the Gold Glove third baseman. In 1949, he became the American League batting champion, when he hit .343.

In a brilliant 15-year career, Kell batted .306 with 2,054 base hits. On defense he led the league in various fielding departments 14 times.

Kell was acknowledged by the Hall of Fame in 1983.

CAREER STATISTICS:

15 Years	Home Runs 78	Strikeouts 287
Games 1,795	Home Run Percentage 1.2	Batting Ave. .306
At Bats 6,702	Runs Scored 881	Slugging Ave. .414
Hits 2,054	RBIs 870	Pinch Hit At Bats 43
Doubles 385	Bases on Balls 620	Pinch Hits 11
Triples 50	Stolen Bases 51	

Joseph James Kelley
(Joe)

B. Dec. 9, 1871, D. Aug. 14, 1943

Bos–NL 1891, Pit–NL 1891–92, Bal–NL 1892–98, Bkn–NL 1899–1901, Bal–AL 1902,
Cin–NL 1902–06, Bos–NL 1908
Manager: Cin–NL 1902–05, Bos–NL 1908

NUMBER OF RECORDS ESTABLISHED AS PLAYER: 2

NATIONAL LEAGUE RECORDS

Career Fielding Records—LF

Highest Fielding Ave.	.961	11

MAJOR LEAGUE RECORDS

Career Fielding Records—LF

Highest Fielding Ave.	.961	11

SUMMARY

Joe Kelley batted over .300 11 seasons. In four consecutive years with Baltimore, he batted .393, .365, .364, and .388.

Despite this feat, Kelley never led the league in any batting categories. Kelley's 194 career triples place him ninth on the all-time list. He had a lifetime batting average of .319.

Hall of Fame honors were bestowed upon Kelley in 1971.

CAREER STATISTICS:

17 Years
Games 1,845
At Bats 7,018
Hits 2,242
Doubles 356
Triples 194 (9th)

Home Runs 65
Home Run Percentage 0.9
Runs Scored 1,426
RBIs 1,193
Bases on Balls 910
Stolen Bases 443

Strikeouts 160
Batting Ave. .319
Slugging Ave. .453
Pinch Hit At Bats 19
Pinch Hits 4

CAREER STATISTICS AS MANAGER:

5 Years
Games 668

Wins 337
Losses 321

Winning Percentage .512
First-place Finishes 0

George Lange Kelly
(High Pockets)
B. Sept. 10, 1895, D. Oct. 13, 1984

NY–NL 1915–17, Pit–NL 1917, NY–NL 1918–26, Cin–NL 1927–30, Chi–NL 1930, Bkn–NL 1932

NUMBER OF RECORDS ESTABLISHED: 8

NATIONAL LEAGUE RECORDS

Season Fielding Records—1B

1920	Most Putouts	1,759		Never Broken
	Most Total Chances	1,873		Never Broken
1921	Most Double Plays	132	2	

MAJOR LEAGUE RECORDS

Season Fielding Records—1B

1921	Most Double Plays	132	2

WORLD SERIES RECORDS

Game Batting Records

1924	Most At Bats	6	49

8-Game Series Batting Records

1921	Most Strikeouts	10	Never Broken

8-Game Series Fielding Records—1B

1921	Most Assists	6	Tied

Career Batting Records—1921–24

	Most Strikeouts	23	8

SUMMARY

George Kelly batted over .300 seven seasons, including six times in a row. In 1920 and 1924 he was a league leader in RBIs. His lifetime batting average was .297 for 16 seasons.

Kelly excelled on defense; he led the league in various fielding categories 12 times.

Kelly was beckoned to the Hall of Fame in 1973.

CAREER STATISTICS:

16 Years	Home Runs 148	Strikeouts 694
Games 1,622	Home Run Percentage 2.5	Batting Ave. .297
At Bats 5,993	Runs Scored 819	Slugging Ave. .452
Hits 1,778	RBIs 1,020	Pinch Hit At Bats 40
Doubles 337	Bases on Balls 386	Pinch Hits 5
Triples 76	Stolen Bases 65	

Michael Joseph Kelly

(King)

B. Dec. 31, 1857, D. Nov. 8, 1894

Cin–NL 1878–79, Chi–NL 1880–86, Bos–NL 1887–89,
Bos–PL 1890, Bos–AA 1891, Bos–NL 1891–92, NY–NL 1893
Manager: Bos–PL 1890, Cin–AA 1891

NUMBER OF RECORDS ESTABLISHED AS PLAYER: 19

NATIONAL LEAGUE RECORDS

Season Batting Records

1882	Most Doubles	37	1
1886	Most Runs Scored	155	8

Season Batting Title Records

1882	Most Doubles Titles	2	2
1885	Most Home Runs Titles	2	1
1886	Most Batting Ave. Titles	2	2
	Most Runs Scored Titles	3	11
1889	Most Doubles Titles	3	12

Career Batting Records

Most Home Runs	63	4
Most Runs Scored	1,209	1
Most RBIs	665	2

Career Fielding Records—RF

Most Games Played	731	2

MAJOR LEAGUE RECORDS

Season Batting Records

1882	Most Doubles	37	1
1886	Most Runs Scored	155	1

Season Batting Title Records

1882	Most Doubles Titles	2	2
1885	Most Runs Scored Titles	2	1
1886	Most Batting Ave. Titles	2	2
	Most Runs Scored Titles	3	11
1889	Most Doubles Titles	3	12

Career Batting Records

Most RBIs	794	4

SUMMARY

"King" Kelly helped popularize sliding in the pioneer days of baseball. Whenever he started running the bases, the fans would yell, "Slide, Kelly, slide!" He introduced the hook slide to baseball and was one of the first to slide on his belly.

Kelly was a marvelous hitter, a two-time batting average king with a lifetime batting average of .307. He had eight seasons of averages over .300, with a high of .388 in 1886, when he led the National League and set a record by scoring 155 runs.

Kelly mostly played right field, but he actually played all nine positions!

Kelly's induction into the Hall of Fame came in 1945.

CAREER STATISTICS:

16 Years	Home Runs 69	Strikeouts 420
Games 1,463	Home Run Percentage 1.2	Batting Ave. .307
At Bats 5,923	Runs Scored 1,363	Slugging Ave. .437
Hits 1,820	RBIs 794	Pinch Hit At Bats 2
Doubles 360	Bases on Balls 550	Pinch Hits 0
Triples 102	Stolen Bases 315	

CAREER STATISTICS AS MANAGER:

2 Years	Wins 124	Winning Percentage .541
Games 232	Losses 105	First-place Finishes 1

Harmon Clayton Killebrew
(Killer)

B. June 29, 1936

Was–AL 1954–60, Min–AL 1961–74, KC–AL 1975

NUMBER OF RECORDS ESTABLISHED: 2

AMERICAN LEAGUE RECORDS

Season Batting Records

1962	Most Strikeouts	142	1

MAJOR LEAGUE RECORDS

Season Batting Records

1962	Most Strikeouts	142	1

SUMMARY

You can't look only at records to see a player's worth. Killebrew's 573 home runs make him the fifth best home run hitter the game has ever had. He is also third in home run percentage and ninth in bases on balls.

Killebrew was a six-time home run champion, a seven-time home run percentage king, a three-time RBI leader, a four-time bases on balls winner, and a two-time slugging champion.

Killebrew led his club to the division title in 1969 and won the MVP Award when he slammed 49 homers and drove in 140 runs that year.

Killebrew entered the Hall of Fame in 1984.

POSTSEASON AWARDS

1969 MVP

CAREER STATISTICS:

22 Years	Home Runs 573 (5th)	Strikeouts 1,699 (7th)
Games 2,435	Home Run Percentage 7.0 (3rd)	Batting Ave. .256
At Bats 8,147	Runs Scored 1,283	Slugging Ave. .509
Hits 2,086	RBIs 1,584	Pinch Hit At Bats 118
Doubles 290	Bases on Balls 1,559 (9th)	Pinch Hits 24
Triples 24	Stolen Bases 19	

☆

Ralph McPherran Kiner

B. Oct. 27, 1922

Pit–NL 1946–53, Chi–NL 1953–54, Cle–AL 1955

NUMBER OF RECORDS ESTABLISHED: 4

NATIONAL LEAGUE RECORDS

Career Batting Records

	Highest Home Run Percentage	7.1		Never Broken

Season Batting Title Records

1951	Most Home Runs Titles	6	1	
1952	Most Home Runs Titles	7		Never Broken

ALL-STAR GAME RECORDS

Career Batting Records—1948–53

	Highest Slugging Ave.	.733	2

SUMMARY

Ralph Kiner was one of baseball's most consistent home run hitters. In his first seven years, he led the league in homers and home run percentage seven times.

Kiner was a league leader in various batting categories 23 times and, in addition to his home run crowns, won three slugging titles. Only Babe Ruth has a higher home run percentage than Kiner.

Since his retirement in 1955, Kiner has been the TV announcer for the New York Mets.

Kiner joined the Hall of Fame in 1975.

CAREER STATISTICS:

10 Years	Home Runs 369	Strikeouts 749
Games 1,472	Home Run Percentage 7.1 (2nd)	Batting Ave. .279
At Bats 5,205	Runs Scored 971	Slugging Ave. .548
Hits 1,451	RBIs 1,015	Pinch Hit At Bats 33
Doubles 216	Bases on Balls 1,011	Pinch Hits 12
Triples 39	Stolen Bases 22	

Charles Herbert Klein

(Chuck)

B. Oct. 7, 1904, D. Mar. 28, 1958

Phi–NL 1928–33, Chi–NL 1934–36, Phi–NL 1936–39, Pit–NL 1939, Phi–NL 1940–44

NUMBER OF RECORDS ESTABLISHED: 7

NATIONAL LEAGUE RECORDS

Season Batting Records

1929	Most Home Runs	43	1	
1930	Most Doubles	59	2	
	Most Extra Base Hits	107		Never Broken

Season Fielding Records—RF

| 1930 | Most Total Chances | 423 | 47 |

MAJOR LEAGUE RECORDS

Season Fielding Records—RF

| 1930 | Most Total Chances | 423 | 47 |

222

ALL-STAR GAME RECORDS

Game Batting Records

1933	Most Games Played	1	1
1934	Most Games Played	2	1

Career Batting Records—1933–34

	Most Games Played	2	1
	Most Singles	2	1

SUMMARY

Chuck Klein led the league 18 times in various batting categories. His lifetime batting average is .320. He batted over .300 nine times and was a three-time slugging average king, a four-time home run champion, a three-time runs scored leader, and a two-time hits, doubles, and RBI leader.

He was also a fine outfielder who led the league six times in fielding. Klein's call to the Hall of Fame came in 1980.

CAREER STATISTICS:

17 Years
Games 1,753
At Bats 6,486
Hits 2,076
Doubles 398
Triples 74

Home Runs 300
Home Run Percentage 4.6
Runs Scored 1,168
RBIs 1,201
Bases on Balls 601
Stolen Bases 79

Strikeouts 521
Batting Ave. .320
Slugging Ave. .543
Pinch Hit At Bats 137
Pinch Hits 28

Sanford Koufax

(Sandy)

B. Dec. 30, 1935

Bkn–NL 1955–57, LA–NL 1958–66

NUMBER OF RECORDS ESTABLISHED: 27

NATIONAL LEAGUE RECORDS

Season Pitching Records

| 1960 | Strikeouts/9 Inn. | 10.1 | 2 |
| 1962 | Strikeouts/9 Inn. | 10.6 | 22 |

Season Pitching Title Records

1963	Cy Young Titles	1	2
	Fewest Hits/9 Inn. Titles	4	1
1964	No-Hit Titles	3	1
	Fewest Hits/9 Inn. Titles	5	1
1965	Cy Young Titles	2	1
	Fewest Hits/9 Inn. Titles	6	Never Broken
1966	Cy Young Titles	3	Tied
	ERA Titles	5	Tied

Career Pitching Records

Strikeouts/9 Inn.	9.3		Never Broken
Fewest Hits/9 Inn.	6.8		Never Broken

MAJOR LEAGUE RECORDS

Season Pitching Records

1960	Strikeouts/9 Inn.	10.1	2	
1962	Strikeouts/9 Inn.	10.6	3	

Season Pitching Title Records

1963	Cy Young Titles	1	2	
	Fewest Hits/9 Inn. Titles	6		Tied
1966	Cy Young Titles	3		Tied

Career Pitching Records

Strikeouts/9 Inn.	9.3		Never Broken
Fewest Hits/9 Inn.	6.8		Never Broken

WORLD SERIES RECORDS

Game Pitching Records

1963	Strikeouts	15	5

4-Game Series Pitching Records

1963	Starts	2		Tied
	Complete Games	2		Tied
	Wins	2		Tied
	Innings	18		Tied
	Strikeouts	23		Never Broken

7-Game Series Pitching Records

1965	Shutouts	2	Tied

Career Pitching Records—1959–66

Strikeouts/9 Inn.	9.64	2	

SUMMARY

After his first seven years in the big leagues, Sandy Koufax's record was 54 wins and 53 defeats. Over the next five years, he became one of the greatest pitchers in baseball, winning 111 and losing only 34 with an ERA of 1.98. His winning percentage was a remarkable .761, and he averaged 288.8 strikeouts per year. He led the National League in ERA four consecutive years and was a league leader 21 times! Sandy was the first man to pitch four no-hitters, one of them a perfect game. He had his greatest year in 1963, when he won 25 and lost 5. He was awarded both the Cy Young and MVP titles.

Koufax was named to the Hall of Fame in 1971.

POSTSEASON AWARDS

1963 MVP
1963 Cy Young Award
1965 Cy Young Award
1966 Cy Young Award

CAREER STATISTICS:

12 Years	Games Started 314	Shutouts 40
Wins 165	Games Completed 137	Relief Appearances 83
Losses 87	Innings 2,324	Relief Wins 6
Winning Percentage .655	Hits 1,754	Relief Losses 2
ERA 2.76	Bases on Balls 817	Saves 9
Total Games 397	Strikeouts 2,396	

Napoleon Lajoie
(Nap, Larry)

B. Sept. 5, 1875, D. Feb. 7, 1959

Phi–NL 1896–1900, Phi–AL 1901–02, Cle–AL 1902–14, Phi–AL 1915–16
Manager: Cle–AL 1905–09

NUMBER OF RECORDS ESTABLISHED AS PLAYER: 70

NUMBER OF RECORDS ESTABLISHED AS MANAGER: 1

TOTAL: 71

PLAYER RECORDS

NATIONAL LEAGUE RECORDS

Career Batting Records—1896–1900

Highest Batting Ave.	.346	1

Career Batting Records—1901–16

Most Games Played	1,989	1
Most At Bats	7,501	1
Most Hits	2,523	12

Most Singles	1,862	12
Most Doubles	511	12
Most Extra Base Hits	661	1
Most Total Bases	3,385	1
Most Runs Scored	1,082	1
Most RBIs	1,141	1
Highest Batting Ave.	.334	4
Highest Slugging Ave.	.448	4
Most Stolen Bases	295	1
Most Home Runs	51	1

Career Fielding Records—2B

Most Games Played	1,721	14
Most Putouts	4,599	14
Most Assists	5,239	14
Most Double Plays	883	14
Most Errors	350	14
Most Total Chances	10,188	14
Highest Fielding Ave.	.967	14

AMERICAN LEAGUE RECORDS

Season Batting Records

1901	Most Hits	229	10
	Most Singles	154	2
	Most Doubles	48	3
	Most Home Runs	14	1
	Highest Home Run Percentage	2.6	1
	Most Extra Base Hits	75	10
	Most Total Bases	345	10
	Most Runs Scored	145	10
	Most RBIs	125	10
	Highest Batting Ave.	.422	Never Broken
	Highest Slugging Ave.	.635	18
1904	Most Doubles	50	6
1910	Most Doubles	51	2

Season Batting Title Records

1901	Most Triple Crowns	1	46
	Most Hits Titles	1	3
	Most Doubles Titles	1	3
	Most Home Runs Titles	1	4
	Batting Ave. Titles	1	2
	Slugging Ave. Titles	1	2
	Most Total Bases Titles	1	3
	Most Runs Scored Titles	1	3

	Most RBI Titles	1	3	
1903	Batting Ave. Titles	2	1	
	Slugging Ave. Titles	2	1	
1904	Batting Ave. Titles	3	6	
	Slugging Ave. Titles	3	6	
	Most Total Bases Titles	2	5	
	Most RBI Titles	2	5	
	Most Doubles Titles	2	2	
	Most Hits Titles	2	5	
1906	Most Hits Titles	3	4	
	Most Doubles Titles	3	4	
1910	Most Hits Titles	4	2	
	Most Doubles Titles	4	10	

Season Fielding Records—2B

1901	Most Putouts	395	4	
	Fewest Errors	32	2	
	Highest Fielding Ave.	.960	3	
1906	Most Double Plays	76	1	
1907	Most Double Plays	86	14	
1908	Most Putouts	450	14	
	Most Assists	538	22	
	Most Total Chances	1,025		Never Broken

MAJOR LEAGUE RECORDS

Career Batting Records—1896–1916

Most Games Played	2,475	1
Most At Bats	9,589	1
Most Doubles	648	1
Most Extra Base Hits	893	1
Most Total Bases	4,471	1

MANAGER RECORDS

American League Career Records

Highest Winning Percentage	.546	9

SUMMARY

Nap Lajoie joined the American League for its first year of operation in 1901. That year he won the Triple Crown. He banged out a career-high 229 hits and led the league in homers, doubles, runs, RBIs, and batting and slugging average. He hit a super .422 (a record that still stands).

He was a league leader 22 times in various batting categories during his 21-year career.

Lajoie had a lifetime batting average of .339, rapping out 3,251 hits. He was a four-time most hits leader, a five-time doubles champion, a three-time RBI king, a three-time batting average leader, and a four-time slugging champion. He also won single crowns in home runs, runs scored, and at bats. In 16 of his 21 years, Nap batted well above .300, including eleven consecutive times from 1896 through 1906.

On defense, he led all second basemen in various fielding categories 26 times.

Nap Lajoie was a player-manager for the Cleveland Indians from 1905 to 1909. As a player, he was one of the game's greatest. As a manager, the best he could do was a second-place finish in 1908. As manager he won 397 games, lost 330, and his .546 winning percentage was a new record that lasted nine years before it was broken.

Lajoie became a Hall of Famer in 1937.

CAREER STATISTICS:

21 Years
Games 2,475
At Bats 9,589
Hits 3,251 (10th)
Doubles 648 (6th)
Triples 163

Home Runs 82
Home Run Percentage 0.9
Runs Scored 1,504
RBIs 1,599
Bases on Balls 516
Stolen Bases 395

Strikeouts 85
Batting Ave. .339
Slugging Ave. .466
Pinch Hits At Bats 35
Pinch Hits 9

CAREER STATISTICS AS MANAGER:

5 Years
Games 740

Wins 397
Losses 330

Winning Percentage .546
First-place Finishes 0

Robert Granville Lemon
(Bob)

B. Sept. 22, 1920

Cle–AL 1941–58

Manager: Was–AL 1968, KC–AL 1970–72, Chi–AL 1977–78, NY–AL 1978–79, 1981–82

NUMBER OF RECORDS ESTABLISHED AS PLAYER: 4

WORLD SERIES RECORDS

4-Game Series Pitching Records

1954	Starts	2	Tied
	Losses	2	Tied
	Highest ERA	6.75	Tied
	Most Bases on Balls	8	Tied

SUMMARY

In a fabulous 15-year career, Bob Lemon won 207 games and lost 128 for a .618 winning percentage. He won 20 or more games 7 times and led the league in various pitching departments 21 times.

Lemon was a three-time most wins champion, a three-time most starts champion, a five-time complete games leader, and a four-time leader in innings pitched, and he won single crowns in strikeouts and shutouts.

In 1948 Lemon helped the Indians win the pennant by posting 20 wins, 10 of which were shutouts. He had another banner year in 1954, with his 23–7 record helping lead his team to another pennant.

Lemon was voted into the Hall of Fame in 1976.

CAREER STATISTICS:

15 Years

Wins 207

Losses 128

Winning Percentage .618

ERA 3.23

Total Games 460

Games Started 350

Games Completed 188

Innings 2,850

Hits 2,559

Bases on Balls 1,251

Strikeouts 1,277

Shutouts 31

Relief Appearances 110

Relief Wins 12

Relief Losses 10

Saves 22

CAREER STATISTICS AS MANAGER:

8 Years

Games 833

Wins 432

Losses 401

Winning Percentage .519

First-place Finishes 1

Frederick Charles Lindstrom
(Freddie)

B. Nov. 21, 1905, D. Oct. 4, 1981

NY–NL 1924–32, Pit–NL 1933–34, Chi–NL 1935, Bkn–NL 1936

NUMBER OF RECORDS ESTABLISHED: 4

WORLD SERIES RECORDS

Game Batting Records

1924	Most Hits	4	59
	Most Singles	4	59

Game Fielding Records—3B

1924	Most Assists	7	16

7-Game Series Fielding Records—3B

1924	Most Assists	18	16

SUMMARY

Freddie Lindstrom was a pure hitter. In 1928 he led the league with 231 hits and batted a solid .358. In his 13-year career, he batted over .300 seven times including a high of .379 in

1930. He batted .300 or over six consecutive seasons. He ended with a career batting average of .311.

Lindstrom earned Hall of Fame honors in 1976.

CAREER STATISTICS:

13 Years	Home Runs 103	Strikeouts 276
Games 1,438	Home Run Percentage 1.8	Batting Ave. .311
At Bats 5,611	Runs Scored 895	Slugging Ave. .449
Hits 1,747	RBIs 779	Pinch Hit At Bats 31
Doubles 301	Bases on Balls 334	Pinch Hits 9
Triples 81	Stolen Bases 84	

Ernesto Natali Lombardi
(Schnozz)

B. Apr. 6, 1908, D. Sept. 26, 1977

Bkn–NL 1931, Cin–NL 1932–41, Bos–NL 1942, NY–NL 1943–47

NUMBER OF RECORDS ESTABLISHED: 1

ALL-STAR GAME RECORDS

Career Batting Records—1938–40

Highest Batting Ave. (Min. 10 At Bats)	.500	Tied

SUMMARY

Ernie Lombardi couldn't run worth a lick, but he could flat out hit.

He set only one record in his 17-year career, but he hit over .300 ten times and retired in 1947 with a lifetime batting average of .306.

Lombardi won the batting crown twice and had several outstanding seasons, with batting averages of .343, .342, .334, and .333. In 1938, he won the MVP Award with a .342 league-leading batting average.

Lombardi was inducted into the Hall of Fame in 1986.

POSTSEASON AWARDS

1938 MVP

CAREER STATISTICS:

17 Years	Home Runs 190	Strikeouts 262
Games 1,853	Home Run Percentage 3.2	Batting Ave. .306
At Bats 5,855	Runs Scored 601	Slugging Ave. .460
Hits 1,792	RBIs 990	Pinch Hit At Bats 281
Doubles 277	Bases on Balls 430	Pinch Hits 66
Triples 27	Stolen Bases 8	

Alfonso Ramon Lopez
(Al)

B. Aug. 20, 1908

Bkn–NL 1928–35, Bos–NL 1936–40, Pit–NL 1940–46
Manager: Cle–AL 1951–56, Chi–AL 1957–65, 1968–69

NUMBER OF RECORDS ESTABLISHED AS PLAYER: 3

NUMBER OF RECORDS ESTABLISHED AS MANAGER: 2
TOTAL: 5

PLAYER RECORDS

NATIONAL LEAGUE RECORDS

Rookie Fielding Records—C

1930	Putouts	465	11

Career Fielding Records—C

	Games	1,861	Never Broken

MAJOR LEAGUE RECORDS

Career Fielding Records—C

Games	1,918	41

MANAGER RECORDS

American League Season Records

1954	Wins	111	Never Broken
	Winning Percentage	.721	Never Broken

SUMMARY

Al Lopez had gone behind the plate more times than any catcher in baseball history until Bob Boone passed him in 1988.

He donned the tools of ignorance for 19 years, belted 1,547 base hits, and batted .261.

Lopez turned to managing in 1951 and won two pennants in his first nine seasons. He finished second ten times in 17 years of managing.

Two of his American League records still remain unbroken: his 1954 Cleveland team won the most games, 111, and finished with the highest winning percentage, .721.

Lopez entered the Hall of Fame in 1977.

CAREER STATISTICS:

19 Years	Home Runs 52	Strikeouts 538
Games 1,950	Home Run Percentage 0.9	Batting Ave. .261
At Bats 5,916	Runs Scored 613	Slugging Ave. .337
Hits 1,547	RBIs 652	Pinch Hit At Bats 19
Doubles 206	Bases on Balls 561	Pinch Hits 6
Triples 42	Stolen Bases 46	

CAREER STATISTICS AS MANAGER:

17 Years	Wins 1,422	Winning Percentage .581 (9th)
Games 2,459	Losses 1,026	First-place Finishes 2

Theodore Amar Lyons
(Ted)
B. Dec. 28, 1900, D. July 25, 1986
Chi–AL 1923–46
Manager: Chi–AL 1946–48

NUMBER OF RECORDS ESTABLISHED: 0

SUMMARY

Ted Lyons established no records, but he won more than 20 games in a season three times and was a league leader 11 times. He was a two-time most wins champion, a two-time complete games leader, a two-time innings leader, and twice led the league in shutouts. He won 260 games over a 21-year career.

Lyons became a Hall of Famer in 1955.

CAREER STATISTICS:

21 Years	Games Started 484	Shutouts 27
Wins 260	Games Completed 356	Relief Appearances 110
Losses 230	Innings 4,161	Relief Wins 17
Winning Percentage .531	Hits 4,489	Relief Losses 21
ERA 3.67	Bases on Balls 1,121	Saves 23
Total Games 594	Strikeouts 1,073	

CAREER STATISTICS AS MANAGER:

3 Years   Wins 185   Winning Percentage .430
Games 434   Losses 245   First-place Finishes 0

Cornelius Mack
(Connie, The Tall Tactician)
B. Dec. 22, 1862, D. Feb. 8, 1956
Was–NL 1886–89, Buf–PL 1890, Pit–NL 1891–96
Manager: Pit–NL 1894–96, Phi–AL 1901–50

NUMBER OF RECORDS ESTABLISHED AS PLAYER: 7

NUMBER OF RECORDS ESTABLISHED AS MANAGER: 22

TOTAL: 29

PLAYER RECORDS

NATIONAL LEAGUE RECORDS

Rookie Fielding Records—C

1887	Putouts	391	3	
	Double Plays	15		Never Broken
	Total Chances	563	3	

Season Fielding Records—C

| 1887 | Double Plays | 15 | 10 | |
| 1888 | Assists | 152 | 2 | |

MAJOR LEAGUE RECORDS

Rookie Fielding Records—C

| 1887 | Double Plays | 15 | 23 | |

Season Fielding Records—C

| 1887 | Double Plays | 15 | 10 | |

MANAGER RECORDS

American League Season Records

1902	Wins	83	1	
	Winning Percentage	.610	1	
	Games Won Pennant By	5	1	
1910	Wins	102	2	
	Winning Percentage	.680	2	
	Games Won Pennant By	14½	13	
1916	Losses	117		Never Broken

American League Career Records

	Years as Manager	50		Never Broken
	Wins	3,627		Never Broken
	Losses	3,891		Never Broken
	Pennants Won	9	10	
	Cons. Pennants Won	3	8	

Major League Season Records

| 1916 | Losses | 117 | 46 | |

Major League Career Records

	Years	53		Never Broken
	Games	7,878		Never Broken
	Wins	3,776		Never Broken
	Losses	4,025		Never Broken

American League World Series Career Records—1905–31

	Series	8	10	
	Games	43	10	
	Losses	19	10	
	Cons. Series Won	3	28	
	(1910–13)			

Major League World Series Career Records

Cons. Series Won   3   28
(1910–13)

SUMMARY

Connie Mack, born Cornelius McGillicuddy, had an unexceptional 11-year career as a player. He finished with a .245 batting average. He gained fame as the manager with the longest career. It is very doubtful whether any human could possibly endure 53 years as a manager in our modern days.

In 1902, he won his first pennant with Hall of Famers Eddie Plank and Rube Waddell. He added another pennant in 1905, when another Hall of Famer, Chief Bender, was added to the pitching staff. Two more pennants followed in 1910 and 1911 with the help of two more Hall of Famers, Eddie Collins and Frank "Home Run" Baker. All these players were still with Mack in 1913 and 1914 to give him two more titles. Mack didn't win again until 1929, but then he won three in a row with the help of Hall of Famers Jimmie Foxx, Mickey Cochrane, Al Simmons, and Lefty Grove.

"The Tall Tactician" retired with records of managing more games and having more wins and more losses than any manager in baseball history.

Mack became a Hall of Famer in 1937.

CAREER STATISTICS:

11 Years   Home Runs 5   Strikeouts 127
Games 723   Home Run Percentage 0.2   Batting Ave. .245
At Bats 2,695   Runs Scored 391   Slugging Ave. .300
Hits 659   RBIs 265   Pinch Hit At Bats 2
Doubles 79   Bases on Balls 169   Pinch Hits 1
Triples 28   Stolen Bases 127

CAREER STATISTICS AS MANAGER:

53 Years (1st)   Wins 3,776 (1st)   Winning Percentage .484
Games 7,878 (1st)   Losses 4,025 (1st)   First-place Finishes 9

Mickey Charles Mantle
(The Commerce Comet, The Mick)

B. Oct. 20, 1931
NY–AL 1951–68

NUMBER OF RECORDS ESTABLISHED: 13

AMERICAN LEAGUE RECORDS

Career Batting Records

Most Strikeouts	1,710	15

MAJOR LEAGUE RECORDS

Career Batting Records

Most Strikeouts	1,710	11

ALL-STAR GAME RECORDS

Career Batting Records

Most Strikeouts	16	Never Broken

WORLD SERIES RECORDS

Game Batting Records

1960	Most RBIs	5	Broken Same Series

7-Game Series Batting Records

1966	Most Runs Scored	8		Tied
	Most RBIs	10	4	

Career Batting Records—1951–64

Most Home Runs	18		Never Broken
Most Runs Scored	42		Never Broken
Most RBIs	40		Never Broken
Most Total Bases	123		Never Broken
Most Extra Base Hits	26		Never Broken
Most Bases on Balls	43		Never Broken
Most Strikeouts	54		Never Broken

SUMMARY

Mickey Mantle was the greatest switch hitter in baseball. He led the league 27 times in various batting categories. He was a four-time home run champion, a two-time home run percentage king, and he won six run-scoring titles and four bases on balls crowns. He was a three-time slugging king, and he won single titles in batting average and RBIs. He is the only switch hitter to win the Triple Crown, and his 536 home runs place him sixth on the all-time list.

Mantle could field his center field position with the best of them. He replaced Joe DiMaggio there—no easy task. He was a league leader in fielding four times.

"The Mick" posted ten World Series records, and eight of them remain unbroken. On the all-time World Series list, Mantle is number one in seven categories and number two in three others. On the all-time major league list, he is fifth in bases on balls and seventh in home run percentage.

Mantle won three MVPs and added the Triple Crown in 1956, when he belted 52 homers, drove in 130 runs, and batted .353.

Mantle was welcomed into the Hall of Fame in 1974.

POSTSEASON AWARDS

1956 MVP
1957 MVP
1962 MVP

CAREER STATISTICS:

18 Years	Home Runs 536 (6th)	Strikeouts 1,710 (6th)
Games 2,401	Home Run Percentage 6.6 (7th)	Batting Ave. .298
At Bats 8,102	Runs Scored 1,677	Slugging Ave. .557
Hits 2,415	RBIs 1,509	Pinch Hit At Bats 106
Doubles 344	Bases on Balls 1,734 (5th)	Pinch Hits 25
Triples 72	Stolen Bases 153	

Henry Emmett Manush
(Heinie)

B. July 20, 1901, D. May 12, 1971

Det–AL 1923–27, StL–AL 1928–30, Was–AL 1930–35,
Bos–AL 1936, Bkn–NL 1937–38,
Pit–NL 1938–39

NUMBER OF RECORDS ESTABLISHED: 2

AMERICAN LEAGUE RECORDS

Career Fielding Records—LF

Highest Fielding Ave.	.980	2

MAJOR LEAGUE RECORDS

Career Fielding Records—LF

Highest Fielding Ave.	.980	2

SUMMARY

Heinie Manush's best season came in 1928, when he slugged 241 base hits, 47 of which were doubles, 20 triples, and 13 homers, with a sizzling .378 batting average.

Manush batted over .300 11 times, with a high of .378 twice. He was a back-to-back doubles champion in 1928 and 1929 and had four seasons with more than 200 hits. He finished with a .330 career batting record.

Manush was named to the Hall of Fame in 1964.

CAREER STATISTICS:

17 Years
Games 2,009
At Bats 7,653
Hits, 2,524
Doubles 491
Triples 160

Home Runs 110
Home Run Percentage 1.4
Runs Scored 1,287
RBIs 1,173
Bases on Balls 506
Stolen Bases 114

Strikeouts 345
Batting Ave. .330
Slugging Ave. .479
Pinch Hit At Bats 146
Pinch Hits 36

Walter James Vincent Maranville
(Rabbit)

B. Nov. 11, 1891, D. Jan. 5, 1954

Bos–NL 1912–20, Pit–NL 1921–24, Chi–NL 1925, Bkn–NL 1926,
StL–NL 1927–28, Bos–NL 1929–35
Manager: Chi–NL 1925

NUMBER OF RECORDS ESTABLISHED AS PLAYER: 20

NATIONAL LEAGUE RECORDS

Rookie Fielding Records—SS

1913	Highest Fielding Ave.	.949	20	

Season Batting Records

1922	Most At Bats	672	9	

Season Fielding Records

1914	Most Assists—SS	574	6	
	Most Total Chances	1,046		Tied
1924	Most Assists—2B	568	2	
	Most Double Plays—2B	109	4	

Career Fielding Records—SS

Most Games Played	2,154		Never Broken
Most Putouts	5,139		Never Broken
Most Double Plays	1,183	23	
Highest Fielding Ave.	.951	1	

MAJOR LEAGUE RECORDS

Rookie Fielding Records—SS

1913	Highest Fielding Ave.	.949	13

Season Batting Records

1922	Most At Bats	672	9

Season Fielding Records—SS

1914	Most Assists	574	6	
	Most Total Chances	1,046		Tied

Career Fielding Records—SS

Most Games Played	2,154	15	
Most Putouts	5,139		Never Broken
Most Double Plays	1,183	15	

WORLD SERIES RECORDS

4-Game Series Fielding Records—SS

1914	Most Putouts	7	14
	Most Errors	1	14
1928	Most Putouts	11	4

SUMMARY

"Rabbit" Maranville has long been considered one of baseball's great all-around shortstops. He laced up his spikes for 23 years, banged out 2,605 hits, and set 20 records.

On defense, "Rabbit" made more putouts than any other shortstop in the major leagues and played more games than any shortstop in the National League. He also played a number of games at second base. He led the league in various fielding departments 23 times.

Maranville entered the Hall of Fame in 1954.

CAREER STATISTICS:

23 Years	At Bats 10,078	Doubles 380
Games 2,670	Hits 2,605	Triples 177

Home Runs 28

Home Run Percentage 0.3

Runs Scored 1,255

RBIs 884

Bases on Balls 839

Stolen Bases 291

Strikeouts 756

Batting Ave. .258

Slugging Ave. .340

Pinch Hit At Bats 7

Pinch Hits 1

CAREER STATISTICS AS MANAGER:

1 Year

Games 53

Wins 23

Losses 30

Winning Percentage .434

First-place Finishes 0

Juan Marichal

B. Oct. 20, 1938
SF–NL 1960–73, Bos–AL 1974, LA–NL 1975

NUMBER OF RECORDS ESTABLISHED: 1

ALL-STAR GAME RECORDS

Career Pitching Records—1962–71

Total Games	8	Tied

SUMMARY

Juan Marichal was a baffling pitcher. His high-kicking motion kept the batters off-stride, and he was a master at changing speeds. In six of seven seasons he won over 20 games. He was a two-time wins leader and a winning percentage leader in 1966 with a splendid .806, based on his 25–6 record.

In 1969, Marichal had the lowest ERA (2.10), and he was a two-time complete games leader, innings leader, and shutouts champion. In 1965 he won 22 games, 10 of them shutouts. He was a league leader 11 times and finished with 243 victories and 142 losses.

Marichal entered the Hall of Fame in 1983.

CAREER STATISTICS:

16 Years

Wins 243

Losses 142

Winning Percentage .631

ERA 2.89

Total Games 471

Games Started 457

Games Completed 244

Innings 3,509

Hits 3,153

Bases on Balls 709

Strikeouts 2,303

Shutouts 52

Relief Appearances 14

Relief Wins 5

Relief Losses 2

Saves 2

Richard William Marquard
(Rube)

B. Oct. 9, 1889, D. June 1, 1980

NY–NL 1908–15, Bkn–NL 1915–20, Cin–NL 1921, Bos–NL 1922–25

NUMBER OF RECORDS ESTABLISHED: 8

WORLD SERIES RECORDS

Game Pitching Records

1912	Fewest Earned Runs (Min. 9 Inn.)	0		Tied

5-Game Series Pitching Records

1916	Losses	2		Tied
	Highest ERA	7.00	20	

6-Game Series Pitching Records

1911	Fewest Bases on Balls (Min. 10 Inn.)	1	37	
	Total Games	3	4	

8-Game Series Pitching Records

| 1912 | Lowest ERA | 0.50 | 9 |

Career Pitching Records—1911–20

| Losses | 5 | 24 |
| Total Games | 11 | 9 |

SUMMARY

In 3 years "Rube" Marquard (1911–13) won 24, 26, and 23 games. In 1911 he led the league in strikeouts with 237 while leading the Giants to the pennant. His record was a blazing 24–7, and his .774 winning percentage was tops in the league.

In 1912, he again led the league with 26 wins and helped the Giants to the pennant. Big Rube won 201 games.

Marquard was inducted into the Hall of Fame in 1971.

CAREER STATISTICS:

18 Years	Games Started 403	Shutouts 30
Wins 201	Games Completed 197	Relief Appearances 133
Losses 177	Innings 3,307	Relief Wins 27
Winning Percentage .532	Hits 3,233	Relief Losses 12
ERA 3.08	Bases on Balls 858	Saves 14
Total Games 536	Strikeouts 1,593	

Edwin Lee Mathews, Jr.
(Eddie)

B. Oct. 13, 1931

Bos–NL 1952, Mil–NL 1953–65, Atl–NL 1966, Hou–NL 1967, Det–AL 1967–68
Manager: Atl–NL 1972–74

NUMBER OF RECORDS ESTABLISHED AS PLAYER: 11

NATIONAL LEAGUE RECORDS

Career Batting Records

Most Strikeouts	1,463	6	

Career Fielding Records—3B

Most Games Played	2,181		Never Broken
Most Assists	4,323	5	
Most Double Plays	369	5	
Most Total Chances	6,665	5	

MAJOR LEAGUE RECORDS

Career Fielding Records—3B

Most Games Played	2,181	9

Most Assists	4,323	5
Most Double Plays	369	5
Most Total Chances	6,665	5

ALL-STAR GAME RECORDS

Game Fielding Records—3B

1960	Most Errors	2	Tied

WORLD SERIES RECORDS

7-Game Series Batting Records

1958	Most Strikeouts	11	Tied

SUMMARY

Eddie Mathews was the greatest left-handed hitting third baseman in the game. His 512 home runs place him tenth on the all-time list and of all third basemen, only Mike Schmidt has more home runs.

Mathews was a league leader in various batting categories ten times. He was a two-time home run king and a three-time home run percentage leader. He led the league in bases on balls four times. Mathews was a 12-time leader in fielding.

Mathews became a Hall of Famer in 1978.

CAREER STATISTICS:

17 Years	Home Runs 512 (10th)	Strikeouts 1,487
Games 2,388	Home Run Percentage 6.0	Batting Ave. .271
At Bats 8,537	Runs 1,509	Slugging Ave. .509
Hits 2,315	RBIs 1,453	Pinch Hit At Bats 70
Doubles 354	Bases on Balls 1,444	Pinch Hits 12
Triples 72	Stolen Bases 68	

CAREER STATISTICS AS MANAGER:

3 Years	Wins 149	Winning Percentage .481
Games 310	Losses 161	First-place Finishes 0

Christopher Mathewson
(Big Six, Christy)
B. Aug. 12, 1880, D. Oct. 7, 1925
NY–NL 1900–16, Cin–NL 1916
Manager: Cin–NL 1916–18

NUMBER OF RECORDS ESTABLISHED AS PLAYER: 51

NATIONAL LEAGUE RECORDS

Season Pitching Title Records

1908	Strikeout Titles	5	2	
1909	ERA Titles	3	2	
1911	ERA Titles	4	2	
1913	ERA Titles	5		Tied

Career Pitching Records

	Most 20-Win Seasons	13		Never Broken
	Wins	373		Tied
	Games	636	14	
	Strikeouts	2,502	49	
	Strikeouts/9 Inn.	4.7	41	
	Winning Percentage	.665		Never Broken
	Shutouts	80	14	

MAJOR LEAGUE RECORDS

Season Pitching Title Records

1909	ERA Titles	3	2	
1911	ERA Titles	4	2	
1913	ERA Titles	5	22	

WORLD SERIES RECORDS

Game Pitching Records

1905	Innings	9	2	
	Innings	9	2	
	Innings	9	2	
	Fewest Bases on Balls	0	7	
	Fewest Bases on Balls	0	7	
	Fewest Earned Runs	0	8	
	Fewest Earned Runs	0	8	
	Fewest Earned Runs	0	8	
1911	Fewest Bases on Balls	0	1	
1912	Fewest Bases on Balls (11 Inn.)	0		Never Broken
1913	Fewest Earned Runs	0	20	

(The above category of records includes extra-inning games.)

5-Game Series Pitching Records

1905	Games	3	69	
	Starts	3		Never Broken
	Complete Games	3		Never Broken
	Wins	3		Never Broken
	Shutouts	3		Never Broken
	Innings	27		Never Broken
	Strikeouts	18		Never Broken
	ERA	0.00		Never Broken
	Fewest Bases on Balls	1	28	

6-Game Series Pitching Records

1911	Games	3	48	
	Starts	3		Never Broken
	Losses	2	70	
	Innings	27		Never Broken
	Most Hits Allowed	25		Never Broken

7-Game Series Pitching Records

1912	Losses	2	7	

Career Pitching Records—1905–13

Games	11	16	
Starts	11	51	
Complete Games	10		Never Broken
Wins	5	1	
Losses	5	51	
Innings	102	51	
ERA	1.15	5	
Strikeouts	48	1	
Shutouts	4		Never Broken
Hits Allowed	76	51	
Series Played	5	18	

SUMMARY

Many call Mathewson the greatest pitcher of all time. Seventeen of "Big Six's" records have never been broken, and he led the league in various pitching departments 30 times. He was amazing as he won 373 games, which places him in a tie for third place on the all-time list. He is third in shutouts with 80 and fifth in ERA at 2.13.

Mathewson has the highest winning percentage of any National League pitcher, and his 13 seasons of winning 20 or more games places him at the top of that National League all-time list. In four of those 13 seasons Matty won 30 or more games.

Mathewson accumulated 37 of his 51 records in World Series play. He teamed up with Joe McGinnity to lead New York to consecutive pennants in 1904 and 1905. Matty won 33 games in 1904 and 31 in 1905.

In the five-game 1905 World Series he started three games and won them all by shutouts, a feat that must go down as one of the most remarkable pitching performances in World Series history!

In 1911, 1912, and 1913, Mathewson teamed up with another Hall of Famer, Rube Marquard, to bring New York three more pennants. During these three years Mathewson and Marquard were the only Hall of Famers on the team. Mathewson was called "Big Six" because he was six feet tall.

Mathewson was welcomed into the Hall of Fame in 1936.

CAREER STATISTICS:

17 Years
Wins 373 (3rd, tie)
Losses 188
Winning Percentage .665 (7th)
ERA 2.13 (5th)
Total Games 636

Games Started 552
Games Completed 435
Innings 4,782
Hits 4,216
Bases on Balls 846
Strikeouts 2,502

Shutouts 80 (3rd)
Relief Appearances 84
Relief Wins 26
Relief Losses 10
Saves 27

CAREER STATISTICS AS MANAGER:

3 Years
Games 346

Wins 164
Losses 176

Winning Percentage .482
First-place Finishes 0

Willie Howard Mays

(Say Hey)

B. May 6, 1931

NY–NL 1951–57, SF–NL 1958–72, NY–NL 1972–73

NUMBER OF RECORDS ESTABLISHED: 20

NATIONAL LEAGUE RECORDS

Career Batting Records

Most Home Runs	660	1
Most Runs Scored	2,062	1
Most Strikeouts	1,526	6

Career Fielding Records—CF

Most Games Played	2,843	Never Broken
Most Putouts	7,095	Never Broken
Most Total Chances	7,431	Never Broken

MAJOR LEAGUE RECORDS

Career Fielding Records—CF

Most Games Played	2,843	Never Broken

Most Putouts	7,095	Never Broken
Most Total Chances	7,431	Never Broken

ALL-STAR GAME RECORDS

Game Batting Records

1960	Most Extra Base Hits	2	Tied
1962	Most Stolen Bases	2	Never Broken
1973	Most Games Played	24	Tied

Career Batting Records—1954–73

Most Games Played	24	Tied
Most At Bats	75	Never Broken
Most Hits	23	Never Broken
Most Singles	15	Never Broken
Most Triples	3	Tied
Most Extra Base Hits	8	Tied
Most Stolen Bases	6	Never Broken

SUMMARY

Willie Mays won the Rookie of the Year Award in 1951 and MVP Awards in 1954 and 1965. He batted .345 to lead the National League and belted 41 homers in 1954, and in 1965 he went downtown 52 times.

Many people call Mays the greatest centerfielder of all time. The "Say Hey Kid" could do everything: hit, hit with power, steal bases, and field. His 1954 catch of Vic Wertz's fly ball in the World Series is remembered as one of the most thrilling fielding plays ever made.

When he retired in 1973, Willie had played more games, made more putouts, and had more total chances than any centerfielder in baseball history. Mays led the league in various batting categories 24 times. He was a five-time slugging king, a home run and home run percentage leader four times, and won the triples title three times. He also scored the most runs twice and led the league in hits once. In all, he batted over .300 ten times and ended his career with a lifetime batting average of .302.

Willie was magnificent in All-Star competition. Willie set 11 records, and none of them have ever been broken!

Willie is third on the all-time list in homers with 660, fifth in runs scored, sixth in games played and at bats, seventh in RBIs, ninth in hits, and tenth in slugging average.

Mays was recognized by the Hall of Fame in 1979.

POSTSEASON AWARDS

1951 Rookie of the Year
1954 MVP
1965 MVP

CAREER STATISTICS:

22 Years
Games 2,992 (6th)
At Bats 10,881 (6th)
Hits 3,283 (9th)
Doubles 523
Triples 140

Home Runs 660 (3rd)
Home Run Percentage 6.1
Runs Scored 2,062 (5th)
RBIs 1,903 (7th)
Bases on Balls 1,463
Stolen Bases 338

Strikeouts 1,526
Batting Ave. .302
Slugging Ave. .557 (10th)
Pinch Hit At Bats 94
Pinch Hits 23

Joseph Vincent McCarthy
(Marse Joe)

B. Apr. 21, 1887, D. Jan. 3, 1978
Manager: Chi–NL 1926–30, NY–AL 1931–46, Bos–AL 1948–50

NUMBER OF RECORDS ESTABLISHED AS MANAGER: 13

American League Career Records

Highest Winning Percentage	.621	10	
Cons. Pennants Won	4	14	
(1936–39)			

Major League Career Records

Highest Winning Percentage	.614		Never Broken
Cons. Pennants Won	4	14	

WORLD SERIES RECORDS

American League Career Records—1931–43

Series	8	10	
Series Won	7		Never Broken
Games Won	29	10	

Cons. Series Won (1932–41)	6		Never Broken
Highest Winning Percentage	.783	38	Never Broken

Major League Career Records—1929–43

Highest Winning Percentage	.698		Never Broken
Series Won	7		Tied
Games Won	30	15	
Cons. Series Won (1932–41)	6		Never Broken

SUMMARY

"Marse Joe" McCarthy was one of the most successful managers in baseball history, and he has the highest winning percentage to prove it. He managed one of the greatest New York Yankee teams in the days of Babe Ruth, Lou Gehrig, and Joe DiMaggio.

He accumulated 13 outstanding records, and seven of them have never been broken. The highlight of his career was during the 1932–41 years, when he won six World Series in six appearances.

McCarthy became a Hall of Famer in 1957.

CAREER STATISTICS AS MANAGER:

24 Years	Wins 2,126 (4th)	Winning Percentage .614 (1st)
Games 3,489 (8th)	Losses 1,335	First-place Finishes 9

Thomas Francis Michael McCarthy
(Little Tom, Tommy)

B. July 24, 1864, D. Aug. 5, 1922

Bos–UA 1884, Bos–NL 1885, Phi–NL 1886–87, StL–AA 1888–91, Bos–NL 1892–95, Bkn–NL 1896
Manager: StL–AA 1890

NUMBER OF RECORDS ESTABLISHED AS PLAYER: 2

NATIONAL LEAGUE RECORDS

Season Fielding Records—LF

1894	Most Double Plays	10	17

MAJOR LEAGUE RECORDS

Season Fielding Records—LF

1894	Most Double Plays	10	17

SUMMARY

Tommy McCarthy was one of the first "little men" in baseball. Standing only 5′7″ and weighing 170 pounds, he was one of the original "scooters." His expertise was stealing bases. In 1888, he stole 93 and in 1890 led the league with 83 steals. In his 13-year career he stole 467 bases.

His best season was 1890, when he batted .350. In 1893 and 1894, he hit .346 and .349. His lifetime batting average was .292.

In the fielding department, "Little Tom" showed a very strong arm by participating in ten double plays in one season, a major league record that stood for 17 years. He was a three-time fielding league leader.

McCarthy was named to the Hall of Fame in 1946.

CAREER STATISTICS:

13 Years
Games 1,275
At Bats 5,128
Hits 1,496
Doubles 192
Triples 58

Home Runs 44
Home Run Percentage 0.9
Runs Scored 1,069
RBIs 665
Bases on Balls 537
Stolen Bases 467

Strikeouts 163
Batting Ave. .292
Slugging Ave. .378
Pinch Hit At Bats 0
Pinch Hits 0

CAREER STATISTICS AS MANAGER:

1 Year
Games 26

Wins 13
Losses 13

Winning Percentage .500
First-place Finishes 0

Willie Lee McCovey
(Stretch)
B. Jan. 10, 1938
SF–NL 1959–73, SD–NL 1974–76, Oak–AL 1976, SF–NL 1977–80

NUMBER OF RECORDS ESTABLISHED: 5

NATIONAL LEAGUE RECORDS

Rookie Batting Records

1959	Highest Home Run Percentage	6.8	Tied
	Highest Slugging Ave.	.656	Never Broken

MAJOR LEAGUE RECORDS

1959	Highest Slugging Ave.	.656	Never Broken

ALL-STAR GAME RECORDS

Game Batting Records

1969	Most Home Runs	2	Tied
	Most Extra Base Hits	2	Tied

SUMMARY

"Stretch" McCovey could hit home runs with the best of them. His career total of 521 places him eighth on the all-time list, and his home run percentage of 6.4 ranks him tenth.

Standing 6'4" and weighing 198 pounds, he was an awesome sight to enemy pitchers. He was a three-time home run champion and a home run percentage leader five times, including four times in a row from 1967 to 1970.

In three consecutive years (1968–70) McCovey led the league in slugging average, and he was a two-time RBI champion in 1968 and 1969. He won the MVP Award in 1969.

McCovey was welcomed into the Hall of Fame in 1986.

POSTSEASON AWARDS

1969 MVP

CAREER STATISTICS:

22 Years	Home Runs 521 (8th)	Strikeouts 1,550
Games 2,588	Home Run Percentage 6.4 (10th)	Batting Ave. .270
At Bats 8,197	Runs Scored 1,229	Slugging Ave. .515
Hits 2,211	RBIs 1,555	Pinch Hit At Bats 254
Doubles 353	Bases on Balls 1,345	Pinch Hits 66
Triples 46	Stolen Bases 26	

Joseph Jerome McGinnity
(Joe, The Iron Man)
B. Mar. 19, 1871, D. Nov. 14, 1929
Bal–NL 1899, Bkn–NL 1900, Bal–AL 1901–02, NY–NL 1902–08

NUMBER OF RECORDS ESTABLISHED: 39

AMERICAN LEAGUE RECORDS

Season Pitching Records

1901	Games	48	3	
	Starts	43	3	
	Complete Games	39	1	
	Innings	382	1	
	Hits Allowed	412		Never Broken

Season Pitching Title Records

1901	Innings Titles	1	2
	Saves Titles	1	9
	Games Titles	1	5
	Complete Games Titles	1	7

NATIONAL LEAGUE RECORDS

Season Pitching Records

1904	Saves	5	1	

Season Pitching Title Records

1903	Wins Titles	3	1	
	Innings Titles	4	1	
1904	Wins Titles	4	2	
	Games Titles	4	1	
	Innings Titles	5	12	
1905	Games Titles	5	1	
1906	Wins Titles	5	14	
	Games Titles	6	1	
1907	Games Titles	7		Never Broken

Career Pitching Records

	Relief Games	75	2
	Relief Wins	19	5
	Saves	22	8
	Wins & Saves	41	8

MAJOR LEAGUE RECORDS

Season Pitching Records

1904	Saves	5	1	

Season Pitching Title Records

1903	Innings Titles	4	1	
	Games Titles	3	1	
1904	Wins Titles	4	2	
	Innings Titles	5	12	
	Games Titles	4	1	
1905	Games Titles	5	1	
1906	Games Titles	6	1	
	Wins Titles	5	14	
1907	Games Titles	7		Never Broken

Career Pitching Records

	Relief Games	85	5
	Relief Wins	21	5
	Relief Losses	13	5
	Saves	23	8
	Wins & Saves	44	8

WORLD SERIES RECORDS

Game Pitching Records

1905	Innings	9	2	
	Fewest Earned Runs	0		Tied
	(9 Inn.)			

SUMMARY

"Iron Man" Joe McGinnity pitched only ten years but he led the league 35 times in various pitching departments and accumulated 39 records! He won 28 games as a rookie in 1899 and then followed with 29, 26, 21, 31, 35, 21, and 27 wins. In 1907 he won only 18 and his arm gave out in 1908 after 11 more wins. He averaged almost 25 wins per season.

McGinnity's best season was in 1904, when he won 35 and lost only 8, with a cool ERA of 1.61. This represents a winning percentage of .814. He started 51 games, pitched 408 innings, spun 9 shutouts, and had 2 wins and 5 saves in relief that year. All these marks were league-leading figures.

In seven of eight years, he led the league in starts, and in six of seven years he was a leader in innings pitched.

McGinnity entered the Hall of Fame in 1946.

CAREER STATISTICS:

10 Years	Games Started 381	Shutouts 32
Wins 247	Games Completed 314	Relief Appearances 85
Losses 144	Innings 3,459	Relief Wins 21
Winning Percentage .632	Hits 3,276	Relief Losses 13
ERA 2.64	Bases on Balls 812	Saves 23
Total Games 466	Strikeouts 1,068	

John Joseph McGraw

(Little Napoleon, Mugsy)

B. Apr. 7, 1873, D. Feb. 25, 1934

Bal–AA 1891, Bal–NL 1892–99, StL–NL 1900, Bal–AL 1901–02, NY–NL 1902–06
Manager: Bal–NL 1899, Bal–AL 1901–02, NY–NL 1902–32

NUMBER OF RECORDS ESTABLISHED AS MANAGER: 24

National League Season Records

1904	Wins	106	2

National League Career Records

	Years	33	Never Broken
	Games	4,681	Never Broken
	Wins	2,744	Never Broken
	Losses	1,885	Never Broken
	Pennants Won	10	Never Broken
	Cons. Pennants Won	4	Never Broken

Major League Season Records

1904	Wins	106	2

Major League Career Records

Years	33	18	
Games	4,879	18	
Wins	2,840	18	
Losses	1,984	18	
Pennants Won	10		Never Broken
Cons. Pennants Won	4	29	

National League World Series Career Records—1899–1932

Series	10		Never Broken
Games	55		Never Broken
Series Won	3	44	
Games Won	26		Never Broken
Games Lost	28		Never Broken

Major League World Series Career Records

Series	10		Never Broken
Games	55	33	
Series Won	3	18	
Games Won	26	18	
Games Lost	28		Never Broken

SUMMARY

John "Mugsy" McGraw was also called the "Little Napoleon" due to his size and toughness; he stood only 5'7" and weighed 155 pounds. In his best seasons he batted .391, .369, .352, .344, .342, and .340. His lifetime batting average was a solid .344. A little-known fact is that McGraw has the second-highest on-base average in baseball history (Ted Williams is number one).

McGraw will go down in baseball history as one of the game's most successful managers. He established 24 records, 13 of which have remained unbroken for more than half a century.

No other National League manager has managed as many years, managed more games, won and lost more games, or has won as many pennants as McGraw. His teams featured such Hall of Fame players as Roger Bresnahan, Joe McGinnity, Christy Mathewson, Joe Kelley, Don Brouthers, Hugh Jennings, Willie Keeler, Wilbert Robinson, Rube Marquard, Bill Mc-Kechnie, Ross Youngs, Frankie Frisch, George Kelly, Dave Bancroft, Casey Stengel, Travis Jackson, Hack Wilson, Bill Terry, Freddie Lindstrom, Rogers Hornsby, Edd Roush, Mel Ott, Burleigh Grimes, Carl Hubbell, and Waite Hoyt. McGraw managed seven future Hall of Famers on his 1925 and 1927 teams.

McGraw was inducted into the Hall of Fame in 1937.

CAREER STATISTICS:

16 Years	Doubles 127	Runs Scored 1,026
Games 1,099	Triples 68	RBIs 462
At Bats 3,922	Home Runs 13	Bases on Balls 836
Hits 1,308	Home Run Percentage 0.3	Stolen Bases 436

Strikeouts 74   Slugging Ave. .411   Pinch Hits 2
Batting Ave. .334   Pinch Hit At Bats 19

CAREER STATISTICS AS MANAGER:

33 Years   Wins 2,840 (2nd)   Winning Percentage .589 (8th)
Games 4,879 (2nd)   Losses 1,984 (3rd)   First-place Finishes 10

William Boyd McKechnie
(Bill, Deacon)

B. Aug. 7, 1886, D. Oct. 29, 1965

Pit–NL 1907–12, Bos–NL 1913, NY–AL 1913,
Ind–FL 1914, Nwk–FL 1915, NY–NL 1916, Cin–NL 1916–17, Pit–NL 1918, 1920
Manager: Nwk–FL 1915, Pit–NL 1922–26, StL–NL 1928–29, Bos–NL 1930–37, Cin–NL 1938–46

NUMBER OF RECORDS ESTABLISHED: 0

SUMMARY

Bill McKechnie, who set no records, played the majority of his major league career as a third baseman but also filled in at first, second, and shortstop. He played for 11 years, mostly for the Pittsburgh Pirates; he also had stints with the Braves, Yankees, Giants, and Reds.

McKechnie was a well-respected manager who put in 25 years at the helm. During that time he won four pennants and two World Series. In four World Series he managed 22 games (10th), winning 8 and losing 14 (6th), and had a winning percentage of .364.

His greatest moment came in 1925, when he led the Pirates to a world championship by defeating the Washington Senators and the great Walter Johnson. In 1928 he led the Cardinals to a pennant over John McGraw's New York Giants. In 1937, he was named manager of the year for leading the hapless Braves to a 78–73 finish. McKechnie was again hired by the Cardinals in 1938, and he led them to two pennants (1939, 1940) and a World Series victory in 1940. Before retiring he coached for the Cleveland Indians (1947–49) and the Boston Red

Sox. He retired in 1953 and was recognized as one of the finest managers in baseball history for his expertise in pitching and defense.

McKechnie was elected to the Hall of Fame in 1962.

CAREER STATISTICS:

11 Years

Games 845

At Bats 2,843

Hits 713

Doubles 86

Triples 33

Homers 8

Home Run Percentage 0.3

Runs Scored 319

RBIs 240

Bases on Balls 188

Stolen Bases 127

Strikeouts 128

Batting Ave. .251

Slugging Ave. .313

Pinch Hit At Bats 35

Pinch Hits 8

CAREER STATISTICS AS MANAGER:

25 Years

Games 3,650 (7th)

Wins 1,898 (8th)

Losses 1,724 (6th)

Winning Percentage .524

First-place Finishes 4

Joseph Michael Medwick
(Joe, Ducky, Muscles)
B. Nov. 24, 1911, D. Mar. 21, 1975

StL–NL 1932–40, Bkn–NL 1940–43, NY–NL 1943–45, Bos–NL 1945, Bkn–NL 1946,
StL–NL 1947–48

NUMBER OF RECORDS ESTABLISHED: 11

NATIONAL LEAGUE RECORDS

Season Batting Records

1936	Most Doubles	64		Never Broken

ALL-STAR GAME RECORDS

Game Batting Records

1934	Most Home Runs	1	7	
	Most RBIs	3	16	
1937	Most Hits	4		Tied
	Most Doubles	2		Tied
	Most Total Bases	6	5	
	Most Extra Base Hits	2		Tied

Career Batting Records—1934–44

Most RBIs	5	6
Most Triples	1	29
Most Extra Base Hits	3	16

WORLD SERIES RECORDS

Game Batting Records

1934	Most Hits	4	48

SUMMARY

"Ducky" Medwick, the man who hit more doubles in a season than any other National League player, completed a marvelous 17-year career with a .324 batting average.

He was a league leader in various batting categories 13 times, which include two most hits titles, three doubles crowns, three RBI titles, and single titles in at bats, triples, homers, runs, batting average, and slugging average. He batted over .300 11 times in succession and 14 times all told. His highest batting averages were .374, .353, and .351.

Medwick enjoyed his finest hour in 1937, when he won both the Triple Crown and the MVP Award. He batted .374, ripped 237 hits, 56 doubles, and 31 homers, drove in 154 runs, and slugged .641.

Medwick entered the Hall of Fame in 1968.

POSTSEASON AWARDS

1937 MVP, Triple Crown

CAREER STATISTICS:

17 Years	Home Runs 205	Strikeouts 551
Games 1,984	Home Run Percentage 2.7	Batting Ave. .324
At Bats 7,635	Runs Scored 1,198	Slugging Ave. .505
Hits 2,471	RBIs 1,383	Pinch Hit At Bats 107
Doubles 540	Bases on Balls 437	Pinch Hits 22
Triples 113	Stolen Bases 42	

John Robert Mize
(Johnny, The Big Cat)
B. Jan. 7, 1913
StL–NL 1936–41, NY–NL 1942–49, NY–AL 1949–53

NUMBER OF RECORDS ESTABLISHED: 4

NATIONAL LEAGUE RECORDS

Rookie Fielding Records—1B

1936	Highest Fielding Ave.	.994	2

WORLD SERIES RECORDS

4-Game Series Fielding Records—1B

1950	Most Assists	3	4

7-Game Series Batting Records

1952	Highest Slugging Ave.	1.106	Never Broken

Career Batting Records—1949–53

	Most Pinch Hits	3	Never Broken

SUMMARY

Few fans realize that Johnny Mize's lifetime slugging average of .562 is the eighth best in baseball. He was a slugging leader four times, winning this crown three times in a row from 1938 to 1940. Mize was also a four-time home run champion, turning the trick back-to-back in 1939 and 1940 and again in 1947 and 1948. He won three RBI titles and all told was a league leader in various batting departments 20 times.

Mize batted over .300 nine consecutive times, with a high of .364 in 1937. His lifetime batting average was .312.

When he was traded from the Giants to the Yankees in 1949, "Big John" led the league in pinch hits three years in a row!

Mize also played well on defense and has 11 league titles to show.

Mize was honored by the Hall of Fame in 1981.

CAREER STATISTICS:

15 Years	Home Runs 359	Strikeouts 524
Games 1,884	Home Run Percentage 5.6	Batting Ave. .312
At Bats 6,443	Runs Scored 1,118	Slugging Ave. .562 (8th)
Hits 2,011	RBIs 1,337	Pinch Hit At Bats 187
Doubles 367	Bases on Balls 856	Pinch Hits 53
Triples 83	Stolen Bases 28	

Stanley Frank Musial
(Stan the Man)
B. Nov. 21, 1920
StL–NL 1941–63

NUMBER OF RECORDS ESTABLISHED: 45

NATIONAL LEAGUE RECORDS

Season Batting Title Records

1946	Most MVP Titles	2	2	
1948	Most MVP Titles	3		Tied
	Most Hits Titles	4	1	
	Most Triples Titles	3	1	
1949	Most Hits Titles	5	3	
	Most Triples Titles	4	2	
1951	Most Triples Titles	5		Never Broken
1952	Most Hits Titles	6	29	
1954	Most Doubles Titles	8		Tied
	Most Runs Scored Titles	5		Tied

Career Batting Records

Most Games Played	3,026	13

Most At Bats	10,972	13	
Most Hits	3,630	13	
Most Doubles	725		Never Broken
Most Extra Base Hits	1,377	13	
Most Total Bases	6,134	13	
Most Runs Scored	1,949	0	
Most RBIs	1,951	13	

Career Fielding Records—LF

Highest Fielding Ave.	.983	1

MAJOR LEAGUE RECORDS

Season Batting Title Records

1954	Most Doubles Titles	8		Tied

Career Batting Records

Most Extra Base Hits	1,377	13
Most Total Bases	6,134	13

ALL-STAR GAME RECORDS

Game Batting Records

1954	Most Games Played	11	1	
1955	Most Games Played	12	1	
1956	Most Games Played	13	1	
1957	Most Games Played	14	1	
1958	Most Games Played	15	1	
1959	Most Games Played	16	1	
1959	Most Games Played	17	1	
1960	Most Games Played	18	1	
1960	Most Games Played	19	1	
1961	Most Games Played	20	1	
1961	Most Games Played	21	1	
1962	Most Games Played	22	1	
1962	Most Games Played	23	1	
1963	Most Games Played	24		Tied

Fielding Records—1B

1958	Most Double Plays	3		Tied

Career Batting Records—1954–63

Most Games Played	24		Tied
Most At Bats	63	10	
Most Hits	20	10	

Most Runs Scored	10	10	
Most Home Runs	6		Never Broken
Most Total Bases	40		Never Broken
Most Extra Base Hits	8		Tied

WORLD SERIES RECORDS

5-Game Series Fielding Records—RF

1943	Most Assists	2	Tied

SUMMARY

Stan "The Man" Musial batted over .300 18 of his 22 years in baseball. He led the National League in various batting categories a remarkable 40 times.

Stan won the most hits crown four times and was an eight-time doubles king and a five-time triples leader; he led in runs scored five times, RBIs twice, and bases on balls once, was a batting average leader seven times, and led the league in slugging six times! These are quite some feats in our difficult modern times.

On the all-time list, Stan "The Man" is third in doubles, fourth in hits, fifth in games played, at bats, and RBIs, sixth in runs scored, eighth in bases on balls, and ninth in slugging average.

On defense he played right field, left field, and first base, and he did very well wherever he was asked to play, eight times leading the league in various fielding departments.

Hall of Fame honors were bestowed on Musial in 1969.

POSTSEASON AWARDS

1943 MVP
1946 MVP
1948 MVP

CAREER STATISTICS:

22 Years	Home Runs 475	Strikeouts 696
Games 3,026 (5th)	Home Run Percentage 4.3	Batting Ave. .331
At Bats 10,972 (5th)	Runs Scored 1,949 (6th)	Slugging Ave. .559 (9th)
Hits 3,630 (4th)	RBIs 1,951 (5th)	Pinch Hit At Bats 126
Doubles 725 (3rd)	Bases on Balls 1,599 (8th)	Pinch Hits 35
Triples 177	Stolen Bases 78	

Charles Augustus Nichols
(Kid)

B. Sept. 14, 1869, D. Apr. 11, 1953

Bos–NL 1890–1901, StL–NL 1904–05, Phi–NL 1905–06
Manager: StL–NL 1904–05

NUMBER OF RECORDS ESTABLISHED AS PLAYER: 14

NATIONAL LEAGUE RECORDS

Season Pitching Title Records

1895	Saves Titles	2	2
1897	Saves Titles	3	1
1898	Saves Titles	4	86
	Wins Titles	3	6

Career Pitching Records

Total Games	621	10
Saves	16	2
Wins	360	10
Wins & Saves	31	2

MAJOR LEAGUE RECORDS

Season Pitching Title Records

1898	Wins Titles	3	5

Career Pitching Records

Relief Games	59	2
Relief Wins	15	2
Relief Losses	9	2
Saves	16	2
Wins & Saves	31	2

SUMMARY

"Kid" Nichols won 360 games, the seventh highest in baseball history. His winning percentage was a marvelous .641, and his 533 complete games rank him fourth on the all-time list. He worked 5,084 innings, which earns him a seventh-place position, and he tossed 48 shutouts. Nichols won 30 or more games seven times. He also had seasons with 29 and 27 wins.

Nichols was a 12-time league leader, and had three consecutive wins titles from 1896 to 1898. He was a three-time shutout king and led the league in saves four times.

Nichols was recognized by the Hall of Fame in 1949.

CAREER STATISTICS:

15 Years	Games Started 562	Shutouts 48
Wins 360 (7th)	Games Completed 533 (4th)	Relief Appearances 59
Losses 202	Innings 5,084 (7th)	Relief Wins 15
Winning Percentage .641	Hits 4,912	Relief Losses 9
ERA 2.94	Bases on Balls 1,282	Saves 16
Total Games 621	Strikeouts 1,885	

CAREER STATISTICS AS MANAGER:

2 Years	Wins 94	Winning Percentage .465
Games 203	Losses 108	First-place Finishes 0

James Henry O'Rourke
(Orator Jim)

B. Aug. 24, 1852, D. Jan. 8, 1919

Bos–NL 1876–78, Pro–NL 1879, Bos–NL 1880, Buf–NL 1881–84, NY–NL 1885–89, NY–PL 1890
Manager: Buf–NL 1881–84, Was–NL 1893

NUMBER OF RECORDS ESTABLISHED AS PLAYER: 22

NATIONAL LEAGUE RECORDS

Rookie Fielding Records—CF

1876	Most Errors	27	12

Season Batting Records

1877	Most Bases on Balls	20	2
	Bases on Balls per Game	0.327	2
1879	Most RBIs	62	2
1884	Most Hits	162	1

Season Batting Title Records

1877	Bases on Balls Titles	1	7
	Most Runs Titles	1	5
1880	Home Runs Titles	1	6
1885	Triples Titles	1	1

Season Fielding Records

| 1876 | Most Errors—CF | 27 | 4 |
| 1888 | Highest Fielding Ave.—LF | .960 | 9 |

MAJOR LEAGUE RECORDS

Rookie Fielding Records

| 1876 | Most Errors—CF | 27 | 8 |

Season Batting Records

1877	Most Bases on Balls	20	2
	Bases on Balls per Game	0.327	2
1879	Most RBIs	62	2
1884	Most Hits	162	2

Season Batting Title Records

1877	Bases on Balls Titles	1	7
	Most Runs Titles	1	5
1880	Most Home Runs Titles	1	6
1885	Most Triples Titles	1	1

Season Fielding Records

| 1876 | Most Errors—CF | 27 | 4 |
| 1888 | Highest Fielding Ave.—LF | .960 | 9 |

SUMMARY

One of the outstanding pioneer players was Jim O'Rourke. Though he mostly played outfield during his 19-year career, he tried all nine positions.

O'Rourke's lifetime batting average was a smart .310, and he batted over .300 11 seasons. He was a league leader in runs scored, bases on balls, and most hits, triples, and home runs.

Hall of Fame honors were bestowed on O'Rourke in 1945.

CAREER STATISTICS:

19 Years	Home Runs 51	Strikeouts 348
Games 1,774	Home Run Percentage 0.7	Batting Ave. .310
At Bats 7,435	Runs Scored 1,446	Slugging Ave. .422
Hits 2,304	RBIs 830	Pinch Hit At Bats 0
Doubles 414	Bases on Balls 481	Pinch Hits 0
Triples 132	Stolen Bases 177	

CAREER STATISTICS AS MANAGER:

5 Years	Wins 246	Winning Percentage .488
Games 509	Losses 258	First-place Finishes 0

Melvin Thomas Ott
(Mel, Master Melvin)
B. Mar. 2, 1909, D. Nov. 21, 1958
NY–NL 1926–47
Manager: NY–NL 1942–48

NUMBER OF RECORDS ESTABLISHED AS PLAYER: 25

NATIONAL LEAGUE RECORDS

Rookie Batting Records

1927	Most Pinch Hit At Bats	46	5

Season Batting Records

1921	Highest Home Run Percentage	7.7	1

Season Batting Title Records

1937	Most Home Run Percentage Titles	6	1
1938	Most Home Run Percentage Titles	7	1
	Most Home Run Titles	5	4

1939	Most Home Run Percentage Titles	8	3	
1942	Most Home Run Percentage Titles	9	2	
	Most Home Run Titles	6	10	
1944	Most Home Run Percentage Titles	10		Never Broken

Career Batting Records

	Most Home Runs	511	21	
	Highest Home Run Percentage	5.4	8	
	Most Runs Scored	1,859	16	
	Most RBIs	1,860	16	
	Most Extra Base Hits	1,071	16	
	Most Total Bases	5,041	16	
	Most Bases on Balls	1,708	41	Never Broken

Career Fielding Records—RF

Most Games Played	2,313	26	
Highest Fielding Ave.	.981	6	

MAJOR LEAGUE RECORDS

Career Fielding Records—RF

Most Games Played	2,313	26

ALL-STAR GAME RECORDS

Game Batting Records

1938	Most Triples	1	40
1944	Most Games Played	11	11

Career Batting Records—1934–44

Most Games Played	11	11
Most Triples	1	29

WORLD SERIES RECORDS

Game Batting Records

1933	Most Hits	4	49

5-Game Series Batting Records

1933	Most Home Runs	2	36

SUMMARY

Mel Ott proved you do not have to be a big man to be a great home run hitter. At 5'9" and 170 pounds, "Master Melvin" pumped 511 balls out of the park and was one of the most feared home run hitters in baseball.

In a marvelous 22-year career, Ott was a 27-time league leader in various batting departments. His lifetime batting average was .304, and he had a healthy slugging average of .533.

Ott was a six-time home run champion, a record-breaking ten-time home run percentage slugger, and a six-time bases on balls leader, and he had single season titles in RBIs, pinch hit at bats, and slugging average. He was also a two-time run-scoring champion.

On the all-time list he is sixth in bases on balls, eighth in RBIs, and ninth in runs scored.

On defense, he was a five-time leader in various fielding categories.

Ott's Hall of Fame honors came in 1951.

CAREER STATISTICS:

22 Years	Home Runs 511	Strikeouts 896
Games 2,732	Home Run Percentage 5.4	Batting Ave. .304
At Bats 9,456	Runs Scored 1,859 (9th)	Slugging Ave. .533
Hits 2,876	RBIs 1,860 (8th)	Pinch Hit At Bats 137
Doubles 488	Bases on Balls 1,708 (6th)	Pinch Hits 32
Triples 72	Stolen Bases 89	

CAREER STATISTICS AS MANAGER:

7 Years	Wins 464	Winning Percentage .467
Games 1,004	Losses 530	First-place Finishes 0

Leroy Robert Paige
(Satchel)

B. July 7, 1906, D. June 8, 1982

Negro Leagues 1926–47, Cle–AL 1948–49, StL–AL 1951–53, KC–AL 1965

NUMBER OF RECORDS ESTABLISHED: 0

SUMMARY

Satchel Paige was easily the best black pitcher of his day. Phenomenally talented and charismatic, he made it a lot easier for other black players to demand better salaries and playing conditions.

When Paige joined the Cleveland Indians in 1948, his first major league team, he was 42 years old, but he won six games and lost only one in helping the Indians to the pennant. Paige was "Black Baseball," and his arrival in the majors marked the beginning of the end for the Negro Leagues, which disbanded for two reasons: attendance was dropping drastically as fans' interest turned more toward the majors, and the majors were stripping the Negro Leagues of their best players. By 1957, 14 major league clubs had 36 of the best black players. Total integration came in 1959, when the Boston Red Sox signed Pumpsie Green.

Paige was without doubt the greatest attraction in Negro baseball. The first time he came to Philadelphia with the Kansas City Monarchs in the thirties, he drew 30,000 fans. Satch was in such demand that he often pitched three innings every day just so fans could get a glimpse of him. In those three innings he sometimes threw nine or ten pitches to strike out the side. He had magnificent control, fantastic speed, and a splendid curve ball.

How great was Satchel Paige? One of those who knew him best was Dizzy Dean, who said, "I know who's the best pitcher I ever saw, and it's old Satchel Paige, that big lanky colored boy." Dean once lost an exhibition heartbreaker to Paige, who beat him 1-0 in 17 innings. Rogers Hornsby also knew Paige well because one day Satch struck him out five times in a row. And Charlie Gehringer and Jimmie Foxx got a taste of Satch, who struck each of them out three times in one game.

Paige was a super showman. Sometimes he toured for a team and other times for himself. For his solo performances he billed himself as "Satchel Paige, World's Greatest Pitcher, Guaranteed to Strike Out the First Nine Men." And he did that more often than not.

Of his days of full flower, Satch remembers, "I threw nothing but bee balls and trouble balls. They couldn't see me. The world knew about my fastball. But my best ones were my looper, nothing ball, bat dodger, and hurry-up ball." His "hesitation pitch" was banned by the American League as "deceitful." Paige says, "I ain't never throwed an illegal pitch, just once in a while I use to toss one that ain't never been seen by this generation."

In one game between Paige's All-Star barnstorming team and Dizzy Dean's All-Stars, Satchel pitched the first 6 innings and struck out 16 of the 18 major leaguers he faced. Sometimes he deliberately walked the first three batters and then struck out the next three.

Paige was 6'4", weighed 190 pounds, and wore a size 14 shoe. He got his nickname from carrying satchels at the railroad station. He said, "I could carry so many satchels, that's all they could see was satchels, they couldn't see no Leroy."

Joe DiMaggio batted against him and said, "He was the best I ever faced. After I got that first hit off him, I knew I was ready for the major leagues."

In 1931 Paige won 31, lost only 4, tossed an amazing 16 shutouts, and averaged 15.4 strikeouts per game! He was known for his "rubber arm" and was said to have pitched about 125 games per year for 20 years. It is estimated that he pitched 2500 games, won 2000, and had 250 shutouts and 100 no-hitters. But he never had a sore arm. He was his own trainer and used olive oil when his arm needed loosening up.

Paige faced Dean ten times in exhibition games and six times came away a winner. After leaving the major leagues in 1953, he continued pitching in the minor leagues and at the age of 52 worked 110 innings for the Miami Marlins and had an ERA of 2.95. He stayed active in the minors until 1966, finally quitting at age 60. In 1965, Satch made a "guest" appearance in the major leagues for the Kansas City A's and pitched three scoreless innings over the Boston Red Sox.

His pitching was a legend among major league hitters, and Satchel Paige is a special part of American folklore.

Paige was inducted into the Hall of Fame in 1971.

CAREER STATISTICS:

26 Years	Games Completed 7	Relief Wins 18
Wins 28	Innings 476	Relief Losses 23
Losses 31	Hits 429	Saves 32
Winning Percentage .475	Bases on Balls 183	
ERA 3.29	Strikeouts 290	
Games 179	Shutouts 4	
Games Started 26	Relief Appearances 153	

Herbert Jefferis Pennock
(Herb, The Knight of Kennett Square)
B. Feb. 10, 1894, D. Jan. 30, 1948
Phi–AL 1912–15, Bos–AL 1916–22, NY–AL 1923–33, Bos–AL 1934

NUMBER OF RECORDS ESTABLISHED: 9

WORLD SERIES RECORDS

4-Game Series Pitching Records

1914	Relief Games	1	8	
1932	Games	2	6	
	Relief Games	2	22	
	Saves	2		Tied

6-Game Series Pitching Records

1923	Games	3	36	
	Saves	1	36	
	Fewest Bases on Balls (Min. 10 Inn.)	1	25	

Career Pitching Records—1914–32

Highest Winning Percentage	1.000		Tied
Saves	3	9	

SUMMARY

In his 22-year career, Herb Pennock tallied 240 victories and 162 defeats. This hard-throwing lefthander is one of the few pitchers who has never lost a World Series game. In four Series, he has a perfect 5-0 record. He created all nine of his records in World Series play, and he ranks fourth in wins and eighth in saves.

Pennock enjoyed his best years while with the New York Yankees between 1923 and 1933. During this span he won 164 and lost only 90. Prior to this, he had been a .500 pitcher with the Boston Red Sox.

Pennock entered the Hall of Fame in 1948.

CAREER STATISTICS:

22 Years	Games Started 421	Shutouts 35
Wins 240	Games Completed 248	Relief Appearances 196
Losses 162	Innings 3,558	Relief Wins 23
Winning Percentage .597	Hits 3,900	Relief Losses 17
ERA 3.61	Bases on Balls 916	Saves 33
Total Games 617	Strikeouts 1,227	

Edward Stewart Plank
(Eddie, Gettysburg Eddie)
B. Aug. 31, 1875, D. Feb. 24, 1926
Phi–AL 1901–14, StL–FL 1915, StL–1916–17

NUMBER OF RECORDS ESTABLISHED: 17

AMERICAN LEAGUE RECORDS

Season Pitching Title Records

1903	Total Game Titles	1	3
1906	Winning Percentage Titles	1	5

Career Pitching Records

Total Games	580	10
Starts	496	10
Complete Games	389	10
Wins	306	10
Innings	4,237	10
Hits Allowed	3,744	10
Strikeouts	2,099	10
Shutouts	63	10
Relief Wins	25	8

WORLD SERIES RECORDS

Game Pitching Records

| 1905 | Innings | 9 | 2 | |
| 1911 | Fewest Bases on Balls/9 Inn. | 0 | | Tied |

5-Game Series Pitching Records

| 1905 | Losses | 2 | | Tied |
| | Hits Allowed | 14 | 2 | |

Career Pitching Records—1905–14

| | Losses | 5 | 50 | |
| | Fewest Hits/9 Inn. | 5.93 | 4 | |

SUMMARY

Eddie Plank was the first American League pitcher to win 300 games; his total of 327 places him ninth on the all-time list. During his 17-year career, Plank tossed 69 shutouts; only four other pitchers have ever done better. "Gettysburg Eddie," from Gettysburg, Pennsylvania, won 20 or more games eight times. He was a seven-time league leader.

In World Series play, he had a super 1.32 ERA, but due to a lack of support by his team-mates he lost 5 of the 7 games in which he appeared.

Plank was welcomed into the Hall of Fame in 1946.

CAREER STATISTICS:

17 Years	Games Started 527	Shutouts 69 (5th)
Wins 327 (9th)	Games Completed 412	Relief Appearances 95
Losses 193	Innings 4,505	Relief Wins 27
Winning Percentage .629	Hits 3,956	Relief Losses 14
ERA 2.34	Bases on Balls 1,072	Saves 23
Total Games 622	Strikeouts 2,246	

Charles Gardner Radbourn
(Old Hoss)
B. Dec. 11, 1854, D. Feb. 5, 1897
Buf–NL 1880, Pro–NL 1881–85, Bos–NL 1886–89, Bos–PL 1890, Cin–NL 1891

NUMBER OF RECORDS ESTABLISHED: 36

NATIONAL LEAGUE RECORDS

Season Pitching Records

Year			
1883	Wins	49	1
	Total Games	76	82
	Relief Losses	2	8
1884	Wins	60	Never Broken
	Strikeouts	441	Never Broken

Season Pitching Title Records

Year			
1884	Total Games Titles	2	5
	Wins Titles	2	5
	Winning Percentage Titles	2	24
	Shutout Titles	2	3
	Strikeout Titles	2	3

Career Pitching Records

Total Games	487	1
Starts	465	1
Complete Games	453	1
Wins	281	1
Innings	4,192	1
Hits Allowed	3,983	1
Most Bases on Balls	775	1
Strikeouts	1,750	1

MAJOR LEAGUE RECORDS

Season Pitching Records

1883	Total Games	76	82	
	Wins	49	1	
1884	Wins	60		Never Broken
	Strikeouts	441	2	
	Relief Losses	2	2	

Season Pitching Title Records

1884	Total Games Titles	2	5
	Wins Titles	2	5
	Winning Percentage Titles	2	6
	Strikeout Titles	2	3
1890	Winning Percentage Titles	3	42

Career Pitching Records

Total Games	528	1
Starts	503	1
Complete Games	489	1
Wins	308	1
Innings	4,535	1
Hits Allowed	4,335	1
Bases on Balls	875	1
Strikeouts	1,830	1

SUMMARY

One of the truly great pioneer pitchers in baseball was "Old Hoss" Radbourn. His name implies a big rugged individual, but in fact "Old Hoss" stood only 5'9" and weighed 168 pounds —a small man by today's standards but a big man on the mound then.

Radbourn was the first hurler to win 300 games, and he was a league leader in various pitching categories 20 times. His most renowned year came in 1884, when he went 60–12 to lead Providence to a pennant (in a 112-game season). In 1884 his ERA was a marvelous 1.38; not only did he finish all 73 games he started, he also picked up a win and a save in the two times he spelled Providence's other pitcher. In 678⅔ innings that year he allowed 528 hits and 98 walks. He struck out 441 men and tossed 11 shutouts.

Radbourn was named to the Hall of Fame in 1939.

CAREER STATISTICS:

12 Years	Games Started 503	Shutouts 35
Wins 308	Games Completed 489 (7th)	Relief Appearances 25
Losses 191	Innings 4,535	Relief Wins 8
Winning Percentage .617	Hits 4,335	Relief Losses 5
ERA 2.67	Bases on Balls 875	Saves 2
Total Games 528	Strikeouts 1,830	

Harold Henry Reese
(Pee Wee, The Little Colonel)
B. July 23, 1918
Bkn–NL 1940–57, LA–NL 1958

NUMBER OF RECORDS ESTABLISHED: 3

NATIONAL LEAGUE RECORDS

Career Fielding Records—SS

	Most Double Plays	1,246	8

ALL-STAR GAME RECORDS

Game Batting Records

1949	Most At Bats	6	1

WORLD SERIES RECORDS

Game Batting Records

1956	Most At Bats	6	17

SUMMARY

"Pee Wee" Reese was one of the National League's most outstanding shortstops. In a 17-year career, he was instrumental in leading the Dodgers to seven pennants.

Reese was a solid-hitting shortstop with a lifetime batting average of .269. He had exceptional power for someone who stood 5'10" and weighed 160 pounds. He belted 126 home runs, 80 triples, and 330 doubles. And he was a good base runner, stealing 232 bases.

In the field, the "Little Colonel" was the team leader. He led all shortstops in various fielding categories 12 times.

In his seven World Series, Reese accumulated 46 base hits, which places him fifth.

Reese entered the Hall of Fame in 1984.

CAREER STATISTICS:

16 Years	Home Runs 126	Strikeouts 890
Games 2,166	Home Run Percentage 1.6	Batting Ave. .269
At Bats 8,058	Runs Scored 1,338	Slugging Ave. .377
Hits 2,170	RBIs 885	Pinch Hit At Bats 34
Doubles 330	Bases on Balls 1,210	Pinch Hits 4
Triples 80	Stolen Bases 232	

Edgar Charles Rice
(Sam)
B. Feb. 20, 1890, D. Oct. 13, 1974
Was–AL 1915–33, Cle–AL 1934

NUMBER OF RECORDS ESTABLISHED: 12

AMERICAN LEAGUE RECORDS

Season Batting Records

1925	Most Singles	182	55

Season Fielding Records—CF

1920	Most Putouts	454	4
	Most Total Chances	498	4

MAJOR LEAGUE RECORDS

Season Fielding Records—CF

1920	Most Putouts	454	4
	Most Total Chances	498	4

WORLD SERIES RECORDS

Game Fielding Records—RF

| 1924 | Most Assists | 2 | | Tied |

7-Game Series Batting Records

1925	Most At Bats	33		Tied
	Most Hits	12	39	
	Most Singles	12		Never Broken

7-Game Series Fielding Records—RF

1924	Most Putouts	13	10	
	Most Assists	4		Never Broken
	Most Errors	1	40	

SUMMARY

Sam Rice had an exceptional 20-year career, and a lifetime batting average of .322. He is yet another example of a "little man who carried a big stick." He was only 5'9" and weighed 150 pounds. He was a splendid base stealer, leading the league in 1920 with 63. He had 351 stolen bases in his career.

Sam was a three-time at bats leader who had six seasons with more than 200 hits. In 1924 and 1926, he was the leader in hits, and in 1923 he won the Triple Crown.

Sam Rice was a fine all-around player who batted over .300 15 times. He led the league in fielding eight times. Rice's Hall of Fame induction came in 1963.

POSTSEASON AWARDS

1923 Triple Crown

CAREER STATISTICS:

20 Years	Home Runs 34	Strikeouts 275
Games 2,404	Home Run Percentage 0.4	Batting Ave. .322
At Bats 9,269	Runs Scored 1,515	Slugging Ave. .427
Hits 2,987	RBIs 79	Pinch Hit At Bats 105
Doubles 497	Bases on Balls 709	Pinch Hits 20
Triples 184	Stolen Bases 351	

Wesley Branch Rickey
(The Mahatma)

B. Dec. 20, 1881, D. Dec. 9, 1965

StL–AL 1905–06, NY–AL 1907, StL–AL 1914
Manager: StL–AL 1913–15, StL–NL 1919–25

NUMBER OF RECORDS ESTABLISHED: 0

SUMMARY

Branch Rickey was not famed for his playing (he got in only 119 games) or for his managing in ten years. His best finishes were third place, by the 1921 and 1922 Cardinals. As a catcher he allowed 13 consecutive runners to steal bases in one game. Rather, Rickey is famed for his time as president of the Brooklyn Dodgers, and his breaking the color line.

In 1945 Rickey asked his chief scout Clyde Sukeforth to set up a meeting with Jackie Robinson, who was playing with the Kansas City Monarchs. When Robinson heard the news he thought Rickey wanted him for the Brooklyn Brown Dodgers, a team in the black Continental League. Instead Rickey told Robinson he wanted him to go to their farm team at Montreal and that perhaps he would join the Brooklyn Dodgers in 1947. Rickey warned Robinson about what it would be like to be the first black in the major leagues. Rickey pretended to be an insulting waiter in a restaurant, a nasty room clerk in a southern hotel, and a sarcastic railway conductor. They went over every possible situation that might arise. "Suppose they throw at your head?" Rickey asked. "Suppose I am an opposing player in the heat of a game and call you a dirty black bastard! What will you do then?" Robinson asked,

"Mr. Rickey, do you want a player who is afraid to fight back?" Rickey replied, "I want a player who has the guts not to fight back. You've got to do this job with base hits, stolen bases, fielding ground balls and nothing else!" When Robinson agreed to turn the other cheek, baseball's most important deal was made.

Branch Rickey is also remembered as the creator of baseball's farm systems, first with the Cardinals, then with the Dodgers, and finally with the Pirates. His many new ideas earned him the reputation as "the brain in baseball." He developed some of the finest talents the game has ever seen and in doing so brought pennants to the Cardinals, Dodgers, and Pirates.

For his long-range vision and innovations, Branch Rickey was inducted into the Hall of Fame in 1967.

CAREER STATISTICS:

4 Years
Games 119
At Bats 343
Hits 82
Doubles 9
Triples 6

Home Runs 3
Home Run Percentage 0.9
Runs Scored 38
RBIs 39
Bases on Balls 27
Stolen Bases 8

Strikeouts 1 (In 1914; prior to 1914 this stat was not kept)
Batting Ave. .239
Slugging Ave. .327
Pinch Hit At Bats 21
Pinch Hits 3

CAREER STATISTICS AS MANAGER:

10 Years
Games 1,277

Wins 597
Losses 664

Winning Percentage .473
First-place Finishes 0

Eppa Rixey
(Jeptha)
B. May 3, 1891, D. Feb. 28, 1963
Phi–NL 1912–20, Cin–NL 1921–33

NUMBER OF RECORDS ESTABLISHED: 0

SUMMARY

Eppa Rixey set no records, but he was an outstanding pitcher who hurled for 21 years and produced 266 victories. Rixey won 20 or more games in a season four times and was a league leader eight times. His best season was in 1922, when he won 25 and dropped 13.

Rixey became a Hall of Famer in 1963.

CAREER STATISTICS:

21 Years	Games Started 552	Shutouts 39
Wins 266	Games Completed 290	Relief Appearances 140
Losses 251 (6th)	Innings 4,495	Relief Wins 20
Winning Percentage .515	Hits 4,633	Relief Losses 17
ERA 3.15	Bases on Balls 1,082	Saves 14
Total Games 692	Strikeouts 1,350	

Robin Evan Roberts

B. Sept. 30, 1926

Phi–NL 1948–61, Bal–AL 1962–65, Hou–NL 1965–66, Chi–NL 1966

NUMBER OF RECORDS ESTABLISHED: 4

ALL-STAR GAME RECORDS

Game Pitching Records

1950	Wild Pitches	1	6
1955	Wild Pitches	1	1

Career Pitching Records—1950–55

Hits Allowed	15	6
Runs Allowed	8	6

SUMMARY

Robin Roberts was a 20-game winner six seasons in a row with Philadelphia, a losing ball club. In six consecutive years he led in starts, and in five of those years he was a leader in complete games. He pitched more innings than any other National League pitcher 5 times and twice led the league in strikeouts and shutouts. In all, he led the league in 31 pitching departments.

Roberts' Hall of Fame honors came in 1976.

CAREER STATISTICS:

19 Years

Wins 286

Losses 245 (7th)

Winning Percentage .539

ERA 3.41

Total Games 676

Games Started 609

Games Completed 305

Innings 4,689

Hits 4,582

Bases on Balls 902

Strikeouts 2,357

Shutouts 45

Relief Appearances 67

Relief Wins 11

Relief Losses 5

Saves 25

Brooks Calbert Robinson, Jr.
(The Vacuum Cleaner)
B. May 18, 1937
Bal–AL 1955–77

NUMBER OF RECORDS ESTABLISHED: 15

AMERICAN LEAGUE RECORDS

Career Fielding Records—3B

Most Games Played	2,870	Never Broken
Most Putouts	2,697	Never Broken
Most Assists	6,205	Never Broken
Most Double Plays	618	Never Broken
Most Total Chances	9,165	Never Broken
Highest Fielding Ave.	.971	Never Broken

MAJOR LEAGUE RECORDS

Career Fielding Records—3B

Most Games Played	2,870	Never Broken
Most Putouts	2,697	Never Broken
Most Assists	6,205	Never Broken

Most Double Plays	618	Never Broken
Most Total Chances	9,165	Never Broken
Highest Fielding Ave.	.971	Never Broken

ALL-STAR GAME RECORDS

Career Batting Records—1960–70

Most Triples	3	Never Broken

WORLD SERIES RECORDS

5-Game Series Batting Records

1970	Most Total Bases	17	Never Broken

5-Game Series Fielding Records

1970	Most Putouts	9	Tied

SUMMARY

Brooks Robinson is probably baseball's greatest defensive third baseman. He led all keystone sackers in various fielding categories 25 times.

Brooks was spectacular during his 23-year career and ranks eighth on the all-time list in games played and seventh in at bats. He clubbed 268 balls out of the park while turning in a respectable .267 batting average.

Robinson became a Hall of Famer in 1983.

CAREER STATISTICS:

23 Years	Home Runs 268	Strikeouts 990
Games 2,896 (8th)	Home Run Percentage 2.5	Batting Ave. .267
At Bats 10,654 (7th)	Runs Scored 1,232	Slugging Ave. .401
Hits 2,848	RBIs 1,357	Pinch Hit At Bats 31
Doubles 482	Bases on Balls 869	Pinch Hits 4
Triples 68	Stolen Bases 28	

Frank Robinson

B. Aug. 31, 1935

Cin–NL 1956–65, Bal–AL 1966–71, LA–NL 1972, Cal–AL 1973–74, Cle–AL 1974–76
Manager: Cle–AL 1975–77, SF–NL 1981–84, Bal–AL 1986–88

NUMBER OF RECORDS ESTABLISHED: 3

NATIONAL LEAGUE RECORDS

Rookie Batting Records

1956	Most Home Runs	38		Tied

MAJOR LEAGUE RECORDS

Rookie Batting Records

1956	Most Home Runs	38	32

WORLD SERIES RECORDS

Game Fielding Records—RF

1969	Most Putouts	7		Tied

SUMMARY

Frank Robinson split his career between the National and American League and was one of the game's great home run hitters. His 586 round-trippers places him fourth on the all-time list, and his 1,829 runs scored gives him a tenth-place finish.

Robinson was an outstanding hitter who led the league in slugging four times, three times in succession from 1960 to 1962. His best season was 1966, when he led the league in home runs, home run percentage, runs scored, RBIs, and batting and slugging average.

He was a league leader 11 times in various batting categories.

He played in five World Series. His 8.7 home run percentage ranks him third and his 8 home runs places him seventh.

He is the only man to win the MVP Award both in the National and American Leagues.

Robinson became a Hall of Famer in 1982.

POSTSEASON AWARDS

1956 Rookie of the Year
1961 MVP National League
1966 MVP American League

CAREER STATISTICS:

21 Years
Games 2,808
At Bats 10,006
Hits 2,943
Doubles 528
Triples 72

Home Runs 586 (4th)
Home Run Percentage 5.9
Runs Scored 1,829 (10th)
RBIs 1,812
Bases on Balls 1,420
Stolen Bases 204

Strikeouts 1,532
Batting Ave. .294
Slugging Ave. .537
Pinch Hit At Bats 87
Pinch Hits 28

CAREER STATISTICS AS MANAGER:

7 Years
Games 916

Wins 450
Losses 466

Winning Percentage .491
First-place Finishes 0

Jack Roosevelt Robinson
(Jackie)
B. Jan. 31, 1919, D. Oct. 24, 1972
Bkn–NL 1947–56

NUMBER OF RECORDS ESTABLISHED: 5

NATIONAL LEAGUE RECORDS

Rookie Fielding Records—1B

1947	Most Double Plays	144		Never Broken

Season Fielding Records—2B

1950	Most Double Plays	133	1
1951	Most Double Plays	137	10
	Highest Fielding Ave.	.991	5

WORLD SERIES RECORDS

Game Batting Records

1952	Most Bases on Balls	4		Tied

SUMMARY

Jackie Robinson will always be remembered as the man who broke the color line in baseball. It took an exceptional human being to do what Robinson did in 1947, to survive the taunts and threats of many people he played with and in front of many who were against him. He controlled his temper and emotions and still played excellent baseball, good enough to win Rookie of the Year honors.

Jackie was an exciting player to watch. He was everywhere, attacking with the bat, on the base paths, and with his glove. And he excelled in all three areas. His .311 career batting average proved he was a solid hitter, and there was no doubt about his fielding talents. Robinson was a fielding league leader ten times at second base, and his rookie double play record at first base still stands.

Robinson was most difficult to strike out. In 4,877 at bats he struck out only 291 times. He won the batting average crown in his third year with a .342 average. He appeared in six World Series and is in the top ten in doubles, runs scored, and bases on balls.

Jackie Robinson entered the Hall of Fame as the first black in 1962.

POSTSEASON AWARDS

1947 Rookie of the Year
1949 MVP

CAREER STATISTICS:

10 Years	Home Runs 137	Strikeouts 291
Games 1,382	Home Run Percentage 2.8	Batting Ave. .311
At Bats 4,877	Runs Scored 947	Slugging Ave. .474
Hits 1,518	RBIs 734	Pinch Hit At Bats 40
Doubles 273	Bases on Balls 740	Pinch Hits 7
Triples 54	Stolen Bases 197	

Wilbert Robinson
(Uncle Robbie)
B. June 2, 1863, D. Aug. 8, 1934

Phi–AA 1886–90, Bal–AA 1891, Bal–NL 1892–99, StL–NL 1900, Bal–AL 1901–02
Manager: Bal–AL 1902, Bkn–NL 1914–31

NUMBER OF RECORDS ESTABLISHED AS PLAYER: 9

NATIONAL LEAGUE RECORDS

Season Fielding Records—C

1895	Highest Fielding Ave.	.979	4

Career Fielding Records—C—1892–1900

	Highest Fielding Ave.	.954	1

MAJOR LEAGUE RECORDS

Season Fielding Records—C

1895	Highest Fielding Ave.	.979	4

Career Fielding Records—C—1886–1902

Most Games	1,316	10
Most Putouts	5,089	10
Most Assists	1,443	1
Most Total Chances	6,946	10
Highest Fielding Ave.	.944	4

SUMMARY

Wilbert Robinson was a major league catcher for 17 years. His best season was in 1894, when he batted .353. He also had fine seasons of .347, .334, and .315.

In his final season as a player, 1902, Robinson became a playing manager for Baltimore of the American League. Bringing his team into seventh place did not help his managerial career, and he did not manage again until 1914, when he secured the manager's job with the Brooklyn Dodgers. He managed the Dodgers for 18 consecutive years, winning only two pennants, in 1916 and 1920. He was denied a World Series ring, first by the Boston Red Sox and then by the Cleveland Indians.

In his 19 seasons of managing, Robinson led his teams for 2,813 games, won 1,397 and lost 1,395.

In his first year as Dodger manager, Robinson had two future Hall of Famers in his line-up. Casey Stengel was in right field, and Zack Wheat was in left. In later years he would have such Hall of Famers as Rube Marquard, Burleigh Grimes, Dazzy Vance, Max Carey, "Rabbit" Maranville, Dave Bancroft, Al Lopez, and Ernie Lombardi.

Robinson entered the Hall of Fame in 1945.

CAREER STATISTICS:

17 Years	Home Runs 18	Strikeouts 178
Games 1,316	Home Run Percentage 0.4	Batting Ave. .273
At Bats 5,077	Runs Scored 640	Slugging Ave. .346
Hits 1,388	RBIs 621	Pinch Hit At Bats 17
Doubles 212	Bases on Balls 286	Pinch Hits 7
Triples 51	Stolen Bases 163	

CAREER STATISTICS AS MANAGER:

19 Years	Wins 1,397	Winning Percentage .500
Games 2,813	Losses 1,395	First-place Finishes 2

Edd J. Roush

B. May 8, 1893, D. Mar. 21, 1988

Chi–AL 1913, Ind–FL 1914, Nwk–FL 1915, NY–NL 1916, Cin–NL 1916–26,
NY–NL 1927–29, Cin–NL 1931

NUMBER OF RECORDS ESTABLISHED: 10

NATIONAL LEAGUE RECORDS

Career Fielding Records—CF

Most Games Played	1,679	16

WORLD SERIES RECORDS

Game Batting Records

1919	Most RBIs	4	17

Game Fielding Records—CF

1919	Most Putouts	8		Tied
	Most Assists	2		Tied
	Most Errors	1	15	

8-Game Series Fielding Records—CF

1919	Most Putouts	31	Never Broken
	Most Assists	3	Never Broken
	Most Errors	2	Tied

Career Fielding Records—CF

	Most Errors	2	Tied

SUMMARY

Edd Roush was an outstanding hitter and a fine centerfielder. He enjoyed an 18-year career, with a lifetime batting average of .323. Roush batted over .300 13 times, including 11 years in a row from 1917 through 1927. He was a league leader in various batting categories five times. When he retired in 1931, he had played more games in center field than any National League player, even though he spent three years with teams in other leagues. Roush created nine of his ten records during World Series play. He starred in the 1919 series, getting 4 RBIs in one game. He really stood out on defense, as his putouts and assists are records that have not been broken in 69 years—in fact three were from the 1919 series.

Roush was welcomed into the Hall of Fame in 1962.

CAREER STATISTICS:

18 Years	Home Runs 68	Strikeouts 215
Games 1,967	Home Run Percentage 0.9	Batting Ave. .323
At Bats 7,363	Runs Scored 1,099	Slugging Ave. .446
Hits 2,376	RBIs 981	Pinch Hit At Bats 94
Doubles 339	Bases on Balls 484	Pinch Hits 24
Triples 182	Stolen Bases 268	

Charles Herbert Ruffing
(Red)
B. May 3, 1904
Bos–AL 1924–30, NY–AL 1930–46, Chi–AL 1947

NUMBER OF RECORDS ESTABLISHED: 11

AMERICAN LEAGUE RECORDS

Career Pitching Records

Most Bases on Balls	1,541	6

ALL-STAR GAME RECORDS

Game Pitching Records

1934	Most Hits/1 Inn.	4	20

Career Pitching Records—1934–40

Hits Allowed	13	15
Highest ERA	12.2	40

WORLD SERIES RECORDS

4-Game Series Pitching Records

1932	Most Bases on Balls	6	22	
1938	Starts	2		Tied
	Wins	2		Tied
	Hits Allowed	17		Never Broken

Career Pitching Records—1932–42

Wins	7	22
Strikeouts	61	9
Series Played	7	22

SUMMARY

In a fabulous 22-year career, "Red" Ruffing registered 273 wins and participated in seven World Series. He tossed 48 shutouts and was an eight-time league leader. Ruffing won 20 or more games four consecutive years (1936–39) in leading the Yankees to four pennants.

"Red" was one of the better-hitting pitchers and batted over .300 eight times, with a high of .364 in 1930. He was often used as a pinch hitter.

Ruffing had one of the worst starts in baseball history. In 135 games with the Red Sox he won only 39 games while losing 96! Yet he went on to become a Hall of Famer.

After being traded to the Yankees in 1930, the big righthander won 226 games while losing only 114.

In World Series play, "Red's" seven wins place him second on the all-time list.

Ruffing became a Hall of Famer in 1967.

CAREER STATISTICS:

22 Years	Games Started 536	Shutouts 48
Wins 273	Games Completed 335	Relief Appearances 88
Losses 225	Innings 4,344	Relief Wins 9
Winning Percentage .548	Hits 4,294	Relief Losses 15
ERA 3.80	Bases on Balls 1,541 (8th)	Saves 16
Total Games 624	Strikeouts 1,987	

Amos Wilson Rusie
(The Hoosier Thunderbolt)
B. May 30, 1871, D. Dec. 6, 1942
Ind–NL 1889, NY–NL 1890–98, Cin–NL 1901

NUMBER OF RECORDS ESTABLISHED: 13

NATIONAL LEAGUE RECORDS

Season Pitching Records

1890	Most Bases on Balls	289		Never Broken

Season Pitching Title Records

1894	Strikeout Titles	4	1	
	Shutout Titles	3	6	
1895	Strikeout Titles	5	25	
	Shutout Titles	4	22	
	Fewest Hits Titles	4	69	

Career Pitching Records

	Most Bases on Balls	1,716		Never Broken

MAJOR LEAGUE RECORDS

Season Pitching Records

1890	Bases on Balls Allowed	289	Never Broken

Season Pitching Title Records

1894	Strikeout Titles	4	1
	Shutout Titles	3	6
1895	Strikeout Titles	5	12
	Fewest Hits Titles	4	31

Career Pitching Records

Most Bases on Balls	1,716	52

SUMMARY

In nine full seasons, Amos Rusie averaged 27 wins per year in winning 243 games and was known as the "Hoosier Thunderbolt" for his lightning fastball. Rusie was a five-time strikeout king, although he also led the league in bases on balls five times.

Rusie's greatest season was 1894, when he won 36 and dropped 13 and led the league in six categories. In all, he was a league leader 23 times.

Rusie became a Hall of Famer in 1977.

CAREER STATISTICS:

10 Years	Games Started 427	Shutouts 30
Wins 243	Games Completed 392	Relief Appearances 35
Losses 160	Innings 3,770	Relief Wins 10
Winning Percentage .603	Hits 3,384	Relief Losses 7
ERA 3.07	Bases on Balls 1,716 (5th)	Saves 5
Total Games 462	Strikeouts 1,957	

George Herman Ruth
(Babe, The Sultan of Swat, The Bambino)
B. Feb. 6, 1895, D. Aug. 16, 1948
Bos–AL 1914–19, NY–AL 1920–34, Bos–NL 1935

TOTAL RECORDS ESTABLISHED: 192 (1st)

AMERICAN LEAGUE RECORDS

Season Batting Records

1915	Most Home Runs by Pitcher	4		Tied
1918	Highest Home Run Percentage	3.5	1	
1919	Most Home Runs	29	1	
	Highest Home Run Percentage	6.7	1	
1920	Most Home Runs	54	1	
	Highest Home Run Percentage	11.8		Never Broken
	Most Extra Base Hits	99	1	
	Highest Slugging Ave.	.847		Never Broken
	Most Bases on Balls	148	3	
1921	Most Home Runs	59	6	
	Most Extra Base Hits	119		Never Broken
	Most Total Bases	457		Never Broken
	Most Runs Scored	177		Tied
	Most RBIs	171	6	

| 1923 | Most Bases on Balls | 170 | | Never Broken |
| 1927 | Most Home Runs | 60 | 34 | |

American League Career Batting Records

	Most Home Runs	708		Never Broken
	Highest Home Run Percentage	8.5		Never Broken
	Most Extra Base Hits	1,350		Never Broken
	Most RBIs	2,199		Never Broken
	Highest Slugging Ave.	690		Never Broken
	Most Bases on Balls	2,036		Never Broken
	Most Strikeouts	1,306	34	

Batting Title Records

1921	Most Home Runs Titles	4	2	
	Most Home Run Percentage Titles	4	1	
1923	Most MVP Titles	1	1	
	Most Home Runs Titles	5	1	
	Most Home Run Percentage Titles	6	1	
	Most RBI Titles	4	3	
1924	Most Home Runs Titles	6	2	
	Most Home Run Percentage Titles	7	2	
	Most Runs Scored Titles	5	2	
1926	Most Home Runs Titles	7	1	
	Most Home Run Percentage Titles	8	1	
	Most Slugging Titles	8	1	
	Most RBI Titles	5	2	
	Most Runs Scored Titles	6	1	
	Most Bases on Balls Titles	5		
1927	Most Home Runs Titles	8	1	
	Most Home Run Percentage Titles	9	1	
	Most Slugging Titles	9	1	
	Most Runs Scored Titles	7	1	
	Most Bases on Balls Titles	6		
1928	Most Home Runs Titles	9	1	
	Most Home Run Percentage Titles	10	1	
	Most Slugging Titles	10	1	
	Most Total Bases Titles	6		
	Most RBI Titles	6		Never Broken
	Most Runs Scored Titles	8		Never Broken

	Most Bases on Balls Titles	7	1
1929	Most Home Runs Titles	10	1
	Most Home Run Percentage Titles	11	1
	Most Slugging Titles	11	1
1930	Most Home Runs Titles	11	1
	Most Home Run Percentage Titles	12	1
	Most Slugging Titles	12	1
	Most Bases on Balls Titles	8	1
	Most Home Runs Titles	12	Never Broken
	Most Home Run Percentage Titles	13	Never Broken
	Most Slugging Titles	13	Never Broken
1931	Most Bases on Balls Titles	9	1
1932	Most Bases on Balls Titles	10	1
1933	Most Bases on Balls Titles	11	Never Broken

Season Fielding Records

1919	Fewest Errors—LF	2	31
	Highest Fielding Ave.—LF	.992	24
1923	Most Putouts—RF	378	38
	Most Total Chances—RF	409	48

MAJOR LEAGUE RECORDS

Season Batting Records

1915	Most Home Runs by Pitcher	4	Tied
1919	Most Home Runs	29	1
	Highest Home Run Percentage	6.7	1
1920	Most Home Runs	54	1
	Highest Home Run Percentage	11.8	Never Broken
	Highest Slugging Ave.	.847	Never Broken
1920	Most Extra Base Hits	99	1
	Most Bases on Balls	148	3
1921	Most Home Runs	59	6
	Most Extra Base Hits	119	Never Broken
	Most Total Bases	457	Never Broken
	Most RBIs	171	6
1923	Most Bases on Balls	170	Never Broken
1927	Most Home Runs	60	34

Batting Title Records

1923	Most Home Runs Titles	5	1
	Most RBI Titles	4	3
	Most MVP Titles	1	1

	Most Home Run Percentage Titles	6	1	
1924	Most Home Runs Titles	6	2	
	Most Home Run Percentage Titles	7	2	
	Most Runs Scored Titles	5	2	
1926	Most Home Runs Titles	7	1	
	Most Home Run Percentage Titles	8	1	
	Most Slugging Titles	8	1	
	Most RBI Titles	5	2	
	Most Runs Scored Titles	6	1	
	Most Bases on Balls Titles	5	1	
1927	Most Home Runs Titles	8	1	
	Most Home Run Percentage Titles	9	1	
	Most Slugging Titles	9	1	
	Most Runs Scored Titles	7	1	
	Most Bases on Balls Titles	6	1	
1928	Most Home Runs Titles	9	1	
	Most Home Run Percentage Titles	10	1	
	Most Slugging Titles	10	1	
	Most Total Bases Titles	6		Tied
	Most RBI Titles	6		Never Broken
	Most Runs Scored Titles	8		Never Broken
	Most Bases on Balls Titles	7	2	
1929	Most Home Runs Titles	10	1	
	Most Home Run Percentage Titles	11	1	
	Most Slugging Titles	11	1	
1930	Most Home Runs Titles	11	1	
	Most Home Run Percentage Titles	12	1	
	Most Slugging Titles	12	1	
	Most Bases on Balls Titles	8	1	
1931	Most Home Runs Titles	12		Never Broken
	Most Home Run Percentage Titles	13		Never Broken
	Most Slugging Titles	13		Never Broken
	Most Bases on Balls Titles	9	1	
1932	Most Bases on Balls Titles	10	1	
1933	Most Bases on Balls Titles	11		Never Broken

Career Batting Records

Most Home Runs	714	41

Highest Home Run Percentage	8.5		Never Broken
Most Extra Base Hits	1,356	28	
Most RBIs	2,211	41	
Highest Slugging Ave.	.690		Never Broken
Most Bases on Balls	2,056		Never Broken
Most Strikeouts	1,330	33	

ALL-STAR GAME RECORDS

Game Batting Records

1933	Most Games Played	1	1
	Most Hits	2	1
	Most Home Runs	1	8
	Most Total Bases	5	4
	Most Extra Base Hits	1	1
	Most Runs Scored	1	1
	Most RBIs	2	1
	Most Strikeouts	2	1
1934	Most Games Played	2	1
	Most Strikeouts	3	33

Career Batting Records—1933–34

Most Games Played	2	1
Most At Bats	8	1
Most RBIs	2	4
Most Bases on Balls	2	4
Most Strikeouts	5	4

WORLD SERIES RECORDS

Game Batting Records

1923	Most Home Runs	2	3
1926	Most Home Runs	3	Tied
	Most Total Bases	12	Tied
	Most Runs Scored	4	Tied
	Most Bases on Balls	4	Tied
1928	Most Home Runs	3	Tied
	Most Total Bases	12	Tied
1932	Most RBIs	4	4

4-Game Series Batting Records

1927	Most Home Runs	2	1
	Most RBIs	7	1
1928	Most Extra Base Hits	6	Never Broken
	Most Runs Scored	9	Tied
	Most Hits	10	Never Broken

Highest Batting Ave.	.625		Never Broken
Most Total Bases	22		Never Broken

6-Game Series Batting Records

1923	Most Home Runs	3	36	
	Most Extra Base Hits	5	54	
	Most Total Bases	19	30	
	Most Runs Scored	8	54	
	Most Bases on Balls	8		Never Broken
	Highest Slugging Ave.	1.000	54	

7-Game Series Batting Records

1926	Most Home Runs	4		Tied
	Most Bases on Balls	11		Tied
	Highest Slugging Ave.	.900	26	

Career Batting Records—1914–32

Most Games Played	41	2	
Most At Bats	129	2	
Most Hits	42	2	
Most Home Runs	15	32	
Highest Home Run Percentage	11.6		Never Broken
Most Runs Scored	37	31	
Most RBIs	33	6	
Most Total Bases	96	31	
Most Extra Base Hits	22	32	
Most Bases on Balls	33	32	
Highest Slugging Ave.	.744	49	
Most Strikeouts	30	27	
Most Series Played	10	31	
Longest Hitting Streak	13	25	

4-Game Series Fielding Records

1927	Most Putouts—RF	10		Tied

Game Pitching Records

1916	Most Innings Pitched	14		Never Broken

5-Game Series Pitching Records

1916	Fewest Hits (Min. 10 Inn.)	6	33	

6-Game Series Pitching Records

1918	Most Shutouts	1		Tied

Career Fielding Records—RF—1918–32

Most Putouts	46	26
Most Total Chances	49	26

Career Pitching Records—1916–18

Most Scoreless Innings	29⅔	44
Fewest Hits/9 Inn.	5.52	2
Lowest ERA	0.87	28

POSTSEASON AWARDS

1923 MVP

CAREER BATTING STATISTICS:

22 Years	Home Runs 714 (2nd)	Strikeouts 1,330
Games 2,503	Home Run Percentage 8.5 (1st)	Batting Ave. .342
At Bats 8,399	Runs Scored 2,174 (2nd)	Slugging Ave. .690 (1st)
Hits 2,873	RBIs 2,211 (2nd)	Pinch Hit At Bats 67
Doubles 506	Bases on Balls 2,056 (1st)	Pinch Hits 13
Triples 136	Stolen Bases 123	

CAREER PITCHING STATISTICS:

10 Years	Games Started 148	Shutouts 17
Wins 94	Games Completed 107	Relief Appearances 15
Losses 46	Innings 1,221	Relief Wins 2
Winning Percentage .671	Hits 974	Relief Losses 2
ERA 2.28	Bases on Balls 441	Saves 4
Total Games 163	Strikeouts 488	

SUMMARY

Babe Ruth's records tell a lot about his phenomenal talent, but they can't tell what he meant to baseball and to the country during his playing years. Not only was he a great pitcher, a great batter, and a fine fielder, not only did he play on some of the best teams ever, he was also a warm human being and a hero to children and adults across the United States.

A breakdown of Ruth's 192 league records follows: Unbroken records 53, American League—67, major league—63, All-Star games—15, World Series—47, club records (Boston Red Sox and New York Yankees)—246. What can one say? He was the best all-around player ever!

Babe Ruth was voted Hall of Fame honors in 1936.

Raymond William Schalk
(Ray, The Cracker)

B. Aug. 12, 1892, D. May 19, 1970
Chi–AL 1912–28, NY–NL 1929
Manager: Chi–AL 1927–28

NUMBER OF RECORDS ESTABLISHED AS PLAYER: 18

AMERICAN LEAGUE RECORDS

Rookie Fielding Records—C

1913	Most Putouts	599	49	
	Most Double Plays	18		Never Broken
	Most Total Chances	768	49	
	Highest Fielding Ave.	.980	12	

Season Fielding Records—C

1922	Highest Fielding Ave.	.989	1	

Career Fielding Records—C

	Most Games Played	1,721	19	
	Most Putouts	7,171	18	
	Most Assists	1,811		Never Broken

Most Double Plays	221		Never Broken
Most Total Chances	9,157	37	

MAJOR LEAGUE RECORDS

Rookie Fielding Records—C

1913	Most Putouts	599	44	
	Most Double Plays	18		Never Broken
	Most Total Chances	768	49	

Career Fielding Records—C

Most Games Played	1,726	12	
Most Putouts	7,171	12	
Most Double Plays	221	12	

WORLD SERIES RECORDS

6-Game Series Fielding Records—C

1917	Most Errors	2		Tied

8-Game Series Fielding Records—C

1919	Most Assists	15	Never Broken

SUMMARY

Ray Schalk was one of the American League's first outstanding catchers. Working behind the plate for 18 years, "The Cracker" caught more games and made more putouts and double plays than any catcher in American League history.

In 1913 Schalk set rookie fielding records for putouts, double plays, and total chances. And he had a higher fielding average than any previous rookie. His putouts and total chances were also major league records that stood for 44 and 49 years before being broken. Schalk's major league double play record still stands. On defense he led the league in various categories 22 times.

Schalk was an adequate hitter with a lifetime batting average of .253.

Schalk was voted into the Hall of Fame in 1955.

CAREER STATISTICS:

18 Years	Home Runs 12	Strikeouts 355
Games 1,760	Home Run Percentage 0.2	Batting Ave. .253
At Bats 5,306	Runs Scored 579	Slugging Ave. .316
Hits 1,345	RBIs 594	Pinch Hit At Bats 28
Doubles 199	Bases on Balls 638	Pinch Hits 5
Triples 48	Stolen Bases 176	

CAREER STATISTICS AS MANAGER:

2 Years	Wins 102	Winning Percentage .449
Games 228	Losses 125	First-place Finishes 0

Albert Fred Schoendienst
(Red)
B. Feb. 2, 1923
StL–NL 1945–56, NY–NL 1956–57, Mil–NL 1957–60, StL–NL 1961–63
Manager: StL–NL 1965–80

NUMBER OF RECORDS ESTABLISHED AS PLAYER: 10

NATIONAL LEAGUE RECORDS

Season Fielding Records—2B

1949	Highest Fielding Ave.	.987	2

Season Batting Records

1954	Most Double Plays	137	7
1962	Most Pinch Hit At Bats	72	8

Career Fielding Records—2B—1945–63

Most Games	1,834	9
Most Double Plays	1,280	9
Highest Fielding Ave.	.983	17

MAJOR LEAGUE RECORDS—2B

Season Batting Records

1962	Most Pinch Hit At Bats	72	8

Season Fielding Records

1949	Highest Fielding Ave.	.987	2

Career Fielding Records—2B

	Highest Fielding Ave.	.983	2

WORLD SERIES RECORDS

Game Batting Records

1946	Most At Bats	6	27

SUMMARY

"Red" Schoendienst led the National League in stolen bases in his rookie year with 26 but never stole more than 12 bases a year for the remainder of his 19-year career. This fine switch-hitting second baseman stole only 89 bases in his entire career.

He was the perfect number-two batter, as he was adept at hitting behind the runner, bunting, and making contact with the ball. In 8,479 at bats, he only struck out 346 times. He batted over .300 five times, with a high of .342 in 1953. For three consecutive years (1952–1954) he batted over .300. In 1947 and 1950 Schoendienst led the league in at bats, and in 1950 he was a league leader in doubles with 43. In 1957 he led the league in hits with an even 200. Because he was a fine contact hitter, he proved valuable as a pinch hitter in the later stage of his career, and in 1962 he led the league in pinch hit at bats with 72 and in pinch hits with 22.

Schoendienst participated in three World Series, played in 19 games, and had 78 at bats and 21 hits for a .269 batting average.

He managed the St. Louis Cardinals for 13 years, winning pennants in 1967 and 1968. He was victorious in the 1967 Series but lost in 1968. He finished second three times and had a .521 career managerial winning percentage.

Schoendienst was inducted into the Hall of Fame in 1988.

CAREER STATISTICS:

19 Years	Home Runs 84	Strikeouts 346
Games 2,216	Home Run Percentage 1.0	Batting Ave. .289
At Bats 8,479	Runs Scored 1,223	Slugging Ave. .387
Hits 2,449	RBIs 773	Pinch Hit At Bats 185
Doubles 427	Bases on Balls 606	Pinch Hits 56
Triples 78	Stolen Bases 89	

CAREER STATISTICS AS MANAGER:

13 Years	Wins 1,028	Winning Percentage .521
Games 1,975	Losses 944	First-place Finishes 2

Joseph Wheeler Sewell
(Joe)
B. Oct. 9, 1898
Cle–AL 1920–30, NY–AL 1931–33

NUMBER OF RECORDS ESTABLISHED: 6

AMERICAN LEAGUE RECORDS
Rookie Fielding Records—SS

1921	Most Double Plays	75	4

MAJOR LEAGUE RECORDS
Rookie Fielding Records—SS

1921	Most Double Plays	75	2

WORLD SERIES RECORDS
Game Batting Records

1932	Most At Bats	6	41

4-Game Series Fielding Records—SS

1932	Most Errors	1	6

7-Game Series Fielding Records—SS

1920	Most Assists	28	11
	Most Errors	6	5

SUMMARY

Joe Sewell was known as the hardest man to strike out. In 7,132 times at bat, enemy pitchers were only able to strike him out 114 times! In 1932 he had 503 official at bats; he walked 68 times and struck out only three times.

Joe averaged .312 over his career and batted over .300 ten times. He was an outstanding doubles hitter and accumulated 436 in all.

He was a star on defense and was the American League's fielding leader 16 times.

Hall of Fame honors came Sewell's way in 1977.

CAREER STATISTICS:

14 Years	Home Runs 49	Strikeouts 114
Games 1,902	Home Run Percentage 0.7	Batting Ave. .312
At Bats 7,132	Runs Scored 1,141	Slugging Ave. .413
Hits 2,226	RBIs 1,051	Pinch Hit At Bats 25
Doubles 436	Bases on Balls 844	Pinch Hits 5
Triples 68	Stolen Bases 74	

Aloysius Harry Simmons
(Al, Bucketfoot)
B. May 22, 1902, D. May 26, 1956

Phi–AL 1924–32, Chi–AL 1933–35, Det–AL 1936, Was–AL 1937–38, Bos–NL 1939,
Cin–NL 1939, Phi–AL 1940–41, Bos–AL 1943, Phi–AL 1944

NUMBER OF RECORDS ESTABLISHED: 19

ALL-STAR GAME RECORDS

Game Batting Records

1933	Most Games Played	1	1	
1934	Most Games Played	2	1	
	Most Hits	3	3	
	Most Doubles	2		Tied
	Most Extra Base Hits	2		Tied
	Most Total Bases	5	3	
	Most Runs Scored	3	12	
1935	Most Games Played	3	1	

Career Batting Records—1933–35

	Most Games Played	3	1
	Most At Bats	13	3

Most Hits	6	3
Most Doubles	3	4
Most Extra Base Hits	3	25
Highest Batting Ave.	.461	3
Highest Slugging Ave.	.692	18

WORLD SERIES RECORDS

Game Batting Records

1929	Most RBIs	4	7

5-Game Series Batting Records

1929	Most Home Runs	2	40	
	Most Runs Scored	6		Tied

7-Game Series Batting Records

1931	Most RBIs	8	25

SUMMARY

Al "Bucketfoot" Simmons, who spent his 20 years in the outfield, and 1 game at first base, averaged .334 and slugged .535. He belted 307 home runs and was a league leader in various batting departments eight times. He batted over .300 13 times, including 11 times in a row from 1924 to 1934. He had highs of .392, .390, .384, .381, .365, and .351.

Simmons played for a lot of clubs, but his prime years were spent with Connie Mack's Philadelphia Athletics, where he teamed with such greats as Jimmie Foxx, Lefty Grove, and Mickey Cochrane.

Simmons became a Hall of Famer in 1953.

CAREER STATISTICS:

20 Years	Home Runs 307	Strikeouts 737
Games 2,215	Home Run Percentage 3.5	Batting Ave. .334
At Bat 8,761	Runs Scored 1,507	Slugging Ave. .535
Hits 2,927	RBIs 1,827	Pinch Hit At Bats 66
Doubles 539	Bases on Balls 615	Pinch Hits 17
Triples 149	Stolen Bases 87	

George Harold Sisler
(Georgeous George)
B. Mar. 24, 1893, D. Mar. 26, 1973
StL–AL 1915–27, Was–AL 1928, Bos–NL 1928–30
Manager: StL–AL 1924–26

NUMBER OF RECORDS ESTABLISHED AS PLAYER: 6

AMERICAN LEAGUE RECORDS

Season Batting Records

1920	Most Hits	257		Never Broken
	Most Singles	171	3	
	Most Total Bases	399	1	

Career Fielding Records—1B

	Most Double Plays	1,131	6	

MAJOR LEAGUE RECORDS

Season Batting Records

1920	Most Hits	257		Never Broken
	Most Total Bases	399	1	

SUMMARY

"Georgeous George" Sisler was one of the finest left-handed hitters in baseball. For 15 years he averaged .340, as he ripped 2,812 hits. In 1920 he amassed 257 hits in 154 games—a record that still stands—and he batted .407. He topped that mark in 1922 by hitting .422. Add to this another 11 seasons of batting over .300, and you have one of the best hitters in the game.

Sisler had six seasons with more than 200 hits and was a league leader in batting 11 times. In addition, he was a tremendous base stealer and won the stolen bases crown four times.

Sisler was also an exceptional first baseman who led the league in various fielding categories 16 times.

The Hall of Fame accepted Sisler in 1939.

CAREER STATISTICS:

15 Years	Home Runs 100	Strikeouts 327
Games 2,055	Home Run Percentage 1.2	Batting Ave. .340
At Bats 8,267	Runs Scored 1,284	Slugging Ave. .468
Hits 2,812	RBIs 1,175	Pinch Hit At Bats 22
Doubles 425	Bases on Balls 472	Pinch Hits 6
Triples 165	Stolen Bases 375	

CAREER STATISTICS AS MANAGER:

3 Years	Wins 218	Winning Percentage .475
Games 461	Losses 241	First-place Finishes 0

Enos Bradsher Slaughter

(Country)

B. Apr. 27, 1916

StL–NL 1938–53, NY–AL 1954–55, KC–AL 1955–56, NY–AL 1956–59, Mil–NL 1959

NUMBER OF RECORDS ESTABLISHED: 4

ALL-STAR GAME RECORDS

Game Batting Records

1950	Most Triples	1	28

WORLD SERIES RECORDS

Game Batting Records

1946	Most At Bats	6	27
	Most Hits	4	36

7-Game Series Fielding Records—RF

1946	Most Putouts	20	29

SUMMARY

Enos "Country" Slaughter had a .300 lifetime batting average and was a league leader in hits, doubles, triples (twice), RBIs, pinch hit at bats, and pinch hits.

Slaughter is perhaps most famous for his role in the 1946 World Series. He gave his Gashouse Gang the win in the seventh game by scoring from first on a single by Harry Walker. Enos batted .300 or over ten times.

Slaughter was welcomed into the Hall of Fame in 1985.

CAREER STATISTICS:

19 Years	Home Runs 169	Strikeouts 538
Games 2,380	Home Run Percentage 2.1	Batting Ave. .300
At Bats 7,946	Runs Scored 1,247	Slugging Ave. .453
Hits 2,383	RBIs 1,304	Pinch Hit At Bats 306
Doubles 413	Bases on Balls 1,019	Pinch Hits 77
Triples 148	Stolen Bases 71	

Edwin Donald Snider
(Duke, The Silver Fox)

B. Sept. 19, 1926

Bkn–NL 1947–57, LA–NL 1958–62, NY–NL 1963, SF–NL 1964

NUMBER OF RECORDS ESTABLISHED: 11

NATIONAL LEAGUE RECORDS

Career Batting Records

Most Strikeouts	1,237	3

WORLD SERIES RECORDS

Game Fielding Records—CF

1959	Most Errors	2	7

5-Game Series Batting Records

1949	Most Strikeouts	8	Tied

7-Game Series Batting Records

1952	Most Home Runs	4	Tied

	Most Extra Base Hits	6	27	
	Most Total Bases	24	27	
	Most RBIs	8	4	
1955	Most Home Runs	4		Tied

Career Batting Records—1949–59

Most Strikeouts	33	5

Career Fielding Records—CF—1949–59

Most Errors	2	Tied

SUMMARY

"Duke" Snider was the Dodgers outstanding centerfielder and home run hitter. In his 18-year career he hit 407 home runs and set ten World Series records. "Duke" was an offensive league leader 11 times and won the run-scoring title three years in a row from 1953 to 1955. He also won titles in hits, RBIs, and bases on balls and was a two-time slugging king. His lifetime batting average was .295, and he had a strong slugging average of .540.

Snider participated in six World Series and clubbed 11 home runs, placing him fourth on the all-time list. He ranks fifth in home run percentage, sixth in doubles, seventh in RBIs, and tenth in runs scored in Series play.

Snider entered the Hall of Fame in 1980.

CAREER STATISTICS:

18 Years	Home Runs 407	Strikeouts 1,237
Games 2,143	Home Run Percentage 5.7	Batting Ave. .295
At Bats 7,161	Runs Scored 1,259	Slugging Ave. .540
Hits 2,116	RBIs 1,333	Pinch Hit At Bats 223
Doubles 358	Bases on Balls 971	Pinch Hits 59
Triples 85	Stolen Bases 99	

Warren Edward Spahn
(Hook, Spahnny)

B. Apr. 23, 1921

Bos–NL 1942–52, Mil–NL 1953–64, NY–NL 1965, SF–NL 1965

NUMBER OF RECORDS ESTABLISHED: 22

NATIONAL LEAGUE RECORDS

Season Pitching Title Records

1957	Cy Young Titles	1	8	
1959	Wins Titles	6	1	
1960	Complete Games Titles	6	1	
	Wins Titles	7	1	
1961	Complete Games Titles	7	1	
	Wins Titles	8		Never Broken
1962	Complete Games Titles	8	1	
1963	Complete Games Titles	9		Never Broken

Career Pitching Records

Total Games	750	4	
Starts	665		Never Broken
Innings	5,244		Never Broken
Strikeouts	2,583	10	

MAJOR LEAGUE RECORDS

Season Pitching Title Records

1959	Wins Titles	6	1	
1960	Complete Games Titles	6	1	
	Wins Titles	7	1	
1961	Complete Games Titles	7	1	
	Wins Titles	8		Never Broken
1962	Complete Games Titles	8	1	
1963	Complete Games Titles	9		Never Broken

ALL-STAR GAME RECORDS

Game Pitching Records

1961	Fewest Hits Allowed (3 Innings)	0		Tied

Career Pitching Records—1947–61

	Most Bases on Balls	6	17

WORLD SERIES RECORDS

6-Game Series Pitching Records

1948	Games	3	11

SUMMARY

Warren Spahn was one of baseball's most durable pitchers. Of modern-time pitchers, Spahnny threw the most complete games. He led the league nine times in complete games, a major league record.

Spahn was very successful in winning most of the games he started. His 363 wins are the most of any left-handed pitcher in baseball history. He was a league leader for most wins eight times, a major league record that remains unbroken.

Spahn started more games and pitched more innings than any National League pitcher. His 63 career shutouts place him sixth on the all-time list. He was a league leader 34 times, won 20 or more games 13 times, and did it six times in a row. "Spahn and Sain and pray for rain"—this was the cry of Braves fans for many years, when not only was Spahn the Braves' best pitcher, but he and Johnny Sain were the Braves' only good pitchers.

Spahn became a Hall of Famer in 1973.

CAREER STATISTICS:

21 Years	Games Started 665	Shutouts 63 (6th)
Wins 363 (5th)	Games Completed 382	Relief Appearances 85
Losses 245 (7th)	Innings 5,244 (5th)	Relief Wins 5
Winning Percentage .597	Hits 4,830	Relief Losses 18
ERA 3.09	Bases on Balls 1,434	Saves 29
Total Games 750	Strikeouts 2,583	

Albert Goodwill Spalding

B. Sept. 2, 1850, D. Sept. 9, 1915

Chi–NL 1876–78
Manager: Chi–NL 1876–77

NUMBER OF RECORDS ESTABLISHED AS PLAYER: 12

NUMBER OF RECORDS ESTABLISHED AS MANAGER: 6

TOTAL: 18

NATIONAL MAJOR LEAGUE RECORDS

Rookie Pitching Records

| 1876 | Wins | 47 | | Never Broken |
| | Winning Percentage | .783 | 11 | |

Season Pitching Records

| 1876 | Wins | 47 | 7 |
| | Winning Percentage | .783 | 4 |

Season Pitching Title Records

| 1876 | Wins Titles | 1 | 2 |
| | Winning Percentage Titles | 1 | 2 |

MANAGER RECORDS

National League Season Records

1876	Wins	52	3
	Winning Percentage	.788	4
	Games Won Pennant By	6	1

Major League Season Records

1876	Wins	52	3
	Winning Percentage	.788	4
	Games Won Pennant By	6	1

SUMMARY

Al Spalding is one of three pitchers in the Hall of Fame with fewer than 50 major league victories (Candy Cummings and Satchel Paige are the others), but he made a major contribution to baseball.

Prior to the formation of the National League, Spalding was the most dominating pitcher in the old National Association. From 1871 to 1874, he won 207 and lost only 56. He averaged 41 wins per year! He had only one successful year in the National League before his arm wore out.

Baseball was on the verge of collapse during those years when businessman William Hulbert encouraged Spalding to help him form a new league. Spalding's influence with the players was a tremendous help in the transition from unorganized team ownership to businessmen as team owners and the new controls that followed.

Baseball was in a bad way because gamblers were in control and players and umpires were paid to throw games. The fans were beginning to boycott the games and lose interest due to this dishonesty. Hulbert set up new rules that prohibited gambling and drinking and cleaned up the game by forming the National League. Al Spalding was his key man.

Spalding became manager and ace pitcher for Hulbert's Chicago team in 1876, which won the first National League pennant. He later formed the Spalding Sporting Goods Company.

Spalding became a Hall of Famer in 1939.

CAREER STATISTICS:

3 Years	Games Started 61	Shutouts 8
Wins 48	Games Completed 53	Relief Appearances 4
Losses 13	Innings 540	Relief Wins 1
Winning Percentage .787	Hits 559	Relief Losses 0
ERA 1.78	Bases on Balls 26	Saves 1
Total Games 65	Strikeouts 41	

CAREER STATISTICS AS MANAGER:

2 Years	Wins 78	Winning Percentage .624
Games 126	Losses 47	First-place Finishes 1

Tristram E. Speaker
(The White Eagle, Spoke)
B. Apr. 4, 1888, D. Dec. 8, 1958
Bos–AL 1907–15, Cle–AL 1916–26, Was–AL 1927, Phi–AL 1928
Manager: Cle–AL 1919–26

NUMBER OF RECORDS ESTABLISHED AS PLAYER: 49

AMERICAN LEAGUE RECORDS

Season Batting Records

1912	Most Doubles	53	11	
1923	Most Doubles	59	3	

Season Batting Title Records

1912	Most MVP Titles	1	12	
1918	Most Doubles Titles	4	2	
1920	Most Doubles Titles	5	1	
1921	Most Doubles Titles	6	1	
1922	Most Doubles Titles	7	1	
1923	Most Doubles Titles	8		Never Broken

Season Fielding Records—CF

1909	Most Assists	35		Tied
1912	Most Assists	35		Tied
1913	Most Total Chances	429	1	
	Most Errors	25		Never Broken
1914	Most Putouts	423	3	
	Most Double Plays	12	5	
	Most Total Chances	467	3	

Career Batting Records

Most Doubles	793		Never Broken
Most Bases on Balls	1,381	2	

Career Fielding Records—CF

Most Games Played	2,700		Never Broken
Most Putouts	6,730		Never Broken
Most Assists	438		Never Broken
Most Errors	222		Never Broken
Most Total Chances	7,390		Never Broken

MAJOR LEAGUE RECORDS

Season Batting Records

1923	Most Doubles	59	3

Season Batting Title Records

1912	Most MVP Titles	1	12	
1923	Most Doubles Titles	8		Tied

Season Fielding Records—CF

1914	Most Putouts	423	3
	Most Double Plays	12	5
	Most Total Chances	467	3

Career Batting Records

Most Doubles	793		Never Broken
Most Bases on Balls	1,381	2	

Career Fielding Records—CF

Most Games Played	2,700	45	
Most Putouts	6,730	45	
Most Assists	438		Never Broken
Most Double Plays	135		Never Broken
Most Total Chances	7,390	45	

WORLD SERIES RECORDS

Game Fielding Records—CF

1912	Most Assists	1	6
	Most Errors	1	22

7-Game Series Batting Records

1912	Most Triples	2	35

7-Game Series Fielding Records—CF

1912	Most Putouts	21	7	
	Most Assists	2	7	
	Most Errors	2		Tied

Career Batting Records—1912–20

Most Triples	4		Tied

Career Fielding Records—CF

Most Putouts	49	31	
Most Assists	2	10	
Most Errors	2		Tied
Most Total Chances	53	31	

SUMMARY

Tris Speaker was one of baseball's most outstanding hitters. His lifetime batting average of .344 places him seventh on the all-time list, and he batted well over .300 18 consecutive years! He batted better than .366 eight times; his high was .389 in 1925.

Speaker was a solid line-drive hitter, and his 793 doubles put him number one on the all-time doubles list. He is fifth in hits, sixth in triples, seventh in batting average, and eighth in runs scored. No one has ever hit more triples in World Series play.

Speaker was recognized by the Hall of Fame in 1937.

POSTSEASON AWARDS

1912 MVP

CAREER STATISTICS:

22 Years	Home Runs 117	Strikeouts 220
Games 2,789	Home Run Percentage 1.1	Batting Ave. .344 (7th)
At Bats 10,208	Runs Scored 1,881 (8th)	Slugging Ave. .500
Hits 3,515 (5th)	RBIs 1,559	Pinch Hit At Bats 60
Doubles 793 (1st)	Bases on Balls 1,381	Pinch Hits 20
Triples 223 (6th)	Stolen Bases 433	

CAREER STATISTICS AS MANAGER:

8 Years	Wins 616	Winning Percentage .542
Games 1,138	Losses 520	First-place Finishes 1

Wilver Dornel Stargell
(Willie, Pops)
B. Mar. 6, 1940
Pit–NL 1962–82

NUMBER OF RECORDS ESTABLISHED: 2

NATIONAL LEAGUE RECORDS

Career Batting Records—1962–82

Most Strikeouts	1,936	Never Broken

MAJOR LEAGUE RECORDS

Career Batting Records—1962–82

Most Strikeouts	1,936	4

SUMMARY

Willie Stargell was a powerful lefthanded hitter who pounded out 475 home runs in his 21-year career with the Pittsburgh Pirates. Most sluggers are vulnerable to the strikeout, and Stargell was no exception.

"Pops" was the player the club looked up to, a team leader who amassed eight club marks, all of which still stand today. He was a league leader six times in batting and three times in fielding. Stargell was the home run champion in 1971 and 1973. In 1973 he was also the doubles king and home run percentage leader. He hit home runs at an 8.4 percent frequency. Stargell was also the slugging leader with a hefty .646 average.

Stargell batted over .300 only three times, but he slugged over .500 13 times. He hit 20 or more homers 15 times.

Stargell entered the Hall of Fame in 1987.

CAREER STATISTICS:

21 Years	Home Runs 475	Strikeouts 1,936
Games 2,360	Home Run Percentage 6.0	Batting Ave. .282
At Bats 7,927	Runs Scored 1,195	Slugging Ave. .529
Hits 2,232	RBIs 1,540	Pinch Hit At Bats 236
Doubles 423	Bases on Balls 937	Pinch Hits 55
Triples 55	Stolen Bases 17	

Charles Dillon Stengel
(Casey, The Ol' Professor)
B. July 30, 1890, D. Sept. 29, 1975

Bkn–NL 1912–17, Pit–NL 1918–19, Phi–NL 1920–21, NY–NL 1921–23, Bos–NL 1924–25
Manager: Bkn–NL 1934–36, Bos–NL 1938–43, NY–AL 1949–60, NY–NL 1962–65

NUMBER OF RECORDS ESTABLISHED AS MANAGER: 16

National League Season Records

1962	Losses	120	Never Broken

American League Career Records

	Winning Percentage	.623	Never Broken
	Pennants Won	10	Never Broken
	Cons. Pennants Won	5	Never Broken

Major League Season Records

1962	Losses	120	Never Broken

Major League Career Records

Pennants Won	10	Tied
Cons. Pennants Won	5	Never Broken

American League World Series Career Records—1949–60

Series	10	Never Broken
Games	63	Never Broken
Series Won	7	Tied
Games Won	37	Never Broken
Games Lost	26	Never Broken

Major League World Series Career Records—1949–60

Series	10	Tied
Games	63	Never Broken
Series Won	7	Tied
Games Won	37	Never Broken

SUMMARY

Casey Stengel was probably the most colorful character ever to wear a baseball uniform. And past all doubt, he was one of the shrewdest. He was a comedian and a genius when it came to baseball. His zany stunts, hilarious one-liners, and famous double talk known as "Stengelese" endeared him to baseball fans. These traits also made him baseball's supreme good-will ambassador. His ability to handle men and his knack for the game made him the standout manager of the modern era.

One of Casey's first breaks came in 1921, when the Philadelphia Phillies traded him to the New York Giants, where he played under John McGraw, who was to influence Stengel's managerial career.

McGraw platooned Stengel, using him against right-handed pitchers (Casey batted left-handed), and Casey had the two best years of his playing career. In 1922 he batted .368 in 84 games, and in 1923 he batted .339 in 75 games. The Giants won the pennant both years, and in the 1923 World Series Casey starred by hitting .417, with two homers in six games. In all, he batted .393 in 12 World Series games.

"The Old Professor" managed 25 years and was the most successful pilot in the American League, leading the Yankees to ten pennants and seven World Series. He was also the hapless Mets' first manager.

Stengel became a Hall of Famer in 1966.

CAREER STATISTICS:

14 Years	Home Runs 60	Strikeouts 453
Games 1,277	Home Run Percentage 1.4	Batting Ave. .284
At Bats 4,288	Runs Scored 575	Slugging Ave. .410
Hits 1,219	RBIs 535	Pinch Hit At Bats 73
Doubles 182	Bases on Balls 437	Pinch Hits 12
Triples 89	Stolen Bases 131	

CAREER STATISTICS AS MANAGER:

League
25 Years
Games 3,812 (4th)

Wins 1,926 (7th)
Losses 1,867 (4th)

Winning Percentage .508
First-place Finishes 10

World Series
10 Years (1st)
Games 63 (1st)

Wins 37 (1st)
Losses 26 (2nd)

Winning Percentage .587 (2nd)

William Harold Terry
(Bill, Memphis Bill)

B. Oct. 30, 1898
NY–NL 1923–36
Manager: NY–NL 1932–41

NUMBER OF RECORDS ESTABLISHED AS PLAYER: 9

NATIONAL LEAGUE RECORDS

Season Batting Records

1930	Most Hits	254		Never Broken

ALL-STAR GAME RECORDS

Game Batting Records

1933	Most Games Played	1	1
	Most Singles	2	4
1934	Most Games Played	2	1
1935	Most Games Played	3	1

Career Batting Records—1933–35

	Most Games Played	3	1
	Most Singles	4	3

WORLD SERIES RECORDS

7-Game Series Batting Records

1924	Highest Batting Ave.	.429	1
	Highest Slugging Ave.	.786	1

SUMMARY

Bill Terry compiled a lifetime batting average of .341. "Memphis Bill" batted over .300 ten times in a row and was the last National League player to hit over .400. Terry rattled the fences for a .401 average in 1930. In the same season, he rapped 254 hits, which represents the most season hits any National League player has ever had.

Terry had seasons of 200 or more hits six times. At first base he led the league 21 times in fielding.

Terry won Hall of Fame honors in 1954.

CAREER STATISTICS:

14 Years
Games 1,721
At Bats 6,428
Hits 2,193
Doubles 373
Triples 112

Home Runs 154
Home Run Percentage 2.4
Runs Scored 1,120
RBIs 1,078
Bases on Balls 537
Stolen Bases 56

Strikeouts 449
Batting Ave. .341
Slugging Ave. .506
Pinch Hit At Bats 113
Pinch Hits 34

CAREER STATISTICS AS MANAGER:

10 Years
Games 1,496

Wins 823
Losses 661

Winning Percentage .555
First-place Finishes 3

Samuel L. Thompson
(Sam, Big Sam)
B. Mar. 5, 1860, D. Nov. 7, 1922
Det–NL 1885–88, Phi–NL 1889–98, Det–AL 1906

NUMBER OF RECORDS ESTABLISHED: 44

NATIONAL LEAGUE RECORDS

Rookie Batting Records

1885	Most Home Runs	7	2
	Highest Home Run Percentage	2.8	2

Season Batting Records

1887	Most Triples	23	3
	Most RBIs	166	43
	Most Total Bases	311	6
	Most Hits	203	2
	Most At Bats	545	1
	Most RBIs per Game	1.31	7
1893	Most Hits	222	1
1894	Most RBIs per Game	1.42	Never Broken

Season Batting Title Records

1890	Most Hits Titles	2	2
1893	Most Hits Titles	3	8
1895	Most Home Runs Titles	2	22

Season Fielding Records—RF

1886	Most Putouts	194	1	
	Most Double Plays	11	8	
	Highest Fielding Ave.	.945	2	
1894	Highest Fielding Ave.	.977	7	

Career Batting Records

Most Home Runs	128	35	
Highest Home Run Percentage	2.1	14	
Most RBIs per Game	0.92		Never Broken

Career Fielding Records—RF

Most Games Played	1,408	12	
Most Putouts	2,042	12	
Most Putouts per Game	1.6	31	
Most Assists	283		Never Broken
Most Double Plays	61		Never Broken
Most Total Chances	2,473	12	
Highest Fielding Ave.	.934	7	

MAJOR LEAGUE RECORDS

Rookie Batting Records

1885	Highest Home Run Percentage	2.8	2

Season Batting Records

1887	Most RBIs	166	34	
	Most RBIs per Game	1.31	7	
1894	Most RBIs per Game	1.42		Never Broken

Season Batting Title Records

1890	Most Hits Titles	2	2
1893	Most Hits Titles	3	14

Season Fielding Records—RF

1886	Highest Fielding Ave.	.945	2
1894	Highest Fielding Ave.	.977	7

Career Batting Records

Most Home Runs	128	21	
Highest Home Run Percentage	2.1	14	
Most RBIs per Game	0.92		Never Broken

Career Fielding Records—RF

Most Games Played	1,408	1
Most Putouts	2,042	11
Most Assists	283	29
Most Double Plays	61	29
Most Total Chances	2,473	11
Highest Fielding Ave.	.934	14

SUMMARY

"Big Sam" Thompson not only batted .331, he also slugged .505 over his career, which is superb for a player of the dead ball era.

Thompson was the first player to get 200 hits in one season, and he was a three-time hits champion. He was also a two-time title winner in slugging average, doubles, home runs, and RBIs. Thompson won single titles in triples, home run percentage, and batting average. He hit over .300 nine times, with a high of .404 in 1894.

He was a five-time league leader among rightfielders.

Thompson was voted into the Hall of Fame in 1974.

CAREER STATISTICS:

15 Years
Games 1,410
At Bats 6,005
Hits 1,986
Doubles 340
Triples 160

Home Runs 128
Home Run Percentage 2.1
Runs Scored 1,263
RBIs 1,299
Bases on Balls 450
Stolen Bases 221

Strikeouts 226
Batting Ave. .331
Slugging Ave. .505
Pinch Hit At Bats 1
Pinch Hits 1

Joseph Bert Tinker

(Joe)

B. July 27, 1880, D. July 27, 1948

Chi–NL 1902–12, Cin–NL 1913, Chi–FL 1914–15, Chi–NL 1916
Manager: Cin–NL 1913, Chi–FL 1914–15, Chi–NL 1916

NUMBER OF RECORDS ESTABLISHED AS PLAYER: 29

NATIONAL LEAGUE RECORDS

Season Fielding Records—SS

1908	Most Assists	570	6
	Highest Fielding Ave.	.958	4
1913	Highest Fielding Ave.	.968	13

MAJOR LEAGUE RECORDS

Season Fielding Records—SS

1908	Most Assists	570	6

WORLD SERIES RECORDS

Game Batting Records

1906	Most Runs Scored	3	20

	Most Bases on Balls	2	3
1907	Most Strikeouts	3	7
1908	Most Bases on Balls	2	1

Game Fielding Records—SS

1907	Most Putouts	5	5
1908	Most Assists	8	13
1910	Most Errors	2	1

Game Base-Running Records

1906	Most Stolen Bases	2	3

5-Game Series Batting Records

1908	Most Home Runs	1	7
	Most RBIs	5	2

5-Game Series Fielding Records—SS

1907	Most Putouts	16		Never Broken
	Most Assists	23	9	
	Most Errors	3	9	

6-Game Series Batting Records

1906	Most Runs Scored	4	5

6-Game Series Base-Running Records

1906	Most Stolen Bases	2	11

6-Game Series Fielding Records—SS

1906	Most Putouts	10	5
	Most Assists	20	12
	Most Errors	2	5

Career Batting Records—1906–10

Most Games Played	21	5
Most Series Played	4	5

Career Fielding Records—SS—1906–10

Most Putouts	44	13
Most Assists	77	13
Most Errors	7	7
Most Total Chances	128	13
Chances w/o Errors	38	13

SUMMARY

"Tinker to Evers to Chance" was the famous double-play cry during the early days of baseball. Joe Tinker was the man who was at the front end of most of those double plays that excited the baseball world. Tinker did very well with the glove, leading all shortstops in various fielding departments 16 times.

Tinker was not a bad hitter for a shortstop, with a .263 career average.

Tinker was inducted into the Hall of Fame in 1946.

CAREER STATISTICS:

15 Years
Games 1,805
At Bats 6,441
Hits 1,695
Doubles 264
Triples 114

Home Runs 31
Home Run Percentage 0.5
Runs Scored 773
RBIs 782
Bases on Balls 416
Stolen Bases 336

Strikeouts 114
Batting Ave .263
Slugging Ave. .354
Pinch Hit At Bats 12
Pinch Hits 1

CAREER STATISTICS AS MANAGER:

4 Years
Games 624

Wins 304
Losses 308

Winning Percentage .497
First-place Finishes 1

Harold Joseph Traynor
(Pie, Pie Man)

B. Nov. 11, 1899, D. Mar. 16, 1972

Pit–NL 1920–37
Manager: Pit—NL 1934–39

NUMBER OF RECORDS ESTABLISHED AS PLAYER: 19

NATIONAL LEAGUE RECORDS

Season Fielding Records—3B

1925	Most Double Plays	41	25	

Career Fielding Records—3B

Most Games Played	1,864	30	
Most Putouts	2,291		Never Broken
Most Assists	3,525	30	
Most Double Plays	308	30	
Most Total Chances	6,140	30	

MAJOR LEAGUE RECORDS

Season Fielding Records—3B

1925	Most Double Plays	41	2

Career Fielding Records—3B

	Most Games Played	1,864	25
	Most Double Plays	308	8

ALL-STAR GAME RECORDS

Game Batting Records

1933	Most Games Played	1	1
	Most Doubles	1	1
	Most Extra Base Hits	1	3
1934	Most Games Played	2	1
	Most Singles	2	3
1935	Most Games Played	3	1

Career Batting Records—1933–35

	Most Games Played	3	1

WORLD SERIES RECORDS

4-Game Series Fielding Records—3B

1927	Most Errors	1	11

7-Game Series Batting Records

1925	Most Triples	2	22

7-Game Series Fielding Records—3B

1925	Most Assists	18	15

SUMMARY

Pie Traynor or Brooks Robinson—one of these players was probably the finest third baseman the game has ever seen. During his era, Pie Traynor was premier among his peers at the hot corner, according to all who saw him. Traynor was a league leader on defense a remarkable 25 times!

For 17 years the "Pie Man" had a composite batting average of .320. In a 12-year span, he batted over .300 ten times and had super seasons with highs of .366, .356, and .342. He won the triples title in 1923.

Pie Traynor became a Hall of Famer in 1948.

CAREER STATISTICS:

17 Years
Games 1,941
At Bats 7,559
Hits 2,416
Doubles 371
Triples 164

Home Runs 58
Home Run Percentage 0.8
Runs Scored 1,183
RBIs 1,273
Bases on Balls 472
Stolen Bases 158

Strikeouts 278
Batting Ave. .320
Slugging Ave. .435
Pinch Hit At Bats 24
Pinch Hits 7

CAREER STATISTICS AS MANAGER:

6 Years
Games 867

Wins 457
Losses 406

Winning Percentage .530
First-place Finishes 0

Clarence Arthur Vance

(Dazzy)

B. Mar. 4, 1891, D. Feb. 16, 1961

Pit–NL 1915, NY–AL 1915–18, Bkn–NL 1922–32, StL–NL 1933–34, Cin–NL 1934, Bkn–NL 1935

NUMBER OF RECORDS ESTABLISHED: 5

NATIONAL LEAGUE RECORDS

Season Pitching Title Records

1927	Strikeout Titles	6	1	
1928	Strikeout Titles	7		Never Broken
1930	Fewest Hits Titles	4	34	

Career Pitching Title Records

| | Strikeout Titles | 7 | | Never Broken |
| | Fewest Hits Titles | 4 | 29 | |

SUMMARY

"Dazzy" Vance was one of the great strikeout pitchers in the early 1920s. He led the league seven consecutive years in strikeouts (1922–28) and was also a three-time ERA champion. His blazing fastball enabled him to win four shutout titles, and in all he was a league leader in pitching categories 18 times.

Vance's best season was 1924, when he won the MVP title by winning 28 and losing 6. He struck out 262 and had a fine 2.16 ERA.

Vance became a Hall of Famer in 1955.

POSTSEASON AWARDS

1924 MVP

CAREER STATISTICS:

16 Years	Games Started 347	Shutouts 30
Wins 197	Games Completed 216	Relief Appearances 95
Losses 140	Innings 2,967	Relief Wins 14
Winning Percentage .585	Hits 2,809	Relief Losses 7
ERA 3.24	Bases on Balls 840	Saves 11
Total Games 442	Strikeouts 2,045	

Joseph Floyd Vaughan
(Arky)
B. Mar. 9, 1912
Pit–NL 1932–41, Bkn–NL 1942–48

NUMBER OF RECORDS ESTABLISHED: 11

ALL-STAR GAME RECORDS

Game Batting Records

1937	Most At Bats	5	12	
1941	Most Home Runs	2		Tied
	Most Total Bases	9	5	
	Most Extra Base Hits	2		Tied
	Most RBIs	4	5	
1942	Most Games Played	7	1	

Career Batting Records—1933–42

	Most Games Played	7	1
	Most Runs Scored	5	8
	Most Home Runs	2	18
	Most Total Bases	15	18
	Most Extra Base Hits	3	18

SUMMARY

Arky Vaughan was one of the top-hitting shortstops in baseball. In a brilliant 14-year career, Vaughan batted .318 and had ten consecutive seasons batting at least .300. In all, he hit .300 or over 12 times.

Vaughan's most outstanding year was in 1935, when he slammed 192 hits, batted a league-leading .385, and slugged .607. In all, he led the league in various batting categories 12 times. He was a three-time triples, runs, and bases on balls champion and had single titles in stolen bases and batting and slugging averages.

Arky could do it with the glove as well as the bat. He led all shortstops in various fielding departments 11 times.

Vaughan was inducted into the Hall of Fame in 1985.

CAREER STATISTICS:

14 Years	Home Runs 96	Strikeouts 276
Games 1,817	Home Run Percentage 1.4	Batting Ave. .318
At Bats 6,622	Runs Scored 1,173	Slugging Ave. .453
Hits 2,103	RBIs 926	Pinch Hit At Bats 71
Doubles 356	Bases on Balls 937	Pinch Hits 21
Triples 128	Stolen Bases 118	

George Edward Waddell

(Rube)

B. Oct. 13, 1876, D. Apr. 1, 1914

Lou–NL 1897–99, Pit–NL 1900–01, Chi–NL 1901, Phi–AL 1902–07, StL–AL 1908–10

NUMBER OF RECORDS ESTABLISHED: 26

AMERICAN LEAGUE RECORDS

Season Pitching Records

1902	Strikeouts	210	1
1903	Strikeouts	302	1
1904	Strikeouts	349	69
1905	Lowest ERA	1.48	3

Season Pitching Title Records

1902	Strikeout Titles	1	1
1903	Strikeout Titles	2	1
1904	Strikeout Titles	3	1
1905	Strikeout Titles	4	1
	Total Games Titles	1	1
	ERA Titles	1	3
	Fewest Hits Titles	1	8

	Saves Titles	1	3
1906	Strikeout Titles	5	1
1907	Strikeout Titles	6	10

Career Pitching Records

Total Games	335	1
Starts	278	1
Wins	163	1
Innings	2,408	1
Bases on Balls	653	3
Strikeouts	1,965	7
Shutouts	47	6
Relief Games	57	4
Relief Wins	22	4
Wins & Saves	26	4

MAJOR LEAGUE RECORDS

Season Pitching Title Records

1906	Strikeout Titles	5	1
1907	Strikeout Titles	6	10

SUMMARY

"Rube" Waddell was one of the American League's first outstanding strikeout pitchers. For six years in a row (1902–07), he led all the league's pitchers in the "K" department. It took the great Walter Johnson ten years to break this remarkable record.

Waddell compiled 28 records, the longest standing of which was his 349 season strikeouts in 1904, which lasted 69 years before Nolan Ryan struck out 383 in 1973.

Waddell led the league in various pitching departments 15 times, and his 2.16 ERA is the sixth best in baseball. He was a four-time 20-game winner (1902–05) with a high of 26 in 1905. In that year he had a sparkling 1.48 ERA and whiffed 287 batters.

Waddell became a Hall of Famer in 1946.

CAREER STATISTICS:

13 Years	Games Started 340	Shutouts 50
Wins 191	Games Completed 261	Relief Appearances 67
Losses 145	Innings 2,961	Relief Wins 22
Winning Percentage .568	Hits 2,460	Relief Losses 6
ERA 2.16 (6th)	Bases on Balls 803	Saves 5
Total Games 407	Strikeouts 2,316	

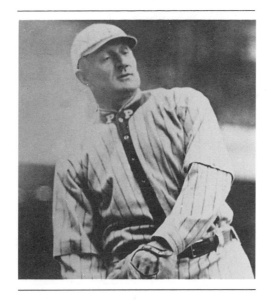

John Peter Wagner
(Honus, The Flying Dutchman)

B. Feb. 24, 1874, D. Dec. 6, 1955

Lou–NL 1897–99, Pit–NL 1900–17
Manager: Pit–NL 1917

NUMBER OF RECORDS ESTABLISHED AS PLAYER: 56

NATIONAL LEAGUE RECORDS

Season Batting Title Records

1903	Most Triples Titles	2	5	
1906	Most Doubles Titles	5	1	
	Batting Ave. Titles	4	1	
1907	Most Doubles Titles	6	1	
	Batting Ave. Titles	5	1	
1908	Most Doubles Titles	7	1	
	Most Triples Titles	3	41	
	Most Total Bases Titles	4	1	
	Batting Ave. Titles	6	1	
1909	Most Doubles Titles	8		Tied
	Most RBI Titles	4		Tied
	Most Total Bases Titles	5	16	

	Batting Ave. Titles	7	2	
	Slugging Ave. Titles	6	16	
1911	Batting Ave. Titles	8		Never Broken

Season Fielding Records–SS

1912	Highest Fielding Ave.	.962	1

Career Batting Records—1897–1917

Most Games Played	2,786	46
Most At Bats	10,427	46
Most Hits	3,430	46
Most Singles	2,426	64
Most Doubles	651	46
Most Triples	252	69
Most Runs Scored	1,740	30
Most RBIs	1,732	30
Most Extra Base Hits	1,004	30
Most Total Bases	4,888	30
Most Stolen Bases	703	11

Career Fielding Records—SS—1901–17

Highest Fielding Ave.	.942	7

MAJOR LEAGUE RECORDS

Season Batting Title Records

1903	Triples Titles	2	5	
1906	Doubles Titles	5	1	
1907	Doubles Titles	6	1	
	Batting Ave. Titles	5	1	
1908	Doubles Titles	7	2	
	Triples Titles	3	41	
	Total Bases Titles	4	1	
	Batting Ave. Titles	6	1	
1909	Doubles Titles	8		Tied
	RBI Titles	4		Tied
	Total Bases Titles	5	16	
	Batting Ave. Titles	7	2	
1911	Batting Ave. Titles	8	4	

Career Batting Records—1897–1917

Most Games Played	2,786	11
Most At Bats	10,427	11
Most Hits	3,430	11
Most Doubles	651	11

Most Extra Base Hits	1,004	11
Most Total Bases	4,888	11
Most Runs Scored	1,740	11
Most RBIs	1,732	11
Most Stolen Bases	703	11

WORLD SERIES RECORDS

Game Batting Records

1903	Most Singles	3		Broken in Same Series
	Most Bases on Balls	1		Broken in Same Series
	Most Stolen Bases	1	6	
1909	Most Stolen Bases	3		Tied

Game Fielding Records—SS

1903	Most Assists	6		Broken in Same Series
	Most Assists	7	3	
	Most Errors	1		Broken in Same Series
	Most Errors	1		Broken in Same Series
	Most Errors	1		Broken in Same Series
	Most Errors	2	8	
1909	Most Errors	2	2	

7-Game Series Batting Records

| 1909 | Most Stolen Bases | 6 | 58 |
| | Most Triples | 1 | 3 |

7-Game Series Fielding Records—SS

| 1909 | Most Putouts | 13 | 31 |
| | Most Assists | 23 | 31 |

8-Game Series Fielding Records—SS

| 1903 | Most Assists | 30 | | Tied |
| | Most Errors | 6 | | Tied |

8-Game Series Base-Running Records

| 1903 | Most Stolen Bases | 3 | | Tied |

Career Batting Records—1907–09

Most RBIs	9	10
Most Bases on Balls	7	1
Most Stolen Bases	9	1

SUMMARY

Honus Wagner, "The Flying Dutchman," is often recognized as the greatest all-around shortstop in baseball history.

In a remarkable 21-year career, he was a league leader a sensational 37 times in various batting categories and had a lifetime batting average of .329, the highest of any shortstop in history.

With his great speed, Honus won five stolen bases titles and belted 651 doubles, which places him fifth on the all-time doubles list. He also earned eight doubles titles, three triples titles, and eight batting average championships while batting over .300 17 consecutive times beginning in his rookie year. He captured five slugging crowns as well.

Wagner was a fine-fielding shortstop who was a fielding leader 11 times. He managed this while not wearing a glove! He was the last of the bare-handed fielders.

Wagner was welcomed into the Hall of Fame in 1936.

CAREER STATISTICS:

21 Years	Home Runs 101	Strikeouts 327
Games 2,786	Home Run Percentage 1.0	Batting Ave. .329
At Bats 10,427 (8th)	Runs Scored 1,740	Slugging Ave. .469
Hits 3,430 (6th)	RBIs 1,732	Pinch Hit At Bats 31
Doubles 651 (5th)	Bases on Balls 963	Pinch Hits 5
Triples 252 (3rd)	Stolen Bases 722 (5th)	

CAREER STATISTICS AS MANAGER:

1 Year	Wins 1	Winning Percentage .200
Games 5	Losses 4	First-place Finishes 0

Rhoderick John Wallace

(Bobby, Rhody)

B. Nov. 4, 1873, D. Nov. 3, 1960

Cle–NL 1894–98, StL–NL 1899–1901, StL–AL 1902–16, StL–NL 1917–18
Manager: StL–AL 1911–12, Cin–NL 1937

NUMBER OF RECORDS ESTABLISHED AS PLAYER: 8

AMERICAN LEAGUE RECORDS

Season Fielding Records—SS

1905	Most Putouts	385	8
	Most Total Chances	953	3

Career Fielding Records—SS

	Most Games Played	1,449	7
	Most Putouts	3,185	7
	Most Assists	4,825	7
	Most Errors	488	7
	Most Double Plays	495	7
	Most Total Chances	8,498	7

SUMMARY

Bobby Wallace had one of the longest careers in baseball. He laced up his spikes for 25 years and left the game as the most active shortstop in American League history.

He was a respectable batter, with a lifetime batting average of .267 on 2,314 hits. He did just as well with the glove, winning 12 fielding crowns. He began as a pitcher and has 25 career wins.

Wallace batted over .300 three times, with a high of .339 in 1897. Wallace became a Hall of Famer in 1953.

CAREER STATISTICS:

25 Years	Home Runs 35	Strikeouts 79
Games 2,386	Home Run Percentage 0.4	Batting Ave. .267
At Bats 8,652	Runs Scored 1,057	Slugging Ave. .360
Hits 2,314	RBIs 1,121	Pinch Hit At Bats 21
Doubles 393	Bases on Balls 774	Pinch Hits 5
Triples 153	Stolen Bases 201	

CAREER STATISTICS AS MANAGER:

3 Years	Wins 62	Winning Percentage .287
Games 217	Losses 154	First-place Finishes 0

Edward Augustin Walsh
(Ed, Big Ed)
B. May 14, 1881, D. May 26, 1959
Chi–AL 1904–16, Bos–NL 1917

NUMBER OF RECORDS ESTABLISHED: 52

AMERICAN LEAGUE RECORDS

Rookie Pitching Records

1904	Winning Percentage	.667	1
	Relief Wins	2	1
	Saves	1	1

Season Pitching Records

1904	Relief Games	10	1
1906	Shutouts	10	2
1907	Games	56	1
	Saves	4	1
1908	Games	66	56
	Shutouts	11	2
	Innings	464	Never Broken

	Saves	6	4	
	Wins & Saves	11	11	
1911	Relief Wins	7	2	
	Relief Losses	5	7	
	Wins & Saves	11	1	
1912	Relief Games	21	1	
	Saves	10	1	
	Wins & Saves	14	5	

Season Pitching Title Records

1907	Saves Titles	1	1	
	ERA Titles	1	1	
1908	Winning Percentage Titles	1	3	
	Saves Titles	2	1	
	Complete Game Titles	2	5	
	Games Titles	2	2	
1908	Innings Titles	2	3	
1909	Shutout Titles	3	9	
1910	ERA Titles	2	8	
	Relief ERA Titles	3	1	
	Saves Titles	3	1	
	Games Titles	3	1	
1911	Innings Titles	3	1	
	Relief ERA Titles	4	1	
	Games Titles	4	1	
1912	Innings Titles	4	4	
	Relief ERA Titles	5		Tied
	Saves Titles	4	20	
	Games Titles	5	20	

Career Pitching Records

	ERA	1.82		Never Broken
	Fewest Hits/9 Inn.	7.12	52	
	Relief Games	114	8	
	Saves	34	16	
	Wins & Saves	56	7	

MAJOR LEAGUE RECORDS

Season Pitching Title Records

1910	Relief ERA Titles	3	1	
1911	Relief ERA Titles	4	1	
1912	Relief ERA Titles	5		Tied

Career Pitching Records

	Lowest ERA	1.82		Never Broken

WORLD SERIES RECORDS

Game Pitching Records

1906	Innings	9	1	
	Strikeouts	12	23	
	Fewest Earned Runs	0	82	Tied

6-Game Series Pitching Records

1906	Wins	2	11	
	Shutouts	1	82	Tied
	Strikeouts	17	5	

SUMMARY

"Big Ed" Walsh was one of the American League's first superstar pitchers. He established 52 records and was a league leader in various pitching categories 34 times. He goes down in history as the pitcher with the lowest ERA of all time, the only pitcher with a lifetime ERA under 2.00.

In addition, Walsh spun 57 shutouts, which places him eighth on the all-time list. His most spectacular season was in 1908, when he won 40 and lost 15 and led the league in ten of the 15 pitching categories! That year he compiled an ERA of 1.42, appeared in 66 games, started 49, completed 42, pitched a record 464 innings, walked only 56 batters, struck out 269, spun 11 shutouts, won 5 games in relief (against 1 loss), and saved 6 others.

Walsh was a workhorse. He was a five-time most games leader, a three-time most starts leader, a two-time complete game champ, a four-time innings king, a two-time strikeout king, a three-time shutout champion, and a seven-time relief pitcher leader.

Walsh was inducted into the Hall of Fame in 1946.

CAREER STATISTICS:

14 Years	Games Started 315	Shutouts 57 (8th)
Wins 195	Games Completed 250	Relief Appearances 115
Losses 126	Innings 2,964	Relief Wins 22
Winning Percentage .607	Hits 2,346	Relief Losses 13
ERA 1.82 (1st)	Bases on Balls 617	Saves 34
Total Games 430	Strikeouts 1,736	

Lloyd James Waner
(Little Poison)

B. Mar. 16, 1906, D. July 22, 1982

Pit–NL 1927–41, Bos–NL 1941, Cin–NL 1941, Phi–NL 1942, Bkn–NL 1944, Pit–NL 1944–45

NUMBER OF RECORDS ESTABLISHED: 15

NATIONAL LEAGUE RECORDS

Rookie Batting Records

1927	Most At Bats	629	4	
	Most Hits	223		Never Broken
	Most Singles	198		Never Broken

Season Batting Records

| 1931 | Most At Bats | 681 | 4 | |

Career Fielding Records—CF

	Most Games Played	1,637	26	
	Most Total Chances	4,804	26	
	Highest Fielding Ave.	.981	15	

MAJOR LEAGUE RECORDS

Rookie Batting Records

1927	Most Hits	223	59
	Most Singles	198	59

Season Batting Records

1931	Most At Bats	681	5

WORLD SERIES RECORDS

Game Fielding Records—CF

1927	Most Errors	1	7
	Most Errors	1	7

4-Game Series Fielding Records—CF

1927	Most Assists	1		Tied
	Most Errors	2	39	

Career Fielding Records—CF

Most Errors	2	39

SUMMARY

"Little Poison" Lloyd Waner stood 5′9″ and weighed all of 150 pounds. His nickname came because to his Brooklyn fans, he was a "little person." Pronounced the local way, though, opponents agreed he was poison indeed.

Waner smacked 2,459 hits and ended his career with a lifetime batting average of .316. He batted over .300 11 times and had a tremendous rookie season, setting three records while batting .355 with 223 hits and 133 runs scored.

Waner was a three-time at bats leader and had single-season winning crowns for most hits, triples, and runs scored. He was a fine outfielder who led the league in various fielding departments seven times.

Waner became a Hall of Famer in 1967.

CAREER STATISTICS:

18 Years
Games 1,992
At Bats 7,772
Hits 2,459
Doubles 281
Triples 118

Home Runs 28
Home Run Percentage 0.4
Runs Scored 1,201
RBIs 598
Bases on Balls 420
Stolen Bases 67

Strikeouts 173
Batting Ave. .316
Slugging Ave. .394
Pinch Hit At Bats 134
Pinch Hits 39

Paul Glee Waner
(Big Poison)
B. Apr. 16, 1903, D. Aug. 29, 1965
Pit–NL 1926–40, Bkn–NL 1941, Bos–NL 1941–42, Bkn–NL 1943–44, NY–AL 1944–45

NUMBER OF RECORDS ESTABLISHED: 16

NATIONAL LEAGUE RECORDS

Rookie Fielding Records—RF

1926	Most Putouts	307	9

Season Batting Records

1932	Most Doubles	62	4

Career Fielding Records—RF

Most Games Played	2,179	2	
Most Putouts	4,631	28	
Most Putouts per Game	2.1		Never Broken
Most Total Chances	4,968	28	
Highest Fielding Ave.	.975	2	

MAJOR LEAGUE RECORDS

Rookie Fielding Records—RF

1926	Most Putouts	307	9	

Career Fielding Records—RF

	Most Putouts	4,631	28	
	Most Putouts per Game	2.1		Tied
	Most Total Chances	4,968	28	

ALL-STAR RECORDS

Game Batting Records

1933	Most Games Played	1	1
1934	Most Games Played	2	1
1935	Most Games Played	3	1
1937	Most At Bats	5	12

Career Batting Records—1933–35

	Most Games Played	3	1

SUMMARY

"Big Poison" stood only 5′8½″ tall and weighed 153 pounds, which made him about the same size as his younger brother, Lloyd.

Paul Waner had a super 20-year career and was one of those rare hitters who compiled more than 3,000 hits. He had 3,152, and a lifetime batting average of .333. He was a league leader in various batting categories 13 times. He batted over .300 his first 12 seasons, and added two more .300-plus seasons later. He had averages of .380, .373, .370, .368, .362, and .354.

Paul belted more than 200 hits in eight seasons and was a two-time most hits champion. He also won two titles in doubles, triples, and runs scored and was a three-time batting average champion.

Waner arrived at the Hall of Fame in 1952.

CAREER STATISTICS:

20 Years	Home Runs 112	Strikeouts 376
Games 2,549	Home Run Percentage 1.2	Batting Ave. .333
At Bats 9,459	Runs Scored 1,626	Slugging Ave. .473
Hits 3,152	RBIs 1,309	Pinch Hit At Bats 164
Doubles 603 (9th)	Bases on Balls 1,091	Pinch Hits 40
Triples 190 (10th)	Stolen Bases 104	

John Montgomery Ward
(Monte)

B. Mar. 3, 1860, D. Mar. 4, 1925

Pro–NL 1878–82, NY–NL 1883–89, Bkn–PL 1890, Bkn–NL 1891–92, NY–NL 1893–94
Manager: NY–NL 1884, Bkn–PL 1890, Bkn–NL 1891–92, NY–NL 1893–94

NUMBER OF RECORDS ESTABLISHED AS PLAYER: 63

NATIONAL LEAGUE RECORDS

Season Batting Records

1887	Most Singles	162	6
	Most Stolen Bases	111	4
	Most At Bats	545	1

Season Pitching Records

1879	Most Wins	47	5
	Most Strikeouts	239	1
	Most Relief Wins	5	12

Season Pitching Title Records

| 1878 | Fewest Hits Titles | 1 | 7 |

	Most ERA Titles	1	1
1879	Most Saves Titles	1	2
1880	Most No-Hit Titles	1	2
1882	Most Saves Titles	2	15

Season Fielding Records—SS

1885	Most Putouts	167	2
1887	Most Putouts	226	2

Season Base-running Title Records

1887	Most Stolen Bases Titles	1	4

Career Batting Records

Most Hits	1,916	1
Most At Bats	7,086	3
Most Games Played	1,697	1
Most Singles	1,592	1
Most Stolen Bases	504	7
Most Runs Scored	1,274	3

Career Pitching Records—1878–84

Lowest ERA	2.10	16
Most Relief Wins	11	27
Most Relief Losses	5	11
Most Wins & Saves	14	24
Highest Relief Winning Percentage	.685	5

Career Fielding Records—SS—1881–91

Most Games Played	698	3
Most Putouts	1,078	3
Most Putouts per Game	1.5	4
Most Assists	2,134	3
Most Assists per Game	3.1	3
Most Errors	405	3
Most Double Plays	230	4
Most Total Chances	3,617	3

MAJOR LEAGUE RECORDS

Season Batting Records

1887	Most Singles	162	6
	Most Stolen Bases	111	4

Season Pitching Records

1879	Most Wins	47	5
	Most Strikeouts	239	1
	Most Relief Wins	5	12

Season Pitching Title Records

1878	Most Fewest Hits Titles	1	7
	Most ERA Titles	1	1
1879	Most Saves Titles	1	2

Season Fielding Records—SS

1885	Most Putouts	167	2
1887	Most Putouts	226	2

Season Base-running Title Records

1887	Most Stolen Bases Titles	1	4

Career Batting Records

Most Hits	2,123	3
Most Singles	1,768	3
Most At Bats	7,647	3
Most Games Played	1,825	3
Most Stolen Bases	504	3

Career Pitching Records—1878–84

Lowest ERA	2.10	26
Most Strikeouts	920	2
Most Relief Wins	11	7
Most Relief Losses	5	11
Most Wins & Saves	14	24
Highest Relief Winning Percentage	.685	5

Career Fielding Records—SS—1881–91

Most Games Played	826	3
Most Putouts	1,381	4
Most Putouts per Game	1.6	8
Most Assists	2,584	4
Most Assists per Game	3.1	4
Most Double Plays	289	4
Most Total Chances	4,475	4

SUMMARY

Monte Ward was one of baseball's first great multi-position players. As a pitcher, he established 26 records and threw a perfect game in 1880. As a batter he set 18 records, and as a shortstop he added another 19 marks for a grand total of 63.

For the first six years of his career, Ward was primarily a pitcher. In 1884, though, he pitched only 9 games and played 47 at second and 59 in the outfield. From 1885 to 1891 he was at shortstop; he then moved back to second base for the years 1892–94. All told, he pitched in 291 games, played short for 826, second for 491, and the outfield for 215. He also had 46 games at third.

Ward was named to the Hall of Fame in 1964.

CAREER STATISTICS (BATTING):

17 Years
Games 1,825
At Bats 7,647
Hits 2,123
Doubles 232
Triples 97
Home Runs 26

Home Run Percentage 0.3
Runs Scored 1,408
RBIs 686
Bases on Balls 420
Stolen Bases 504
Strikeouts 326

Batting Ave. .278
Slugging Ave. .344
Pinch Hit At Bats 1
Pinch Hits 0

CAREER STATISTICS (PITCHING):

7 Years
Wins 161
Losses 101
Winning Percentage .615
ERA 2.10 (4th)
Total Games 291
Games Started 261

Games Completed 244
Innings 2,462
Hits 2,317
Bases on Balls 253
Strikeouts 920
Shutouts 25

Relief Appearances 30
Relief Wins 11
Relief Losses 5
Saves 3

CAREER STATISTICS AS MANAGER:

6 Years
Games 717

Wins 394
Losses 307

Winning Percentage .562
First-place Finishes 0

Michael Francis Welch
(Mickey, Smiling Mickey)
B. July 4, 1859, D. July 30, 1941
Tro–NL 1880–82, NY–NL 1883–92

NUMBER OF RECORDS ESTABLISHED: 7

NATIONAL LEAGUE RECORDS

Season Pitching Records

| 1884 | Most Bases on Balls | 146 | 2 |
| 1886 | Most Bases on Balls | 163 | 4 |

Career Pitching Records

| | Most Bases on Balls | 1,297 | 9 |
| | Most Strikeouts | 1,850 | 2 |

MAJOR LEAGUE RECORDS

Season Pitching Records

| 1884 | Most Bases on Balls | 146 | 2 |

Career Pitching Records

Most Bases on Balls	1,297	2
Most Strikeouts	1,850	1

SUMMARY

Mickey Welch was one of the first two pitchers to retire with more than 300 wins. ("Pud" Galvin was the other. Galvin had 361, and Welch came in with 311. Both retired in 1892.)

Welch was a 21-year-old rookie when he won 34 games in 1880. In all, he won over 30 games in one season four times, with a high of 44 in 1885. His 525 complete games is sixth on the all-time list, and his 4,802 innings rank him tenth. Welch was very wild and set a major league bases on balls record, but he made up for it by also setting the strikeout record.

Welch entered the Hall of Fame in 1973.

CAREER STATISTICS:

13 Years
Wins 311
Losses 207
Winning Percentage .600
ERA 2.71
Total Games 564

Games Started 549
Games Completed 525 (6th)
Innings 4,802 (10th)
Hits 4,587
Bases on Balls 1,297
Strikeouts 1,850

Shutouts 40
Relief Appearances 15
Relief Wins 3
Relief Losses 2
Saves 4

Zachary Davis Wheat
(Zack, Buck)
B. May 23, 1888, D. Mar. 11, 1972
Bkn–NL 1909–26, Phi–AL 1927

NUMBER OF RECORDS ESTABLISHED: 15

NATIONAL LEAGUE RECORDS

Rookie Batting Records

| 1910 | Most Games Played | 156 | 43 |
| | Most Doubles | 36 | 3 |

Career Batting Records

| | Most Home Runs | 131 | 11 |

Career Fielding Records—LF

	Most Games Played	2,288	Never Broken
	Most Putouts	4,837	Never Broken
	Most Total Chances	5,349	Never Broken

MAJOR LEAGUE RECORDS

Career Fielding Records—LF

Most Games Played	2,350	Never Broken
Most Putouts	4,942	Never Broken
Most Total Chances	5,411	Never Broken

WORLD SERIES RECORDS

Game Fielding Records—LF

1916	Most Errors	1	Tied
1920	Most Errors	1	Tied
	Most Errors	1	Tied

5-Game Series Fielding Records—LF

1916	Most Putouts	14	Tied

7-Game Series Batting Records

1920	Most Hits	9	2

7-Game Series Fielding Records—LF

1920	Most Errors	1	Tied

SUMMARY

When Zack Wheat retired in 1927, he had hit more home runs than any other player in National League history. His mark stood for 11 years before Rogers Hornsby passed him.

Zack Wheat played more games, made more putouts, and had more total chances than any leftfielder in the history of baseball. These major league records are still unbroken.

In a fabulous 19-year career, Zack batted .317, including 14 seasons with batting averages over .300. He batted .375 in 1923 and 1924 and had other great years with averages of .359, .358, and .335 (twice).

Hall of Fame honors were bestowed on Wheat in 1959.

CAREER STATISTICS:

19 Years	Home Runs 132	Strikeouts 559
Games 2,410	Home Run Percentage 1.4	Batting Ave. .317
At Bats 9,106	Runs Scored 1,289	Slugging Ave. .450
Hits 2,884	RBIs 1,261	Pinch Hit At Bats 68
Doubles 476	Bases on Balls 650	Pinch Hits 17
Triples 172	Stolen Bases 205	

James Wilhelm
(Hoyt)
B. July 26, 1923
NY–NL 1952–56, StL–NL 1957, Cle–AL 1957–58, Bal–AL 1958–62, Chi–AL 1963–68, Cal–AL 1969, Atl–NL 1969–70, Chi–NL 1970, Atl–NL 1971, LA–NL 1971–72

NUMBER OF RECORDS ESTABLISHED: 14

NATIONAL LEAGUE RECORDS

Rookie Relief Pitching Records

1952	Relief Games	71	24	
	Relief Wins	15		Never Broken

AMERICAN LEAGUE RECORDS

Career Relief Pitching Records

	Relief Games	570	13
	Relief Losses	66	13
	Saves	157	13
	Wins & Saves	229	13

MAJOR LEAGUE RECORDS

Rookie Relief Pitching Records

| 1952 | Relief Games | 71 | 24 | |
| | Relief Wins | 15 | | Never Broken |

Career Relief Pitching Records

	Total Games	1,070		Never Broken
	Relief Games	1,018		Never Broken
	Relief Wins	123		Never Broken
	Relief Losses	102		Never Broken
	Saves	227	12	
	Wins & Saves	350	12	

SUMMARY

The first pitcher to make the Hall of Fame as a reliever was Hoyt Wilhelm. For 19 of his 21 years in baseball he was a full-time relief pitcher, appearing in more games than any pitcher in history.

He started his career in 1952 by setting a major league record of 15 wins in relief, a mark that still stands today. He also led the league in winning percentage, ERA, and relief games.

Wilhelm is a ten-time league leader and had six seasons with ERAs lower than 2.00! On the all-time pitching list he is number one in total games, first in relief wins, and number five in saves.

Wilhelm entered the Hall of Fame in 1985.

CAREER STATISTICS:

21 Years	Games Started 52	Shutouts 5
Wins 143	Games Completed 20	Relief Appearances 918
Losses 122	Innings 2,254	Relief Wins 123 (1st)
Winning Percentage .540	Hits 1,757	Relief Losses 102
ERA 2.52	Bases on Balls 778	Saves 227 (5th)
Total Games 1,070 (1st)	Strikeouts 1,610	

Billy Leo Williams

B. June 15, 1938

Chi–NL 1959–74, Oak–AL 1975–76

NUMBER OF RECORDS ESTABLISHED: 0

SUMMARY

Outfielder Billy Williams was one of the most consistent hitters of modern times. For 18 seasons he banged enemy pitchers for 2,711 base hits, 426 of which were round-trippers.

Williams also slammed 434 doubles and rattled the fences with 88 triples. He was considered a pure hitter in every sense of the word.

Billy batted over .300 five times and won the batting title in 1972 with .333 and the slugging crown with .606. In 1970, he produced the most hits and scored the most runs.

Williams entered the Hall of Fame in 1987.

CAREER STATISTICS:

18 Years	Home Runs 426	Strikeouts 1,046
Games 2,488	Home Run Percentage 4.6	Batting Ave. .290
At Bats 9,350	Runs Scored 1,410	Slugging Ave. .492
Hits 2,711	RBIs 1,475	Pinch Hit At Bats 59
Doubles 434	Bases on Balls 1,045	Pinch Hits 15
Triples 88	Stolen Bases 90	

Theodore Samuel Williams
(Ted, The Splendid Splinter, The Thumper)

B. Aug. 30, 1918

Bos–AL 1939–60
Manager: Was–AL 1969–70

NUMBER OF RECORDS ESTABLISHED AS PLAYER: 26

AMERICAN LEAGUE RECORDS

Rookie Batting Records

1939	Most RBIs	145		Never Broken
	Most Bases on Balls	107		Never Broken

Rookie Fielding Records—RF

1939	Most Putouts	318	38	
	Most Total Chances	348		Never Broken

Season Batting Title Records

1942	Most Triple Crowns	1	5	
1947	Most Triple Crowns	2		Tied
1951	Most Total Bases Titles	6		Tied

MAJOR LEAGUE RECORDS

Rookie Batting Records

1939	Most RBIs	145		Never Broken

ALL-STAR GAME RECORDS

Game Batting Records

1941	Most RBIs	4	5	
1946	Most Hits	4		Tied
	Most Home Runs	2		Tied
	Most RBIs	5		Tied
	Most Runs Scored	4		Never Broken
	Most Extra Base Hits	2		Tied
	Most Total Bases	10		Never Broken
1951	Most Triples	1	27	
1957	Most At Bats	7		Tied

Career Batting Records—1939–60

Most Hits	14	3	
Most Runs Scored	10	13	
Most RBIs	12		Never Broken
Most Home Runs	4	3	
Most Total Bases	30	3	
Extra Base Hits	7	3	
Most Bases on Balls	10		Never Broken
Most Strikeouts	9	8	

WORLD SERIES RECORDS

7-Game Fielding Records—LF

1946	Most Assists	2		Tied

SUMMARY

Starring for the Boston Red Sox for 19 years, Ted Williams is considered by many to be the purest hitter in baseball history. He was the last modern player to hit over .400, a feat he accomplished in 1941, when he batted .406. Considering the tough relief pitching of his era, this is one of baseball's greatest achievements.

The "Splendid Splinter" led the American League in various batting departments an astonishing 43 times. He won back-to-back doubles crowns in 1948 and 1949 and did the same in home runs in 1941 and 1942. In all, Ted won four home run titles and four home run percentage crowns. He led the league 6 times in runs scored, including five times in a row from 1940 to 1947. "The Thumper" led in RBIs 4 times with a high of 159 in 1949.

With the eyes of an eagle, Williams refused to swing at balls out of the strike zone and won the bases on balls title eight times, six times in succession from 1941 to 1949. It was said that if Williams did not swing at a pitch, the umpires automatically called a ball.

Williams has the lowest ratio of strikeouts among sluggers with more than 500 homers. He won the batting average title six times and had nine slugging championships. Williams has the highest on base percentage of any player in baseball history.

Ted Williams became a Hall of Famer in 1966.

CAREER STATISTICS:

19 Years	Home Runs 521 (8th)	Strikeouts 709
Games 2,292	Home Run Percentage 6.8 (6th)	Batting Ave. .344 (6th)
At Bats 7,706	Runs Scored 1,798	Slugging Ave. .634 (2nd)
Hits 2,654	RBIs 1,839 (10th)	Pinch Hit At Bats 111
Doubles 525	Bases on Balls 2,019 (2nd)	Pinch Hits 33
Triples 71	Stolen Bases 24	

CAREER STATISTICS AS MANAGER:

4 Years	Wins 273	Winning Percentage .429
Games 637	Losses 364	First-place Finishes 0

Lewis Robert Wilson
(Hack)
B. Apr. 26, 1900, D. Nov. 23, 1948
NY–NL 1923–25, Chi–NL 1926–31, Bkn–NL 1932–34, Phi–NL 1934

NUMBER OF RECORDS ESTABLISHED: 9

NATIONAL LEAGUE RECORDS

Season Batting Records

1930	Most Home Runs	56	Never Broken
	Highest Home Run Percentage	9.6	Never Broken
	Most RBIs	190	Never Broken

MAJOR LEAGUE RECORDS

Season Batting Records

1930	Most RBIs	190		Never Broken

WORLD SERIES RECORDS

Game Batting Records

1924	Most At Bats	6	49

Game Fielding Records—CF

1929	Most Errors	1	5

5-Game Series Fielding Records—CF

1929	Most Errors	1	14

7-Game Series Batting Records

1924	Most Strikeouts	9	34

7-Game Series Fielding Records—CF

1924	Most Assists	1	22

SUMMARY

"Hack" Wilson had the greatest RBI year of any player in baseball history. The year was 1930, and this slugger enjoyed his greatest season. He led the National League in six categories: 56 home runs, a 9.6 home run percentage, 190 RBIs, 105 bases on balls, a .723 slugging average, and a percentage of 1.23 RBIs per game. He also led in strikeouts with 84.

Wilson won four home run titles, two home run percentage titles, two RBI crowns, and two bases on balls titles. His batting average was a solid .307, and he batted over .300 5 consecutive seasons. His lifetime slugging average was .545.

Hall of Fame honors came to Wilson in 1979.

CAREER STATISTICS:

12 Years	Home Runs 244	Strikeouts 713
Games 1,348	Home Run Percentage 5.1	Batting Ave. .307
At Bats 4,760	Runs Scored 884	Slugging Ave. .545
Hits 1,461	RBIs 1,062	Pinch Hit At Bats 64
Doubles 266	Bases on Balls 674	Pinch Hits 16
Triples 67	Stolen Bases 52	

George Wright

B. Jan. 28, 1847, D. Aug. 21, 1937

Bos–NL 1876–78, Pro–NL 1879, Bos–NL 1880–81, Pro–NL 1882
Manager: Pro–NL 1879

NUMBER OF RECORDS ESTABLISHED AS PLAYER: 24

NUMBER OF RECORDS ESTABLISHED AS MANAGER: 2

TOTAL: 26

PLAYER RECORDS

MAJOR LEAGUE RECORDS

National League Rookie Batting Records

1876	At Bats	335	3
	Games	70	3

Rookie Fielding Records—SS

1876	Assists	251	4
	Double Plays	16	4

Season Batting Records

1876	At Bats	335	3
	Games	70	3

Season Fielding Records—SS

1876	Assists	251	3
	Double Plays	16	1
1878	Double Plays	24	1
	Fielding Ave.	.947	25
1879	Assists	319	1
	Total Chances	449	1

MANAGER RECORDS

National League Season Records

1879	Wins	59	1

Major League Season Records

1879	Wins	59	1

SUMMARY

George Wright was one of the first great shortstops in professional baseball. The old National Association played from 1871 to 1875, and Wright, as a member of the Boston Red Stockings, batted .409, .336, .378, .345, and .337. So good was he at scooping up ground balls with his bare hands that his fielding average of .947 in 1878 lasted a quarter of a century. It is safe to say he was the greatest bare-handed shortstop the game ever saw.

George Wright won the pennant in his first year of managing and then never managed again. He led his Providence team to victory in 1879 as a player-manager.

Wright was welcomed into the Hall of Fame in 1937.

CAREER STATISTICS:

7 Years	Home Runs 2	Strikeouts 103
Games 329	Home Run Percentage 0.1	Batting Ave. .256
At Bats 1,494	Runs Scored 264	Slugging Ave. .323
Hits 383	RBIs 123	Pinch At Bats 0
Doubles 54	Bases on Balls 43	
Triples 20	Stolen Bases—Not Recorded	

CAREER STATISTICS AS MANAGER:

1 Year	Wins 59	Winning Percentage .702
Games 85	Losses 25	First-place Finishes 1

William Henry Wright
(Harry)

B. Jan. 10, 1835, D. Oct. 3, 1895

Bos–NL 1876–77
Manager: Bos–NL 1876–81, Pro–NL 1882–83, Phi–NL 1884–93

NUMBER OF RECORDS ESTABLISHED AS MANAGER: 11

MANAGER RECORDS

National League Season Records

1877	Games Won Pennant By	7	3

National League Career Records

Years		18	5
Games		1,917	5
Wins		1,042	5
Losses		848	5
Cons. Pennants Won		2	4

Major League Season Records

1877	Games Won Pennant By	7	3

Major League Career Records

Years	18	5
Games	1,917	5
Wins	1,042	5
Losses	848	5

SUMMARY

Harry Wright, who was born in Sheffield, England, was the first professional manager in baseball history. He was paid $1,200 to manage and play center field for the Cincinnati Red Stockings in 1869. This team toured the country and won 56 games with one tie and no losses. It was the beginning of big-league baseball.

When the National Association was formed in 1871, Harry Wright was the manager for the Boston Red Stockings until the league folded in 1875. He then became the manager for the Boston team in the newly formed National League. In all, he managed 18 years in the National League, and when he retired in 1893 he had managed more years, more games, and had more wins and losses than any manager to that date.

Wright became a Hall of Famer in 1953.

CAREER STATISTICS:

2 Years	Home Runs 0	Strikeouts 2
Games 2	Home Run Percentage 0	Batting Ave. .000
At Bats 7	Runs Scored 0	Slugging Ave. .000
Hits 0	RBIs 0	No Pinch Hit At Bats
Doubles 0	Bases on Balls 0	
Triples 0	Stolen Bases 0	

CAREER STATISTICS AS MANAGER:

18 Years	Wins 1,042	Winning Percentage .551
Games 1,917	Losses 848	First-place Finishes 2

Early Wynn
(Gus)
B. Jan. 6, 1920
Was–AL 1939, 1941–44, 1946–48, Cle–AL 1949–57, Chi–AL 1958–62, Cle–AL 1963

NUMBER OF RECORDS ESTABLISHED: 3

AMERICAN LEAGUE RECORDS

Career Pitching Records

Most Bases on Balls	1,775	Never Broken

MAJOR LEAGUE RECORDS

Career Pitching Records

Most Bases on Balls	1,775	21

ALL-STAR GAME RECORDS

Career Pitching Records—1955–60

Total Games	7	6

SUMMARY

Early Wynn's best years were with the Cleveland Indians from 1950 to 1956. During that span he won 20-plus games four times, with an overall record of 138 wins and 76 losses. His best year came in 1956, when he was 20–9 and had a career low ERA of 2.72. He led the league in various pitching departments 16 times.

Although he was a little on the wild side, he struck out 559 more batters than he walked, winning two strikeout titles.

Wynn entered the Hall of Fame in 1972.

CAREER STATISTICS:

23 Years	Games Started 612	Shutouts 49
Wins 300	Games Completed 290	Relief Appearances 79
Losses 244 (9th)	Innings 4,564	Relief Wins 11
Winning Percentage .551	Hits 4,291	Relief Losses 12
ERA 3.54	Bases on Balls 1,775 (2nd)	Saves 15
Total Games 691	Strikeouts 2,334	

Carl Michael Yastrzemski
(Yaz)
B. Aug. 22, 1939
Bos–AL 1961–83

TOTAL NUMBER OF RECORDS: 6

AMERICAN LEAGUE RECORDS

Season Fielding Records—LF

1977	Highest Fielding Ave.	1.000	Never Broken

Career Batting Records—1961–83

	Most Games Played	3,308	Never Broken
	Most At Bats	11,988	Never Broken

MAJOR LEAGUE RECORDS

Season Fielding Records—LF

1977	Highest Fielding Ave.	1.000	Never Broken

ALL-STAR RECORDS

Game Batting Records

1970	Most Hits	4	Never Broken
	Most Singles	3	Never Broken

SUMMARY

Carl Yastrzemski is the only player in baseball history to accumulate more than 400 home runs *and* 3,000 hits. Playing all 23 years of his fabulous career with the Boston Red Sox, Yaz created 19 Boston club records, 13 of which remain unbroken. His 3,308 games played rank number two, his 11,988 at bats have been bettered only by Pete Rose's 14,053, and his keen eye at the plate earned him 1,845 bases on balls, which ranks him fourth.

Yaz is also seventh in hits (3,419) and doubles (646) and ninth in RBIs with 1,844. He slammed 452-round trippers, batted .285, and slugged .462.

He led the league 18 times in various batting categories. He was a two-time hits champion, three times won the doubles crown, was the home run king in 1967, led the league three times in runs, batting average, and slugging average, was a two-time bases on balls leader, and drove in more runs than any other American Leaguer in 1967.

He batted over .300 6 times and slugged over .500 5 times. Yaz gained fame for his outstanding mastery of the Green Monster (left field) at Fenway Park and led the league in assists seven times. In all, he accumulated ten fielding titles.

His ten hits in All-Star Games rank him sixth on the all-time list, his five RBIs rank him seventh, and his two doubles place him second. Yaz also set two All-Star Game records, when in 1970 he had 4 hits in one game, 3 of which were singles.

Carl Yastrzemski became a Hall of Famer in 1988.

CAREER STATISTICS:

23 Years	Home Runs 452	Strikeouts 1,393
Games 3,308 (2nd)	Home Run Percentage 3.8	Batting Ave. .285
At Bats 11,988 (3rd)	Runs Scored 1,816	Slugging Ave. .462
Hits 3,419 (7th)	RBIs 1,844 (9th)	Pinch Hit At Bats 52
Doubles 646 (7th)	Bases on Balls 1,845 (4th)	Pinch Hits 8
Triples 59	Stolen Bases 168	

Denton True Young

(Cy)

B. Mar. 29, 1867, D. Nov. 4, 1955

Cle–NL 1890–98, StL–NL 1899–1900, Bos–AL 1901–08, Cle–AL 1909–11, Bos–NL 1911
Manager: Bos–AL 1907

NUMBER OF RECORDS ESTABLISHED AS PLAYER: 93

NATIONAL LEAGUE RECORDS

Season Pitching Records

1891	Relief Losses	3	1	

Season Pitching Title Records

1896	Fewest Bases on Balls Titles	5	1	
	Most Shutout Titles	3	4	
1897	Fewest Bases on Balls Titles	6	1	
1898	Fewest Bases on Balls Titles	7	1	
1899	Fewest Bases on Balls Titles	8	1	
1900	Fewest Bases on Balls Titles	9		Never Broken
	Shutout Titles	4	17	

Career Pitching Records

	Most 20-Wins Seasons	10	5	
	Relief Wins	17	8	

	Saves	8	6
	Wins Plus Saves	25	8
	Relief Games	60	8

AMERICAN LEAGUE RECORDS

Season Pitching Records

1901	Lowest ERA	1.62	3
	Wins	33	3
	Strikeouts	158	1
	Shutouts	5	2
1902	Starts	43	2
	Complete Games	41	1
	Innings	385	1
1904	Shutouts	10	2

Season Pitching Title Records

1901	Shutout Titles	1	2
	Wins Titles	1	2
	Strikeout Titles	1	2
	Fewest Hits Titles	1	12
	Fewest Bases on Balls Titles	1	2
	ERA Titles	1	7
1902	Wins Titles	2	1
	Innings Titles	1	1
	Complete Games Titles	1	7
	Games Titles	1	4
1903	Wins Titles	3	15
	Fewest Bases on Balls Titles	2	1
	Winning Percentage Titles	1	1
	Innings Titles	2	8
	Complete Games Titles	2	5
	Shutout Titles	2	1
	Shutout Titles	3	14
	Fewest Bases on Balls Titles	3	1
1905	Fewest Bases on Balls Titles	4	1
1906	Fewest Bases on Balls Titles	5	Never Broken

Career Pitching Records—1901–11

Most Games	390	2
Starts	358	2
Complete Games	321	2
Wins	222	6
Losses	141	1
Innings	3,236	2
Hits	2,823	2
Saves	8	1

MAJOR LEAGUE RECORDS

Season Pitching Records

1891	Relief Losses	3	3	

Season Pitching Title Records

1896	Fewest Bases on Balls Titles	5	1	
1897	Fewest Bases on Balls Titles	6	1	
1898	Fewest Bases on Balls Titles	7	1	
1899	Fewest Bases on Balls Titles	8	1	
1900	Fewest Bases on Balls Titles	9	1	
	Shutout Titles	4	1	
1901	Fewest Bases on Balls Titles	10	1	
	Shutout Titles	5	2	
1902	Wins Titles	3	1	
1903	Wins Titles	4	3	
	Fewest Bases on Balls Titles	11	1	
	Complete Games Titles	3	11	
	Shutout Titles	6	1	
1904	Fewest Bases on Balls Titles	13	1	
1906	Fewest Bases on Balls Titles	14		Never Broken

Career Pitching Records

Games	906	61	
Starts	815		Never Broken
Complete Games	751		Never Broken
Wins	511		Never Broken
Losses	313		Never Broken
Innings	7,356		Never Broken
Strikeouts	2,799	16	
Hits	7,092		Never Broken
Relief Games	91	5	
Relief Wins	30	5	
Relief Losses	18	5	
Wins Plus Saves	46	5	
20-Wins Seasons	16		Never Broken

WORLD SERIES RECORDS

Game Pitching Records

1903	Fewest Hits	6		Broken Same Series
	Most Hits	12	7	
	Most Innings	9	4	

Fewest Bases on Balls	0	9
Most Bases on Balls	3	Broken Same Series
Fewest Earned Runs	0	10
Most Earned Runs	3	Broken Same Series

8-Game Series Pitching Records

1903	Lowest ERA	1.59	9
	Most Relief Games	1	9

Career Pitching Records

	Lowest ERA	1.59	10
	Most Hits	31	6
	Most Innings w/o Bases on Balls	22	6

SUMMARY

In a sensational 22-year career, Cy Young created many records that will never be broken. It is doubtful that any pitcher will ever win more than 511 games, complete more than 751, or pitch more than 7,356 innings.

In all, Young established 93 records, more than any pitcher in baseball history. He was a league leader in 31 pitching departments; the most impressive of these records is his 14 seasons of allowing the fewest bases on balls. He simply was baseball's greatest control pitcher.

Another remarkable feat that makes Young tops in pitching is his wins of 20 or more games 16 times, also more than any pitcher in baseball history. He won 30 or more games in a season 5 times.

Young was inducted into the Hall of Fame in 1937.

CAREER STATISTICS:

22 Years	Games Started 815	Shutouts 76 (4th)
Wins 511 (1st)	Games Completed 751 (1st)	Relief Appearances 91
Losses 313 (1st)	Innings 7,356 (1st)	Relief Wins 30
Winning Percentage .620	Hits 7,092	Relief Losses 18
ERA 2.63	Bases on Balls 1,217	Saves 16
Total Games 906 (3rd)	Strikeouts 2,799	

CAREER STATISTICS AS MANAGER:

1 Year	Wins 3	Winning Percentage .429
Games 7	Losses 4	First-place Finishes 0

Ross Middlebrook Youngs

B. Apr. 10, 1897, D. Oct. 22, 1927

NY–NL 1917–26

NUMBER OF RECORDS ESTABLISHED: 9

WORLD SERIES RECORDS

Game Batting Records

1924	Most Bases on Balls	4	Tied

Game Fielding Records—RF

1922	Most Errors	2	Tied
1923	Most Errors	2	Tied

5-Game Series Fielding Records—RF

1922	Most Assists	2	Tied
	Most Errors	2	Tied

8-Game Series Batting Records

1921	Most Bases on Balls	7	Tied

Career Batting Records—1921–24

    Most Bases on Balls   17   8

Career Fielding Records—RF—1921–24

Most Errors	4	Never Broken
Most Assists	5	Never Broken

SUMMARY

In nine years of his ten-year career, Ross Youngs batted over .300. He averaged a solid .322. In 1919 he led the league in doubles and in 1923 scored more runs than any other National League player.

    Ross had fine seasons of .356, .351, .346, .336, .331, and .327. He was a scrappy rightfielder who led the league eight times in various fielding categories.

    Youngs entered the Hall of Fame in 1972.

CAREER STATISTICS:

10 Years	Home Runs 42	Strikeouts 390
Games 1,211	Home Run Percentage 0.9	Batting Ave. .322
At Bats 4,627	Runs Scored 812	Slugging Ave. .441
Hits 1,491	RBIs 592	Pinch Hit At Bats 9
Doubles 236	Bases on Balls 550	Pinch Hits 3
Triples 93	Stolen Bases 153	

2

NON-PLAYER PROFILES

☆

Albert Joseph Barlick
(Al)
1915–

In 1936, Al Barlick entered baseball as umpire in the Class D league. Barlick's ability, efficiency, and hard work earned him rapid promotions in various minor leagues from 1937 to 1940.

During September 1940, Barlick joined the National League umpires as a replacement for the ailing Bill Klem. He became a regular National League umpire in 1941 and remained one until his retirement in 1971.

During his active career he umpired in seven World Series and seven All-Star Games. Since his retirement, he has served as a National League consultant.

Barlick frequently was called the loudest, most colorful, and best umpire in baseball. Unique, vigorous "out" gestures and booming "strr-ruck-huh" calls identified him unmistakably. His total commitment, unerring accuracy, and complete control of the game made him a truly great arbiter. When *The Sporting News* writers' poll in 1961 voted Barlick the best National League umpire, he protested his displeasure of the results as a slur on his peers by persons not competent to judge the arbiters' professionalism. He accepted an Umpire of the Year award in 1970, however, because the balloting had been conducted among umpires.

Barlick was inducted into the Hall of Fame in 1988.

☆

Edward Grant Barrow
(Cousin Ed)
1868–1953
Manager: Det–AL 1903–04, Bos–AL 1918–20

Ed Barrow's name is synonymous with the success of the New York Yankees from 1921 to 1945. With Barrow as general manager, the Yankees won 14 pennants and ten World Series. Barrow organized and developed the farm system that established the Yankees as the kings of baseball.

Barrow was considered a genius at evaluating talent. He discovered and developed Honus Wagner and was quoted as saying, "Honus Wagner was without question the best all-around player that ever lived."

Perhaps what Barrow is most famous for is playing Babe Ruth in the outfield when he was not pitching. Barrow was then the manager of the Boston Red Sox and led them to a pennant and World Series in 1918. Prior to managing the Red Sox, he was the manager for the Detroit Tigers in 1903 and 1904.

Barrow managed for five years and won 310 and lost 320, with a winning percentage of .492.

Barrow was inducted into the Hall of Fame in 1953.

☆

James Bell
(Cool Papa)
1903–
Negro Leagues: 1922–46

James (Cool Papa) Bell's career began with the Negro Leagues' St. Louis Stars in 1922. Bell starred with this team through 1931 and then went to the Detroit Senators in 1932. The Senators soon folded, but Bell hooked on with the Homestead Grays. After a month and a half with the Grays, Bell finished the season with the Kansas City Monarchs.

In 1933, "Cool Papa" played with the Pittsburgh Crawfords and was a mainstay of the club until 1936. He traveled to Santo Domingo in the Dominican Republic for the Trujillo All-Stars in 1937 and helped win the championship. From 1938 through 1941, he played in Mexico, and in 1942 he played for the Chicago American Giants. From 1943 to 1946, Bell was again with the Homestead Grays.

Bell began his career as a pitcher but was moved to the outfield because of his tremendous speed. The fastest runner in 1922 was Jimmy Lyons, and when Bell defeated him in a race, he became known as the fastest black player in the history of Negro baseball.

Pitcher Dick Coffman was quoted as saying, " 'Cool Papa' Bell can walk faster than Don Gutteridge the St. Louis Cardinals infielder can run."

Eddie Gottlieb, Negro League team owner of the Philadelphia Stars, said, "Bell was the black Willie Keeler at bat and the black Tris Speaker in center field." Buck Leonard, one of Bell's teammates, said, "Bell was the fastest thing I ever saw on a baseball field. I roomed with him for five years. Even though he was in the evening of his career, he could still fly."

Bell played 20 summer and 21 winter seasons of baseball. His best year was in 1933, when he stole 175 bases in an estimated 200-game schedule. He was a natural righthanded hitter, but he taught himself to switch-hit.

In all his years of baseball, he was approached by a major league team only once. In 1935, Bell played against a team in Mexico City managed by Connie Mack's son, Earle. This Mexican League team had Rogers Hornsby, Doc Cramer, Heinie Manush, Jimmie Foxx, and Max Bishop. Hornsby hit a home run his first time up and in his second at bat drove a ball over Bell's head in deep centerfield. No one thought Bell had a chance for the ball but, using his blazing speed, he caught the ball over his shoulder. After the game Hornsby told Bell it was the hardest ball he had ever hit in his life and wanted to know how he caught it. Bell's response was, "I just ran back and caught it." Earle Mack congratulated Bell after the game and said, "If the doors were open to black players, you would be the first one I'd get."

Few people know that Bell was instrumental in Jackie Robinson's career. In 1945, when Robinson was playing for the Kansas City Monarchs, Frank Duncan, his manager, asked Bell if he would teach Jackie some of his tricks about stealing bases. In addition, Robinson wanted to be a shortstop, but he was weak at going to his right. In a one-on-one game, Bell deliberately hit two ground balls to Jackie's right and easily beat the throws to first base. After that game, Bell was able to convince Robinson that shortstop was not his position. Bell also gave Maury Wills tips on stealing bases.

Bell's composite batting average (from the records we have) was .341 with 418 hits and 88 home runs in 1,227 at bats. In 46 big-league exhibition games, Bell batted .395, getting 67 hits, including 4 home runs, in 169 at bats. He also stole 15 bases.

In 1940 he had a career-high batting average of .437 and led the Negro League in every offensive category. He was considered faster than Ty Cobb and perhaps even Jesse Owens. He routinely scored from second on ground balls and once scored from first on a bunt in a 1948 game against Bob Lemon's barnstorming All-Stars.

Paul Waner and Bill Veeck included Bell on their all-time list of outfielders.

Bell entered the Hall of Fame in 1974, the fifth black player to do so.

Morgan Gardner Bulkeley
1837–1922

Morgan Bulkeley was the first president of the National League when it was founded in 1876. The National Association had just folded after five years of baseball riddled with drinking, gambling, and the throwing of games. Bulkeley played a vital part in reducing gambling and drinking at the games. National League owners praised him for his "invaluable aid" as "a founder of the national game."

Bulkeley was elected to the Hall of Fame as a pioneer and executive in 1937.

☆

Alexander Joy Cartwright
1820–92

Alexander J. Cartwright was the man responsible for the game we call our national pastime.

Cartwright was an amateur player and a surveyor by trade. As a youth in the 1840s he played a game with a stick and ball that was sometimes called "round ball" or "cats." The bases did not have any set distances, an inning was not completed until every member of the opposing team was put out, the game was over when one team scored 21 aces (runs), and in order for a fielder to register an out on a ground ball he had to hit the runner with the ball.

Cartwright decided to refine this game and experimented with the bases until he found that a distance of 90 feet apart was a fair match for the batter and the fielder. In order for a fielder to get an out on a ground ball in Cartwright's new game, he had to field the ball cleanly and make an accurate throw to first base before the runner arrived. Cartwright also created the three outs to an inning rule. Prior to this a team sometimes had to stay in the field for hours before the entire line-up was put out.

In Cartwright's game, it was no longer necessary for one team to score 21 runs to win. He invented the 9-inning game, in which each team had equal turns at bat and the team with the most runs at the end of 9 innings was the winner. Prior to Cartwright's vision of baseball, there existed no shortstops or second basemen. Instead, there were five outfielders who were called "rovers." Three of whom played deep while two played shallow. Cartwright decided to move the shallow outfielders into what we now call the second base and shortstop positions.

On June 19, 1846, two amateur teams met on the Elysian Fields in Hoboken, New Jersey, and played a form of baseball no one had ever seen before. In that game, Cartwright was the umpire and fined a player sixpence for swearing. The New York Knickerbockers were beaten by the New York Nine, 23–1.

At about this time, the gold rush in California was on, and Cartwright headed for the gold. But as he crossed the United States he taught the game everywhere he went. Amateur teams sprang up all across the country, and by 1869 the first professional team, the Cincinnati Red Stockings, was formed.

Cartwright was inducted into the Hall of Fame as "The Inventor of Modern Baseball" in 1938.

☆

Henry Chadwick

1824–1908

Henry Chadwick—"the Father of Baseball"—was the earliest promoter, shaper, chronicler, and conscience of the national pastime. He began his journalistic career for the Brooklyn Long Island *Star* in 1844 and was with Alexander Cartwright in 1847 and 1848, when he was quick to recognize baseball's potential for becoming America's national game. Over the next 50 years,

Chadwick wrote voluminously about baseball in newspapers, magazines, pamphlets, and books. He reported its games, chronicled its development, taught its skills, recommended rule changes, and battled the drinking and gambling that threatened its integrity.

He originated the annual baseball guide in 1860 and edited *DeWitt's Guide* from 1869 to 1880 and the Spaldings' *Base Ball Guide* from 1881 to 1908. In 1868 he wrote the first hardcover book devoted entirely to baseball, *The Game of Base Ball.*

Chadwick influenced baseball's development unofficially through his writings and officially as a rules committee member of the National Association of Base Ball Players (1858–70) and the National League. To improve record keeping, he perfected the box score and devised the system for scoring games that is essentially still used today.

Chadwick was a guardian of baseball's image and well-being, inveighing against drinking and rowdiness by players and fans and opposing disruptive influences. His opposition to gambling helped baseball officials to stand firm against gamblers' persistent threats to corrupt players and umpires and to reduce baseball to a betting medium.

Chadwick was elected to the Hall of Fame in 1938.

☆

Albert Benjamin Chandler
(Happy)
1898–

After earning his law degree at the University of Kentucky, "Happy" Chandler became the governor of Kentucky from 1935 to 1939 and then again from 1955 to 1959.

In 1945 Leland MacPhail, Sr., promoted Chandler's selection as baseball commissioner, a position left vacant by the death of Judge Kenesaw Mountain Landis in 1944. Chandler became the good-will ambassador baseball needed. He was the commissioner when Jackie Robinson integrated baseball. He acted with fair-mindedness and spoke in favor of integration when anything less might have denied Robinson his opportunity. Chandler suspended Leo Durocher for an accumulation of unpleasant incidents detrimental to baseball. He helped the players' association secure radio and television revenue to bolster the new pension plan and supported a player's minimum salary of $5,000.

Chandler entered the Hall of Fame in 1982.

☆

Oscar Charleston

1896–1954

Negro Leagues: 1915–37

Among his own peers, when a vote was taken for the best black players at each position, Oscar Charleston's name came out on top in center field. No other centerfielder in Negro baseball— with the possible exception of Cool Papa Bell—could match Charleston, and old-timers say it is subject to debate whether Tris Speaker, Willie Mays, Joe DiMaggio, and Terry Moore were his superiors. Charleston was a marvelous defensive outfielder who combined hitting ability with tremendous speed and a powerful throwing arm.

Prior to Jackie Robinson, black players only played against major leaguers in exhibition games. From 1915 through 1936, Charleston appeared in 53 games, came to bat 195 times, and belted 62 hits for a batting average of .318. He slammed 11 home runs, the most any black player had ever hit off major league pitchers.

During his career he played in 1,028 games, had 3,479 at bats, 1,228 hits, 183 doubles, 70 triples, 136 home runs, and 144 stolen bases, and batted .353.

Charleston entered the Hall of Fame in 1976.

☆

John Bertrand Conlan
(Jocko)

1899–1988

As a youngster, "Jocko" Conlan served as batboy for the Chicago White Sox from 1912 to 1913. He enjoyed some good seasons in the minor leagues before a knee injury prevented him from having a shot with the Cincinnati Reds in 1926. However, he was called out of retirement by the injury-ridden White Sox in 1934 and batted .249 in 63 games. He returned in 1935 and hit .286 in 65 games.

Between games of a July 1935 double-header between the White Sox and St. Louis Browns, umpire "Red" Ormsby suffered heat prostration and could not continue. Conlan, sidelined by a sprained thumb, volunteered to take his place. He was so good at umpiring he decided to make a career of it and worked in the minors from 1936 to 1940 before coming up to the National League in 1941. He quickly established his authority by ejecting 26 players in his first season. He umpired in six World Series, six All-Star Games, and four pennant-deciding National League play-off games before retiring in 1967.

Besides being the only big-league arbiter of his time to make all his signals with his left hand, he was the only National League umpire to wear an outside chest protector.

Conlan was inducted into the Hall of Fame in 1974.

☆

Thomas Henry Connolly
(Tommy, Tom)
1870–1961

Thomas Henry Connolly was the dean of American League arbiters and the nation's leading authority on the rule book. He umpired in the minor leagues from 1894 to 1897 and joined the National League in 1898.

In 1901, Connolly was hired by "Ban" Johnson, president of the newly formed American League. Connolly umpired the very first game in American League history, between Cleveland and Chicago at Comiskey Park. He also officiated the first game at Yankee Stadium, the Philadelphia Athletics' Shibe Park, and Fenway Park in Boston. He called the first modern World Series in 1903 and the seven subsequent Series.

Connolly described an umpire as a man "with poise and without rabbit ears." He commanded great respect from players for his fairness. Although he ejected ten players his first year, he went ten full seasons without ousting a protester. Ty Cobb said of Connolly, "You can go just so far with Tommy. Once you see his neck getting red it's time to lay off."

In 1931 Connolly was appointed American League umpire-in-chief. He supervised umpires, scouted the minor leagues for talent, and advised league president Will Harridge on playing rules. He retired in 1954 at the age of 83.

Connolly became the first umpire to be elected into the Hall of Fame in 1953.

☆

Raymond Dandridge
(Hooks)
1913–
Negro Leagues: 1933–55

Ray Dandridge was a squat, bow-legged third baseman who fielded like Brooks Robinson and hit like "Pie" Traynor. He was proclaimed the greatest third baseman *never* to make the major leagues. Dandridge regretted never having had the opportunity to play. He said, "The only thing I ever wanted to do was hit major league pitching. I just wanted to put my left foot in there. I just would have liked to have been up there for only one day, even if it was only to get a cup of coffee."

Against major league pitching in 13 exhibition games, he batted .347 on 17 hits in 49 at bats. In his career in the Negro Leagues he appeared in 2,189 games, had 7,879 at bats and 2,527 hits, slammed 74 home runs, and stole 171 bases.

One of the highest compliments ever paid him was by Monte Irvin, who said, "Ray Dandridge was fantastic. Best I've ever seen at third. I saw all the greats—Brooks, Nettles—but I've never seen a better third baseman than Ray Dandridge. He had the best hands. In a season he seldom made more than one or two errors. If the ball took a bad hop, his glove took a bad hop. He came in on a swinging bunt, grabbed the ball barehanded and threw to first without looking and got his man. And a good number two hitter. He was particularly good at hitting behind the runner. He hit like a shot to right field. I never saw 'Judy' Johnson in his prime or Marcelle at all, but a lot of people who saw both would give it to Ray Dandridge because of his hitting, fielding, and speed. Once you saw him, you never would forget him."

Dandridge was inducted into the Hall of Fame in 1987.

☆

Martin DiHigo

1905–71

Negro Leagues: 1922–47

Hall of Famer "Judy" Johnson said, "The average player on the Pittsburgh Crawfords could have played in the major leagues. There was one guy who, if it boiled down to being the first black in the major leagues in my time, I would say it would have to be Martin DiHigo. He was the greatest all-around ballplayer I ever saw."

After watching the 1941 major league All-Star Game, a sportswriter for the Washington *Post* wrote, "I just saw the best white men play the game and a month before I saw the best black players in action. And there is no comparison. One player in particular was Martin DiHigo. He was playing with the Cuban Stars, and he could do it all. Terry Moore couldn't touch him."

DiHigo was considered the most versatile black performer. He excelled as a batter and pitcher and played all positions except catcher. He batted .307 in 1925, .331 in 1927, and won batting titles by hitting .386 in 1929, .372 in 1935, and .387 in 1938. He hit over .400 twice (years not recorded) and led the league in home runs in 1926 and 1927.

DiHigo had an extremely powerful throwing arm, wide range, and considerable speed. His manager "Cum" Posey said, "DiHigo's gifts have not been approached by any man—black or white."

As a pitcher he won 234 games and lost 117. Teammate "Buck" Leonard said, "DiHigo was the greatest all-around player in any league, black or white." And John McGraw agreed, "He was the greatest all-around player I ever saw."

DiHigo appeared in 1,679 games and had 5,496 at bats, 1,660 hits, 193 doubles, 50 triples, 134 home runs, 152 stolen bases, and a lifetime batting average of .304. Against major league pitchers, he appeared in 17 exhibition games and had 61 at bats, 15 hits, 3 doubles, 1 home run, and a batting average of .246.

DiHigo was inducted into the Hall of Fame in 1977.

☆

William George Evans
(Billy)
1884–1956

Billy Evans began his major league umpiring career in the American League at the age of 22, the youngest umpire in the history of baseball. He began in 1906 and lasted until 1927. He worked six World Series and encouraged using four arbiters in the fall classics.

When on-field fights occurred, Evans substituted diplomacy for belligerency. He was lauded for his fairness and high integrity and provided an excellent model for future umpires.

From 1926 to 1936 he served as general manager of the Cleveland Indians. From 1936 to 1940 he was farm director for the Boston Red Sox. In 1941 he became general manager of the Cleveland Rams of the American Football Conference, and from 1942 to 1946 he was president of the Double A minor leagues. During his stay in the minor leagues, attendance increased from 700,000 to over 2 million. From 1947 to 1951, Evans served as general manager of the Detroit Tigers.

Evans was inducted into the Hall of Fame in 1973.

☆

Andrew Foster
(Rube)
1879–1930
Negro Leagues: 1897–1920

"Rube" Foster got his nickname one day in 1902 when he pitched an exhibition game against the Philadelphia A's "Rube" Waddell (who also went on to become a Hall of Famer). Foster beat Waddell, and his teammates began to call him "Rube" as an affectionate acknowledgment that he was as capable as any pitcher around.

Foster was a giant, a powerful man who could pitch almost

endlessly. Honus Wagner said, "He was one of the greatest pitchers of all time. He was the smartest pitcher I had ever seen in all my years in baseball."

Foster supplemented his ability with a knowledge of baseball that comes to few men. In 1905 it was reported that Foster won 51 games in 55 exhibition contests against major and minor league teams. In Chicago he organized and pitched for one of the great Negro teams, the Leland Giants, which later became the Chicago American Giants. When he retired as an active player, he became the Giants' manager and operated in the same aggressive way that John McGraw did with the National League Giants.

In 1920, Foster accomplished what men had failed to do for three decades: he formed a Negro professional league. Foster won the cooperation of "Ban" Johnson, founder of the white American League. With Foster as president, the league had franchises in Kansas City, Indianapolis, Chicago, Detroit, and St. Louis. Foster also had a traveling team of Cuban All-Stars. Foster died in 1930, but he lived long enough to see the results of his efforts. His league survived the Great Depression and lasted until black players made their way into the major leagues.

Foster arrived in the Hall of Fame in 1981.

☆

Ford Christopher Frick
(1894–1978)

Ford Frick began his career as a sportswriter for the New York *Journal,* assigned to cover the New York Yankees from 1923 to 1934. He ghost-wrote newspaper articles for Babe Ruth and subsequently wrote *Babe Ruth's Own Book of Baseball.* Between 1930 and 1934, Frick combined sportswriting with radio announcing and shared in the first radio broadcast of the Brooklyn Dodgers in 1931.

In 1934 he became the National League service bureau publicity chief and began his climb to the top of baseball's hierarchy. Nine months later he was named National League president, where he stayed until 1951. He stabilized National League affairs, found new capital for financing weak teams, and promoted the creation of the Hall of Fame Museum at Cooperstown, New

York in 1939. He supported Jackie Robinson in 1947 and warned St. Louis Cardinal players who were threatening not to play that they would be barred from baseball. In 1951, Frick became the third commissioner of baseball and served two seven-year terms.

Frick retired in 1965 and was elected into the Hall of Fame in 1970.

☆

Joshua Gibson
(Josh)
1912–47
Negro Leagues: 1930–46

Josh Gibson played in the Negro Leagues from 1930 to 1946. He was a sensational hitting catcher who hit more home runs than Babe Ruth and Hank Aaron. Records compiled by the Society of American Baseball Research show that Gibson came to bat 1,860 times and hit safely 818 times for a fantastic batting average of .440. Against major league pitching in exhibition games, Gibson had 28 hits in 66 at bats for a .424 batting average.

Bill Veeck said, "If they ever let him play in small parks like Ebbets Field or Fenway Park, he would have re-wrote the record books. Gibson, at a minimum, was two Yogi Berras."

Teammate "Buck" Leonard averred: "He was the greatest ballplayer of all time. There were better defensive catchers like Roy Campanella and Biz Mackey, but when it came to running, hitting, and throwing, I don't know anyone who could beat him. Josh was easily the most powerful hitter in the Negro Leagues. I saw him almost hit one out of Yankee Stadium. At the Polo Grounds I saw him hit one between the upper deck and the roof. It hit an elevated train track outside the park. Josh hit seventy to seventy-two home runs one year. In 1939 he hit more home runs in Griffith Stadium than all the righthanded hitters in the American League combined."

In 1931, while playing with the Homestead Grays, Gibson was credited with 75 home runs as the team barnstormed through New York State. Gibson's plaque in Cooperstown, New York, says he hit almost 800 home runs. But Satchel Paige said, "He was not only a home run hitter, he hit for a high average as well. I'd rate him in power over Ted Williams, Joe DiMaggio, and Stan Musial, in that order." Gibson did indeed hit for average. He was the Negro batting king in 1936 with .457 and in 1938 with .440. He also was the batting champion in 1942 and 1945.

Probably Gibson's greatest compliment came from Roy Campanella, who said, "Knowing Josh Gibson and knowing Hank Aaron and playing against both, I think Josh Gibson was the greatest home run hitter I ever saw. I know records have not been kept to show how many home runs he hit and not taking anything away from Babe Ruth, I think Josh Gibson is the greatest home run hitter that ever lived."

Gibson was inducted into the Hall of Fame in 1972.

☆

Warren Crandall Giles
1896–1979

Warren Giles began his career in the minor leagues as a manager and, after winning the pennant in 1921, served as an aide to Branch Rickey of the St. Louis Cardinals in searching for young players. When Rickey organized his farm system, Giles managed his top team in Syracuse in 1926 and 1927 and in Rochester from 1928 to 1936. In nine years, Rochester won four pennants and two championships.

Challenged to save a debt-ridden team, Giles joined the Cincinnati Reds as general manager from 1937 to 1947 and as president until 1952. Under his leadership, the Reds regained financial strength and improved on the field with manager Bill McKechnie and stars like Ernie Lombardi and Bucky Walters. Cincinnati won pennants in 1939 and 1940 and the 1940 World Series.

In 1952 Giles became the eleventh National League president and held that position until 1969. An active president, he thought that teams not well supported in one city could go elsewhere. He facilitated the move of the Braves from Boston to Milwaukee in 1953 and to Atlanta in 1966 and the shift of the Brooklyn Dodgers and New York Giants to California in 1957. He added new franchises in New York, Houston, San Diego, and Montreal and favored the construction of new stadiums. In a strategy with long-range implications, Giles cooperated with efforts of National League teams to sign black and Latin American players, jumping ahead of the rival American League. During his 18-year presidency, the National League won ten World Series and 15 All-Star games.

A principal figure in shaping modern baseball administration, the affable, strong-willed Giles was inducted into the Hall of Fame in 1979.

William Harridge
(Will)
1883–1971

Will Harridge was employed by the Wabash Railroad in Chicago when "Ban" Johnson, the president of the American League, noticed his skill at scheduling transportation. Johnson hired the surprised clerk as his secretary, and Harridge served in this position from 1911 to 1927, when Johnson was ousted from office. The American League then named Harridge its secretary.

In 1931 Harridge was elected as third president of the American League and was so effective that he was reelected three times and remained the league's top executive for a record 28 years. After resigning in 1958 he chaired the American League board until his death in 1971.

Throughout his long tenure, Harridge concentrated on administrative matters and avoided publicity for himself and his office. His penchant for discreetly handling American League matters behind closed doors won him the respect and loyalty of team owners.

In 1933 Harridge actively promoted participation in the first All-Star Game and championed the annual spectacle during his presidency. Besides firing and suspending players and managers for "baiting" umpires, in 1948 he dismissed umpire Ernest Stewart for trying to unionize American League umpires and he stopped Bill Veeck from further using a midget pinch hitter, Eddie Gaedel, for the 1951 St. Louis Browns. He also established new departments within his office to promote attendance.

Harridge was inducted into the Hall of Fame in 1971.

☆

Cal Hubbard
(Robert)
1900–1977

Cal Hubbard had careers as a professional football player and as a major league umpire. In 1927 he joined the National Football League's New York Giants and developed into one of the game's best linemen. Although Hubbard had grown to 265 pounds, the Giants installed a screen pass, making the mobile tackle an eligible receiver. When Hubbard asked the Giants to trade him to Green Bay, owner Tim Mara granted him his wish, and Hubbard helped the Packers win three consecutive championships. He played both offensive and defensive tackle in those pre-free-substitution days and made the NFL's All-Pro team from 1928 to 1933.

He umpired baseball games in the minor leagues in the off season and from 1936 to 1951 in the American League. After a hunting accident left him with impaired sight in his right eye, the American League made the highly respected Hubbard supervisor of umpires, a position he held until retiring in 1969.

Hubbard was voted the NFL's greatest tackle for the league's first 50 years. He is the only player to be named to the College Hall of Fame, Pro Football Hall of Fame, and Baseball Hall of Fame.

Hubbard was elected to the Hall of Fame in 1969.

☆

Byron Bancroft Johnson
(Ban)
1863–1931

"Ban" Johnson began his baseball career as a sportswriter for the Cincinnati *Gazette* from 1887 to 1894. He met many baseball figures and developed a deep knowledge of the game. He disliked rowdy behavior on the field and umpire abuse and sought to correct those problems.

For the next six years, Johnson served as president of the minor leagues and aspired to head a major league. In the winter of 1899–1900 he saw his opportunity. The National League had dropped the bottom four teams from its 12-club membership, which opened up important free territory.

In 1901, Johnson formed the American League and unsuccessfully pressed the National League to accept it as a major league. A two-year war broke out during which 87 National Leaguers jumped to the American League because it offered a higher base salary. After the American League won the attendance battle in 1902, the National League sought peace. The "peace conference" created the basic structure governing organized baseball for over half a century.

Johnson was called the "Czar of Baseball," and during his era (1903–20) baseball prospered as never before and became known as the national pastime. His creation of a second major league, along with his efforts to upgrade umpires, crack down on rowdy players and fans, and make baseball "respectable family entertainment," contributed to the game's success.

Johnson was elected to the Hall of Fame in 1937.

☆

William J. Johnson
(Judy)
1899–
Negro Leagues: 1920–38

Connie Mack on Judy Johnson: "If Judy were only white, he could name his price."

A lean 5'11½" 145-pounder, Johnson played in the Negro Leagues from 1920 until 1938 with the Hilldale Daisies, Homestead Grays, Darby Daisies, and Pittsburgh Crawfords.

For the seven years that statistics were kept in the Negro Leagues, Johnson's batting average was in the mid-.340's, and he was considered their best-fielding third baseman. He was called the black Pie Traynor.

When asked what the caliber of the Negro Leagues were, Johnson replied, "They were not of major league quality but you could easily pick a team of black players who could beat the hell out of the white Major Leaguers any day. On a whole, the Negro League was a triple 'A' league."

From 1920 to 1938, available statistics show Johnson belting 596 hits in 1,720 at bats for a .349 average. Against major league pitching, Johnson appeared in 20 games, getting 20 hits for a batting average of .263.

Johnson was inducted into the Hall of Fame in 1975.

☆

William Joseph Klem
(Bill, The Old Arbitrator, Catfish)
1874–1951

Before coming to the National League, Bill Klem umpired for three years (1902–04) in the minor leagues. His major league umpiring career lasted from 1905 to 1941. He arbitrated in a record 18 World Series. From 1941 until his death, he served as the National League umpire-in-chief.

At Klem's initiative, the dignity of umpires was upgraded by increasing salaries, using multiple arbiters, providing adequate quarters, and compelling managers to bring their line-ups to home plate before a game. Klem gave verbal and visual definition to many of an umpire's functions, including audible strike calls, hand-waving on foul-line calls, and the sweeping gesture of the thumb on the close "out." Enhancing the integrity of umpires, Klem always asserted, "I never missed one in my life!" At a ceremony honoring him at the Polo Grounds on September 2, 1949, "The Old Arbitrator" declared, "Baseball to me is not a game; it is a religion."

Klem was elected to the Hall of Fame in 1953.

☆

Kenesaw Mountain Landis
1866–1944

Named for the June 1864 Civil War battle of Kennesaw Mountain, Georgia, where his father was wounded, Landis was the first sole commissioner of baseball (1920–44). Named commissioner in 1920 amid the collapse of the old National Commission and the Chicago "Black Sox" scandal, he ruled baseball with an iron hand. Some believe he restored the game to respectability.

Landis won the sympathy of the baseball establishment in 1915, when the Federal League antitrust suit against organized baseball was argued in his court. By refusing to render a decision until the Federal League war was over and the suit was dropped, he preserved baseball's unique monopoly status. When the National Commission collapsed, baseball leaders turned to Landis to restore integrity to the game. He accepted the post of commissioner on November 12, 1920.

On assuming office, Landis demanded and received absolute power. No appeals of his rulings or public criticisms of his actions by owners were permitted. Although zealous in defense of players' rights, Landis in March 1921 barred the Philadelphia Phillies' pitcher Eugene Paulette from the game for life for consorting with gamblers. In June 1921 he similarly blacklisted Cincinnati Reds pitcher Ray Fisher for negotiating with an "outlaw" team. He also banned New York Giants outfielder Benny Kauff, who had been indicted for and acquitted of auto theft. On August 3, 1921, the day after a jury acquitted the eight Chicago "Black Sox" of throwing the 1919 World Series, Landis banished the players permanently from organized baseball. In 1922 he blacklisted Giants pitcher "Shufflin' Phil" Douglas, who in a drunken state had hinted willingness to throw a game. In 1924 Landis permanently barred outfielder Jimmy O'Connell and pitcher "Cozy" Dolan for complicity in a bribe plot between the New York Giants and the Phillies. Phillies owner William D. Cox was expelled from the game in 1943 for betting on his own team.

In the last game of the 1934 World Series, Landis ordered from the field hard-hitting St. Louis leftfielder "Ducky" Medwick, who had been bombarded with fruit and garbage by Detroit fans. Landis could not break up baseball's farm system, which he strongly opposed.

He proclaimed as free agents close to 200 players whom he believed parent clubs were "covering up." He also waged unceasing war against baseball personnel with racetrack connections. Landis made the dedicatory address officially opening the National Baseball Hall of Fame in Cooperstown, New York, on June 12, 1939.

Landis entered the Hall of Fame in 1944.

Walter Leonard

(Buck)

1907–

Negro Leagues: 1933–49

The consensus is that "Buck" Leonard was the greatest black first baseman in Negro League history. A fancy fielder and a powerful hitter, he was steady, smooth, smart, and consistently batted above .300. From 1933 to 1949, of the records kept, Leonard hit safely 316 times in 927 at bats for a .341 average.

At the peak of his career Buck Leonard was a svelte 5'10" 185-pounder who frequently batted clean-up behind the more publicized Josh Gibson. He dug into the batters' box with a certain defiance, crouching menacingly in a slightly open stance.

Eddie Gottlieb, owner of the Philadelphia Stars of the Negro League, is quoted as saying, " 'Buck' Leonard was as smooth a first baseman as I ever saw. In those days, the first baseman on a team in the Negro League often played the clown. They had a funny way of catching the ball so the fans would laugh, but Leonard was strictly baseball: a great glove, a hell of a hitter, and drove in runs."

Leonard played for the Homestead Grays and the Brooklyn Royal Giants from 1933 to 1950. His best years in the Negro National League were in 1941 and 1942. In 1941 he batted .392 to lead the league. The following year he hit 42 home runs. From 1937 to 1945 Leonard and Gibson, who formed the greatest home run-hitting combination in Negro League history, led their teams to nine consecutive pennants. Against major league pitching he had five hits in 7 games for a batting average of .333. Monte Irvin reported, "Satchel Paige and Josh Gibson got more publicity but Buck Leonard was just as good."

Leonard entered the Hall of Fame in 1972.

☆

John Henry Lloyd

(Pop)

1884–1965

Negro Leagues: 1908–31

In a vote among his peers, "Pop" Lloyd was voted the most outstanding black shortstop of them all. He stood 5'11" and weighed

180 pounds. He was tall for a shortstop, and he ranged all over the field. His long arms and big hands enabled him to get to balls other shortstops could not reach, and he had tremendous presence at the plate.

From the records available, Lloyd played from 1908 through 1931. He had 2,893 recorded at bats, with 988 hits, for a batting average of .342. Against major league pitching in 29 exhibition games, he batted .321, with 106 at bats and 34 hits.

Honus Wagner said about Lloyd, "They called him the black Honus Wagner and I was anxious to see him play. Well, one day, I had the opportunity to see him play, and after I saw him I felt honored that they would name such a great player after me."

Lloyd entered the Hall of Fame in 1976.

☆

Leland Stanford MacPhail, Sr.
(Larry)
1890–1975

Larry MacPhail became involved with baseball after several unsuccessful business ventures in Ohio. He obtained an option on the impoverished American Association baseball club in Columbus and turned it into a farm team for the St. Louis Cardinals. St. Louis bought the club and made MacPhail president of the team, although he had no previous experience. The Cardinals built a new ball park and installed lights at Columbus. MacPhail implemented innovative, successful promotions, but was fired for his personal actions in and out of baseball.

In 1934, MacPhail was hired by the Cincinnati Reds, who were struggling financially. He obtained financial backing and immediately instituted several changes in the stadium, obtained new players, and persuaded club owners to permit night baseball for the first time in major league history. MacPhail convinced President Franklin D. Roosevelt in May 1935 to touch the signal in the White House turning on the lights for the historic first night game. Night baseball, along with MacPhail's mammoth fireworks displays, attracted near-capacity crowds.

In 1938, after leaving Cincinnati, MacPhail was called on to rescue the Brooklyn Dodgers from severe financial problems. His first move was to have lights installed in Ebbets Field. He ended the agreement with the New York Yankees and New York Giants barring play-by-play broadcasts of baseball games in the New York area and brought Red Barber from Cincinnati to announce the Dodger games. He bought new players such as Dolf Camilli, Mickey Owen, Pee Wee Reese, Whit Wyatt, Dixie Walker, Billy Herman, "Ducky" Medwick, and Kirby Higbe. He then hired Leo Durocher as manager and made the Dodgers into a contender for the top National League spot.

After World War II, MacPhail formed a partnership with Dan Topping and Del Webb to buy the New York Yankees from the heirs of the late Colonel Jacob Ruppert for $2.8 million. The bargain deal included Yankee Stadium, the team's minor league farm system, and considerable real estate. MacPhail received one-third interest in the partnership and a ten-year contract to administer the ball club. Once more he instituted many innovations, including installing lights in Yankee Stadium for the first time.

MacPhail was inducted into the Hall of Fame in 1978.

☆

George Martin Weiss
1895–1973

When George Weiss bought a minor league franchise at the age of 24, he became the youngest owner in organized baseball. For nine years, his club played in Weiss Park, ranked among the best in the minors, and sent many players to the major leagues.

Weiss displayed his talents as general manager of the Baltimore Orioles from 1929 to 1931 by reviving the ailing team through player sales. His Baltimore success impressed New York Yankee owner Jacob Ruppert, who hired Weiss in 1932 and instructed him to develop a farm system modeled on clubs already organized by Branch Rickey. A tireless worker, Weiss assembled a premier farm system that sent Joe DiMaggio, Charlie Keller, and other stars to the Yankees. During the 15 years Weiss directed the Yankee system, New York won nine pennants and eight World Series and sold an estimated $2 million worth of players to other teams.

As general manager from 1948 to 1960, Weiss built a dynasty that won ten pennants and seven world championships in 13 seasons and a record five straight championships from 1949 to 1953. He hired Casey Stengel to manage the Yankees from 1949 to 1960 and provided him with stars like Mickey Mantle, Yogi Berra, and Whitey Ford.

He shrewdly obtained such players as Bob Turley, Don Larsen, Enos Slaughter, and Roger Maris in trades that helped keep the Yankees on top. For this uncanny ability, Weiss won a record four Major League Executive of the Year awards.

After being retired by the Yankees in 1960, he was hired by the New York Mets and produced the first world championship by an expansion club.

Weiss was elected to the Hall of Fame in 1971.

☆

Thomas Austin Yawkey
(Tom)
1903–76

Tom Yawkey purchased the struggling Boston Red Sox in 1933 and spent heavily to build winning teams. During the depressed 1930s, his wealth enabled the Red Sox to secure star players from poorer teams. Yawkey acquired Lefty Grove and Jimmie Foxx from the A's and shortstop Joe Cronin for $25,000 from the Senators. In 1950, he tried to buy Herb Score from the Indians for one million dollars. His large investments in the Boston farm system produced some exceptional players, including Ted Williams, Carl Yastrzemski, and Jim Rice. The popular owner revived fan interest in the Red Sox and increased attendance at Fenway Park, which he had rebuilt in 1934.

Yawkey was a paternal employer who exhibited personal interest in his players' welfare. He proved a strong voice in major league councils and served as American League vice-president from 1956 to 1973.

Tom Yawkey became a Hall of Famer in 1980.

3

ALL-TIME RECORDS LIST

ALL-TIME LONGEVITY LIST—Everyday Players

#	Player	Yrs	#	Player	Yrs	#	Player	Yrs
1	Eddie Collins	25	32	Jim O'Rourke	19	77	King Kelly	16
1	Bobby Wallace	25	32	Enos Slaughter	19	77	John McGraw	16
3	Ty Cobb	24	32	Zack Wheat	19	77	Pee Wee Reese	16
4	Hank Aaron	23	32	Ted Williams	19	85	Lou Boudreau	15
4	Rogers Hornsby	23	46	Luis Aparicio	18	85	Billy Herman	15
4	Brooks Robinson	23	46	Roberto Clemente	18	85	Travis Jackson	15
4	Rabbit Maranville	23	46	Roger Connor	18	85	George Kell	15
4	Carl Yastrzemski	23	46	Kiki Cuyler	18	85	Johnny Mize	15
9	Cap Anson	22	46	Johnny Evers	18	85	George Sisler	15
9	Al Kaline	22	46	Buck Ewing	18	85	Sam Thompson	15
9	Harmon Killebrew	22	46	Rick Ferrell	18	85	Joe Tinker	15
9	Willie Mays	22	46	Goose Goslin	18	93	Jimmy Collins	14
9	Willie McCovey	22	46	Mickey Mantle	18	93	Billy Hamilton	14
9	Stan Musial	22	46	Edd Roush	18	93	Joe Sewell	14
9	Mel Ott	22	46	Ray Schalk	18	93	Casey Stengel	14
9	Babe Ruth	22	46	Duke Snider	18	93	Bobby Doerr	14
9	Tris Speaker	22	46	Lloyd Waner	18	93	Bill Terry	14
18	Fred Clarke	21	46	Billy Williams	18	93	Arky Vaughan	14
18	Frank Robinson	21	60	Johnny Bench	17	100	Earl Averill	13
18	Nap Lajoie	21	60	Wilbert Robinson	17	100	Frank Baker	13
18	Willie Stargell	21	60	Roger Bresnahan	17	100	Mickey Cochrane	13
18	Honus Wagner	21	60	Frank Chance	17	100	Charlie Comiskey	13
23	Luke Appling	20	60	Bill Dickey	17	100	Joe DiMaggio	13
23	Jake Beckley	20	60	Hugh Duffy	17	100	Elmer Flick	13
23	Max Carey	20	60	Lou Gehrig	17	100	Hank Greenberg	13
23	Joe Cronin	20	60	Harry Heilmann	17	100	Chick Hafey	13
23	Jimmie Foxx	20	60	Harry Hooper	17	100	Miller Huggins	13
23	Gabby Hartnett	20	60	Hugh Jennings	17	100	Freddie Lindstrom	13
23	Sam Rice	20	60	Joe Kelley	17	100	Tommy McCarthy	13
23	Al Simmons	20	60	Chuck Klein	17	111	Earle Combs	12
23	Paul Waner	20	60	Ernie Lombardi	17	111	Bucky Harris	12
32	Ernie Banks	19	60	Heinie Manush	17	111	Hack Wilson	12
32	Yogi Berra	19	60	Eddie Mathews	17	114	Connie Mack	11
32	Lou Brock	19	60	Joe Medwick	17	115	Roy Campanella	10
32	Red Schoendienst	19	60	Pie Traynor	17	115	Ralph Kiner	10
32	Dan Brouthers	19	60	Monte Ward	17	115	Jackie Robinson	10
32	Sam Crawford	19	77	Dave Bancroft	16	115	Ross Youngs	10
32	Frankie Frisch	19	77	Jim Bottomley	16	115	Monte Irvin	8
32	Charlie Gehringer	19	77	Jesse Burkett	16	120	George Wright	7
32	Willie Keeler	19	77	Ed Delahanty	16	121	Harry Wright	2
32	Al Lopez	19	77	George Kelly	16			

ALL-TIME LONGEVITY LIST—Pitchers

1	Early Wynn	23	19	Eddie Plank	17	31	Ed Walsh	14
2	Cy Young	22	19	Bob Gibson	17	38	Rube Waddell	13
2	Herb Pennock	22	19	Lefty Grove	17	38	Mickey Welch	13
2	Red Ruffing	22	19	Christy Mathewson	17	40	John Clarkson	12
5	Eppa Rixey	21	23	Chief Bender	16	40	Dizzy Dean	12
5	Waite Hoyt	21	23	Whitey Ford	16	40	Hoss Radbourn	12
5	Walter Johnson	21	23	Carl Hubbell	16	40	Sandy Koufax	12
5	Ted Lyons	21	23	Juan Marichal	16	44	Jack Chesbro	11
5	Warren Spahn	21	23	Dazzy Vance	16	45	Amos Rusie	10
5	Clark Griffith	21	28	Catfish Hunter	15	45	Joe McGinnity	10
5	Hoyt Wilhelm	21	28	Bob Lemon	15	47	Addie Joss	9
12	Red Faber	20	28	Kid Nichols	15	48	Satchel Paige	6
12	Grover Alexander	20	31	Three Finger Brown	14	49	Al Spalding	3
14	Burleigh Grimes	19	31	Stan Coveleski	14	50	Candy Cummings	2
14	Jesse Haines	19	31	Don Drysdale	14			
14	Robin Roberts	19	31	Pud Galvin	14			
17	Bob Feller	18	31	Lefty Gomez	14			
17	Rube Marquard	18	31	Tim Keefe	14			

This list represents only Hall of Fame pitchers. Of non-Hall of Famers, Tommy John has 25 years.

ALL-TIME LONGEVITY LIST—Managers

1	Connie Mack	53	20	Frank Chance	11	41	Johnny Evers	3
2	John McGraw	33	22	Bill Terry	10	41	Christy Mathewson	3
3	Bucky Harris	29	23	Hugh Duffy	8	41	George Sisler	3
4	Casey Stengel	25	23	Bob Lemon	8	44	Max Carey	2
5	Joe McCarthy	24	23	Tris Speaker	8	44	Burleigh Grimes	2
6	Walter Alston	23	26	Walter Johnson	7	44	Kid Nichols	2
7	Clark Griffith	20	26	Frank Robinson	7	44	Ray Schalk	2
8	Cap Anson	20	28	Monte Ward	6	44	Al Spalding	2
9	Fred Clarke	19	28	Yogi Berra	6	49	Cy Young	1
9	Wilbert Robinson	19	28	Ty Cobb	6	49	Honus Wagner	1
11	Harry Wright	18	28	Jimmy Collins	6	49	Jim Bottomley	1
12	Miller Huggins	17	28	Pie Traynor	6	49	Three Finger Brown	1
12	Al Lopez	17	33	Roger Bresnahan	5	49	Roger Connor	1
14	Lou Boudreau	16	33	Mickey Cochrane	5	49	Bill Dickey	1
14	Frankie Frisch	16	33	Joe Kelley	5	49	Pud Galvin	1
16	Joe Cronin	15	33	Nap Lajoie	5	49	Rabbit Maranville	1
17	Hugh Jennings	14	33	Jim O'Rourke	5	49	Tommy McCarthy	1
18	Rogers Hornsby	13	38	Dave Bancroft	4	49	George Wright	1
18	Red Schoendienst	13	38	Billy Herman	4			
20	Charlie Comiskey	11	38	Joe Tinker	4			

ALL-TIME AMERICAN LEAGUE BATTING AND FIELDING RECORDS LIST

1	Babe Ruth	67	12	Bobby Wallace	8	23	Carl Yastrzemski	3
1	Ty Cobb	67	13	Ted Williams	7	23	Sam Rice	3
3	Nap Lajoie	63	13	Elmer Flick	7	23	Earle Combs	3
4	Sam Crawford	26	15	Brooks Robinson	6	27	Charlie Gehringer	2
5	Tris Speaker	23	15	Goose Goslin	6	27	Willie Keeler	2
6	Frank Baker	15	15	Joe DiMaggio	6	27	Mickey Cochrane	2
7	Lou Gehrig	12	15	Al Kaline	6	27	George Kell	2
8	Luis Aparicio	10	15	Harry Hooper	6	31	Joe Sewell	1
8	Eddie Collins	10	20	Lou Boudreau	5	31	Heinie Manush	1
8	Ray Schalk	10	21	Yogi Berra	4	31	Harmon Killebrew	1
8	Jesse Burkett	10	21	George Sisler	4	31	Mickey Mantle	1
12	Jimmy Collins	8	23	Bill Dickey	3	31	Rick Ferrell	1

ALL-TIME AMERICAN LEAGUE UNBROKEN BATTING AND FIELDING RECORDS LIST

1	Babe Ruth	20	6	Al Kaline	5	15	Yogi Berra	2
2	Tris Speaker	11	9	Joe DiMaggio	4	15	Sam Crawford	2
3	Ty Cobb	10	9	Goose Goslin	4	15	Nap Lajoie	2
4	Luis Aparicio	7	11	Lou Gehrig	3	18	Frank Baker	1
5	Brooks Robinson	6	11	Carl Yastrzemski	3	18	George Sisler	1
6	Ted Williams	5	11	Harry Hooper	3	18	Rick Ferrell	1
6	Eddie Collins	5	11	Ray Schalk	3			

ALL-TIME NATIONAL LEAGUE BATTING AND FIELDING RECORDS LIST

1	Cap Anson	48	14	King Kelly	11	26	Dave Bancroft	6
2	Monte Ward	40	14	Jim O'Rourke	11	32	Eddie Mathews	5
3	Dan Brouthers	34	14	Fred Clarke	11	32	Kiki Cuyler	5
4	Sam Thompson	30	19	Rabbit Maranville	10	34	Roy Campanella	4
5	Rogers Hornsby	26	19	Hugh Duffy	10	34	Johnny Bench	4
6	Stan Musial	24	21	Willie Keeler	9	34	Gabby Hartnett	4
6	Honus Wagner	24	22	Frankie Frisch	8	34	Chuck Klein	4
8	Billy Hamilton	19	23	Lloyd Waner	7	34	Jackie Robinson	4
9	Mel Ott	18	23	Paul Waner	7	39	Lou Brock	3
10	Max Carey	17	23	Hugh Jennings	7	39	Joe Tinker	3
11	Ed Delahanty	16	26	Willie Mays	6	39	Hack Wilson	3
11	Roger Connor	16	26	Pie Traynor	6	39	George Kelly	3
11	Jake Beckley	16	26	Zack Wheat	6	39	Ralph Kiner	3
14	Jesse Burkett	11	26	Buck Ewing	6	44	Jimmy Collins	2
14	Hank Aaron	11	26	Billy Herman	6	44	Roger Bresnahan	2

44	Johnny Evers	2	49	Joe Medwick	1	49	Frank Robinson	1
44	Ernie Banks	2	49	Edd Roush	1	49	Pee Wee Reese	1
44	Willie McCovey	2	49	Elmer Flick	1	49	Roberto Clemente	1
49	Nap Lajoie	1	49	Bill Terry	1	49	Joe Kelley	1
49	Chick Hafey	1	49	Jim Bottomley	1	49	Tommy McCarthy	1
49	Duke Snider	1	49	Johnny Mize	1	49	Willie Stargell	1

ALL-TIME NATIONAL LEAGUE UNBROKEN BATTING AND FIELDING RECORDS LIST

1	Cap Anson	7	9	Dave Bancroft	3	26	Billy Herman	1
2	Hank Aaron	6	9	Hack Wilson	3	26	Paul Waner	1
2	Rogers Hornsby	6	17	Mel Ott	2	26	Gabby Hartnett	1
4	Stan Musial	5	17	Frankie Frisch	2	26	Eddie Mathews	1
5	Billy Hamilton	4	17	Fred Clarke	2	26	Joe Medwick	1
5	Hugh Jennings	4	17	Ralph Kiner	2	26	Chuck Klein	1
5	Sam Thompson	4	17	Ed Delahanty	2	26	Bill Terry	1
5	Willie Keeler	4	17	Lloyd Waner	2	26	Ernie Banks	1
9	Jake Beckley	3	17	Lou Brock	2	26	Jackie Robinson	1
9	Honus Wagner	3	17	George Kelly	2	26	Frank Robinson	1
9	Willie Mays	3	17	Willie McCovey	2	26	Roberto Clemente	1
9	Rabbit Maranville	3	17	Monte Ward	2	26	Jimmy Collins	1
9	Zack Wheat	3	26	Roy Campanella	1	26	Willie Stargell	1
9	Johnny Bench	3	26	Pie Traynor	1	26	Max Carey	1

ALL-TIME MAJOR LEAGUE BATTING AND FIELDING RECORDS LIST

1	Babe Ruth	63	17	Jesse Burkett	8	30	Hugh Jennings	4
2	Cap Anson	48	20	Sam Crawford	7	30	Joe DiMaggio	4
3	Ty Cobb	38	20	Rabbit Maranville	7	39	Luis Aparicio	3
3	Monte Ward	38	22	Ray Schalk	6	39	Frankie Frisch	3
5	Dan Brouthers	34	22	Nap Lajoie	6	39	Willie Mays	3
6	Sam Thompson	17	22	Brooks Robinson	6	39	Pie Traynor	3
6	Billy Hamilton	17	22	Honus Wagner	6	39	Lloyd Waner	3
8	Jake Beckley	15	22	Rogers Hornsby	6	39	Stan Musial	3
9	Tris Speaker	13	27	Hugh Duffy	5	39	Zack Wheat	3
10	Roger Connor	11	27	Dave Bancroft	5	39	Lou Brock	3
10	Jim O'Rourke	11	27	Lou Gehrig	5	39	Bill Dickey	3
12	Fred Clarke	10	30	Yogi Berra	4	48	Roy Campanella	2
13	Max Carey	9	30	Jimmy Collins	4	48	Frank Baker	2
13	Ed Delahanty	9	30	Harry Hooper	4	48	Goose Goslin	2
13	Eddie Collins	9	30	Paul Waner	4	48	Johnny Bench	2
13	Willie Keeler	9	30	Eddie Mathews	4	48	Charlie Gehringer	2
17	Hank Aaron	8	30	Buck Ewing	4	48	Gabby Hartnett	2
17	King Kelly	8	30	Al Kaline	4	48	Sam Rice	2

48	Lou Boudreau	2	59	Carl Yastrzemski	1	59	Hack Wilson	1
48	Luke Appling	2	59	Joe Kelley	1	59	George Kelly	1
48	George Sisler	2	59	Billy Herman	1	59	Chuck Klein	1
48	Mickey Cochrane	2	59	Harmon Killebrew	1	59	Joe Sewell	1
59	Joe Tinker	1	59	Chick Hafey	1	59	Ernie Banks	1
59	Frank Robinson	1	59	Heinie Manush	1	59	Willie McCovey	1
59	Mel Ott	1	59	Mickey Mantle	1	59	George Kell	1
59	Ted Williams	1	59	Tommy McCarthy	1	59	Willie Stargell	1
59	Roberto Clemente	1	59	Elmer Flick	1			

ALL-TIME MAJOR LEAGUE UNBROKEN BATTING AND FIELDING RECORDS LIST

1	Babe Ruth	15	14	Sam Crawford	2	28	Harry Hooper	1
2	Cap Anson	6	14	Frankie Frisch	2	28	Ray Schalk	1
2	Brooks Robinson	6	14	Fred Clarke	2	28	Paul Waner	1
4	Ty Cobb	5	14	Johnny Bench	2	28	Hugh Duffy	1
5	Hank Aaron	4	14	Yogi Berra	2	28	Hack Wilson	1
5	Eddie Collins	4	14	Rabbit Maranville	2	28	Willie McCovey	1
5	Tris Speaker	4	14	Willie Keeler	2	28	Rogers Hornsby	1
5	Billy Hamilton	4	14	Ed Delahanty	2	28	Willie Stargell	1
5	Al Kaline	4	14	Lou Brock	2	28	Roy Campanella	1
10	Jake Beckley	3	14	Hugh Jennings	2	28	Max Carey	1
10	Luis Aparicio	3	14	Dave Bancroft	2	28	Stan Musial	1
10	Zack Wheat	3	14	Monte Ward	2	28	Ted Williams	1
10	Joe DiMaggio	3	14	Lou Gehrig	2	28	Carl Yastrzemski	1
14	Honus Wagner	2	28	Sam Thompson	1			

ALL-TIME ALL-STAR GAME RECORDS LIST

1	Stan Musial	22	12	Hack Wilson	9	23	Chuck Klein	2
1	Lou Gehrig	22	12	Joe Medwick	9	23	Carl Yastrzemski	2
3	Charlie Gehringer	19	14	Pie Traynor	7	23	Willie McCovey	2
4	Frankie Frisch	18	14	Billy Herman	7	26	Brooks Robinson	1
5	Ted Williams	17	14	Joe DiMaggio	7	26	Mickey Mantle	1
6	Joe Cronin	16	17	Gabby Hartnett	6	26	Eddie Mathews	1
7	Babe Ruth	15	17	Bill Terry	6	26	Enos Slaughter	1
7	Al Simmons	15	19	Jimmie Foxx	5	26	Ralph Kiner	1
9	Willie Mays	11	19	Paul Waner	5	26	Pee Wee Reese	1
9	Arky Vaughan	11	21	Mel Ott	4			
11	Earl Averill	10	22	Ernie Banks	3			

ALL-TIME ALL-STAR GAME UNBROKEN RECORDS LIST

1	Willie Mays	11	4	Joe Cronin	3	13	Billy Herman	1
2	Ted Williams	9	4	Ernie Banks	3	13	Brooks Robinson	1
3	Stan Musial	5	9	Lou Gehrig	2	13	Mickey Mantle	1
4	Charlie Gehringer	3	9	Carl Yastrzemski	2	13	Eddie Mathews	1
4	Arky Vaughan	3	9	Al Simmons	2	13	Earl Averill	1
4	Joe Medwick	3	9	Willie McCovey	2		

ALL-TIME WORLD SERIES RECORDS LIST

1	Babe Ruth	47	20	Duke Snider	9	41	Hank Greenberg	2
2	Eddie Collins	29	20	Johnny Evers	9	41	Monte Irvin	2
3	Joe Tinker	25	20	Edd Roush	9	41	Jim Bottomley	2
4	Frank Baker	24	20	Ross Youngs	9	41	Jimmie Foxx	2
5	Honus Wagner	22	26	Bill Dickey	8	41	Bill Terry	2
6	Jimmy Collins	21	27	Sam Rice	7	48	Travis Jackson	1
7	Sam Crawford	19	28	Zack Wheat	6	48	Pee Wee Reese	1
8	Frank Chance	19	29	Lloyd Waner	5	48	Joe Medwick	1
9	Ty Cobb	17	29	Hack Wilson	5	48	Kiki Cuyler	1
9	Frankie Frisch	17	31	Max Carey	4	48	Mickey Cochrane	1
11	Goose Goslin	15	31	Al Simmons	4	48	Jackie Robinson	1
11	Fred Clarke	15	31	George Kelly	4	48	Frank Robinson	1
13	Tris Speaker	12	31	Earle Combs	4	48	Stan Musial	1
13	Yogi Berra	12	31	Freddie Lindstrom	4	48	Rogers Hornsby	1
13	Lou Gehrig	12	31	Joe Sewell	4	48	Ted Williams	1
13	Roger Bresnahan	12	37	Rabbit Maranville	3	48	Billy Herman	1
17	Joe DiMaggio	11	37	Pie Traynor	3	48	Gabby Hartnett	1
17	Chick Hafey	11	37	Enos Slaughter	3	48	Al Kaline	1
19	Mickey Mantle	10	37	Johnny Mize	3	48	Eddie Mathews	1
20	Harry Hooper	9	41	Mel Ott	2		
20	Lou Brock	9	41	Ray Schalk	2		

ALL-TIME WORLD SERIES UNBROKEN RECORDS LIST

1	Babe Ruth	18	11	Lou Gehrig	5	22	Ray Schalk	2
2	Ross Youngs	8	11	Frankie Frisch	5	22	Frank Chance	2
2	Frank Baker	8	11	Harry Hooper	5	22	Lloyd Waner	2
4	Mickey Mantle	8	15	Honus Wagner	4	22	Brooks Robinson	2
4	Lou Brock	7	15	Fred Clarke	4	22	George Kelly	2
4	Goose Goslin	7	15	Chick Hafey	4	22	Earle Combs	2
4	Eddie Collins	7	15	Sam Rice	4	22	Johnny Mize	2
8	Yogi Berra	6	15	Duke Snider	4	30	Stan Musial	1
8	Zack Wheat	6	20	Tris Speaker	3	30	Rogers Hornsby	1
8	Edd Roush	6	20	Sam Crawford	3	30	Joe Tinker	1
11	Joe DiMaggio	5	22	Jimmy Collins	2	30	Ted Williams	1

30	Al Simmons	1	30	Eddie Mathews	1	30	Jim Bottomley	1
30	Billy Herman	1	30	Al Kaline	1	30	Frank Robinson	1
30	Gabby Hartnett	1	30	Mickey Cochrane	1	30	Monte Irvin	1
30	Bill Dickey	1	30	Jackie Robinson	1			

ALL-TIME LEAGUE LEADERS
BATTING RECORDS LIST *†

1	Babe Ruth	69	35	Charlie Gehringer	11	75	Ross Youngs	3
2	Ty Cobb	52	35	Cap Anson	11	75	Pee Wee Reese	3
3	Rogers Hornsby	43	35	Jesse Burkett	11	75	Frank Chance	3
3	Ted Williams	43	35	Roger Connor	11	75	Billy Herman	3
5	Stan Musial	40	42	Frank Baker	10	75	Jake Beckley	3
6	Honus Wagner	37	42	Luis Aparicio	10	75	Jimmy Collins	3
7	Mickey Mantle	27	42	Hugh Duffy	10	75	Buck Ewing	3
7	Jimmie Foxx	27	42	Eddie Collins	10	75	Earl Averill	3
7	Mel Ott	27	46	Eddie Mathews	9	83	Jackie Robinson	2
10	Dan Brouthers	26	47	King Kelly	8	83	Luke Appling	2
11	Willie Mays	25	47	Kiki Cuyler	8	83	Tommy McCarthy	2
12	Hank Aaron	24	47	Elmer Flick	8	83	Brooks Robinson	2
13	Ralph Kiner	23	47	Al Simmons	8	83	Zack Wheat	2
13	Harmon Killebrew	23	51	Ernie Banks	7	88	Joe Sewell	1
15	Nap Lajoie	22	51	Jim Bottomley	7	88	Freddie Lindstrom	1
15	Lou Gehrig	22	51	Sam Rice	7	88	Monte Irvin	1
17	Billy Hamilton	19	51	Enos Slaughter	7	88	Gabby Hartnett	1
18	Hank Greenberg	18	55	Lloyd Waner	6	88	Chick Hafey	1
18	Carl Yastrzemski	18	55	Willie Keeler	6	88	Pie Traynor	1
18	Ed Delahanty	18	55	Roberto Clemente	6	88	Rabbit Maranville	1
18	Chuck Klein	18	55	Harry Heilmann	6	88	Roy Campanella	1
22	Monte Ward	17	55	Heinie Manush	6	88	Roger Bresnahan	1
22	Max Carey	17	60	Jim O'Rourke	5	97	Yogi Berra	0
24	Hack Wilson	16	60	George Kelly	5	97	Dave Bancroft	0
24	Johnny Mize	16	60	Frankie Frisch	5	97	Joe Tinker	0
24	Sam Thompson	16	60	Earle Combs	5	97	Hugh Jennings	0
27	Sam Crawford	15	60	Goose Goslin	5	97	Mickey Cochrane	0
28	Tris Speaker	14	60	Al Kaline	5	97	Bill Dickey	0
28	Willie McCovey	14	60	Johnny Bench	5	97	Johnny Evers	0
30	Lou Brock	13	60	George Kell	5	97	Rick Ferrell	0
30	Paul Waner	13	60	Bill Terry	5	97	Bobby Wallace	0
30	Duke Snider	13	60	Edd Roush	5	97	Ray Schalk	0
30	Joe Medwick	13	70	Fred Clarke	4	97	Joe Kelley	0
34	Arky Vaughan	12	70	Lou Boudreau	4	97	Travis Jackson	0
35	Joe DiMaggio	11	70	Willie Stargell	4	97	Harry Hooper	0
35	George Sisler	11	70	Joe Cronin	4			
35	Frank Robinson	11	70	Billy Williams	4			

* Includes the batting categories of at bats, hits, doubles, triples, home runs, home run percentage, runs scored, RBIs, bases on balls, strikeouts, stolen bases, batting and slugging average, pinch hit at bats, and pinch hits.

† Thirteen Hall of Famers never led the league in any batting categories.

ALL-TIME LEAGUE LEADERS COMPOSITE FIELDING RECORDS LIST*†

1	Cap Anson, 1B	32	36	George Kelly, OF	12	70	Hank Aaron, RF	4
2	Yogi Berra, C	30	36	Pee Wee Reese, SS	12	70	Jesse Burkett, LF	4
2	Gabby Hartnett, C	30	40	Honus Wagner, SS	11	70	Mickey Mantle, CF	4
4	Eddie Collins, 2B	28	40	Willie Mays, CF	11	70	Al Kaline, RF	4
5	Nap Lajoie, 2B	26	40	Arky Vaughan, SS	11	75	Tommy McCarthy, LF	3
5	Max Carey, CF	26	40	Johnny Mize, 1B	11	75	Freddie Lindstrom, OF	3
5	Tris Speaker, CF	26	40	Rick Ferrell, C	11	75	Willie Stargell, OF	3
5	Billy Herman, 2B	26	41	Jackie Robinson, 2B	10	75	Sam Crawford, RF	3
9	Charlie Gehringer, 2B	25	41	Carl Yastrzemski, LF	10	79	Harry Heilmann, 1B	2
9	Pie Traynor, 3B	25	43	Frankie Frisch, 2B	9	79	Harmon Killebrew, 3B	2
9	Brooks Robinson, 3B	25	43	Rogers Hornsby, 2B	9	79	Joe Medwick, OF	2
12	Luis Aparicio, SS	24	43	Buck Ewing, C	9	79	Edd Roush, CF	2
12	Bobby Doerr, 2B	24	43	Jimmie Foxx, 1B	9	79	Earle Combs, CF	2
14	Rabbit Maranville, SS	23	43	Roberto Clemente, RF	9	79	Hack Wilson, OF	2
15	Ray Schalk, C	22	48	Ty Cobb, CF	8	79	Billy Hamilton, CF	2
15	Ernie Banks, SS–1B	22	48	Stan Musial, OF–1B	8	79	King Kelly, OF	2
17	Bill Dickey, C	21	48	Sam Rice, CF	8	79	Ted Williams, LF	2
17	Bill Terry, 1B	21	48	Ross Youngs, RF	8	79	Willie Keeler, RF	2
19	Luke Appling, SS	20	48	Jim Bottomley, 1B	8	79	Frank Chance, 1B	2
19	Mickey Cochrane, C	20	53	Johnny Evers, SS	7	79	Zack Wheat, LF	2
21	Roy Campanella, C	19	53	Enos Slaughter, RF	7	79	Paul Waner, RF	2
22	Roger Connor, 1B	18	53	Lou Gehrig, 1B	7	79	Roger Bresnahan, C	2
22	Lou Boudreau, SS	18	53	Lloyd Waner, CF	7	93	Kiki Cuyler, OF	1
24	Jimmy Collins, 3B	17	53	Willie McCovey, 1B	7	93	Ralph Kiner, LF	1
24	Jake Beckley, 1B	17	58	Lou Brock, LF	6	93	Frank Robinson, OF	1
26	Frank Baker, 3B	16	58	Johnny Bench, C	6	93	Babe Ruth, RF	1
26	Joe Tinker, SS	16	58	Dan Brouthers, OF	6	93	Jim O'Rourke, OF	1
26	Dave Bancroft, SS	16	58	Fred Clarke, LF	6	93	Ed Delahanty, LF	1
26	Joe Cronin, SS	16	58	Chuck Klein, RF	6	94	Hugh Duffy, OF	0
26	George Sisler, 1B	16	63	Earl Averill, CF	5	94	Chick Hafey, RF	0
26	Joe Sewell, SS	16	63	Hank Greenberg, 1B	5	94	Duke Snider, CF	0
32	George Kell, 3B	14	63	Sam Thompson, OF	5	94	Elmer Flick, CF	0
32	Travis Jackson, SS	14	63	Mel Ott, RF	5	94	Monte Irvin, LF	0
32	Monte Ward, SS	14	63	Joe DiMaggio, CF	5	94	Joe Kelley, LF	0
35	Hugh Jennings, SS	13	63	Goose Goslin, LF	5	94	Heinie Manush, LF	0
36	Eddie Mathews, 3B	12	63	Harry Hooper, RF	5	94	Billy Williams, LF	0
36	Bobby Wallace, SS	12	70	Al Simmons, LF	4			

* This list represents players who have led the league in one or more positions.
† Eight Hall of Famers never led the league in any fielding category.

ALL-TIME MOST SEASONS BATTING OVER .300 LIST

#	Name		#	Name		#	Name		#	Name	
1	Ty Cobb	23*	33	Mel Ott	11	72	George Kelly	7			
2	Cap Anson	20	33	Joe DiMaggio	11	72	Freddie Lindstrom	7			
3	Rogers Hornsby	19	33	Goose Goslin	11	75	Frank Baker	6			
4	Stan Musial	18	33	Jim O'Rourke	11	75	Gabby Hartnett	6			
4	Tris Speaker	18	33	Lloyd Waner	11	75	Carl Yastrzemski	6			
4	Eddie Collins	18	33	Buck Ewing	11	75	Jackie Robinson	6			
4	Ted Williams	18	33	Bill Dickey	11	75	Travis Jackson	6			
8	Babe Ruth	17	33	Joe Cronin	11	80	Jimmy Collins	5			
8	Honus Wagner	17	33	Bill Terry	11	80	Harry Hooper	5			
10	Luke Appling	16	33	Joe Kelley	11	80	Frank Chance	5			
10	Dan Brouthers	16	33	Heinie Manush	11	80	Hugh Jennings	5			
10	Nap Lajoie	16	48	Willie Mays	10	80	Dave Bancroft	5			
13	Sam Rice	15	48	Pie Traynor	10	80	Hack Wilson	5			
13	Willie Keeler	15	48	Mickey Mantle	10	80	Rick Ferrell	5			
15	Lou Gehrig	14	48	Kiki Cuyler	10	80	Billy Williams	5			
15	Hank Aaron	14	48	Enos Slaughter	10	88	Yogi Berra	4			
15	Charlie Gehringer	14	48	Joe Sewell	10	88	Roger Bresnahan	4			
15	Zack Wheat	14	54	Chick Hafey	9	88	Lou Boudreau	4			
15	Paul Waner	14	54	Al Kaline	9	88	Tommy McCarthy	4			
15	Joe Medwick	14	54	Ross Youngs	9	92	Monte Ward	3			
15	Jimmie Foxx	14	54	Chuck Klein	9	92	Willie Stargell	3			
22	Frankie Frisch	13	54	Earle Combs	9	92	Roy Campanella	3			
22	Jake Beckley	13	54	Mickey Cochrane	9	92	Eddie Mathews	3			
22	Al Simmons	13	54	Frank Robinson	9	92	Bobby Wallace	3			
22	Hugh Duffy	13	54	George Kell	9	92	Ernie Banks	3			
22	Edd Roush	13	54	Jim Bottomley	9	92	Ralph Kiner	3			
22	George Sisler	13	54	Sam Thompson	9	92	Monte Irvin	3			
22	Roberto Clemente	13	54	Johnny Mize	9	99	Brooks Robinson	2			
29	Billy Hamilton	12	54	Hank Greenberg	9	99	Johnny Evers	2			
29	Ed Delahanty	12	66	Billy Herman	8	99	Willie McCovey	2			
29	Arky Vaughan	12	66	Lou Brock	8	102	Rabbit Maranville	1			
29	Harry Heilmann	12	66	Earl Averill	8	102	Luis Aparicio	1			
33	Sam Crawford	11	66	Elmer Flick	8	102	Pee Wee Reese	1			
33	Fred Clarke	11	66	Max Carey	8	102	Johnny Bench	1			
33	Jesse Burkett	11	66	King Kelly	8	102	Harmon Killebrew	1			
33	Roger Connor	11	72	Duke Snider	7	107	Ray Schalk	0†			

ALL-TIME MOST SEASONS BATTING OVER .300 CONSECUTIVELY LIST‡

1	Ty Cobb	23	2	Stan Musial	17	5	Dan Brouthers	16
2	Honus Wagner	17	2	Ted Williams	17	6	Cap Anson	15

* Ty Cobb played 24 seasons and batted over .300 in 23 seasons. He did not bat over .300 in his rookie year.
† In 18 years Ray Schalk never batted over .300. His highest batting average was .282 in 1919.
‡ 16 Hall of Famers never hit over .300 two years in a row.

7	Willie Keeler	14	35	Heinie Manush	7	73	Mel Ott	3
8	Rogers Hornsby	13	42	Jake Beckley	6	73	Harry Hooper	3
9	Lou Gehrig	12	42	Pie Traynor	6	73	Lou Brock	3
9	Billy Hamilton	12	42	Lloyd Waner	6	73	Gabby Hartnett	3
9	Paul Waner	12	42	Zack Wheat	6	73	Al Kaline	3
9	Harry Heilmann	12	42	Bill Dickey	6	73	Dave Bancroft	3
9	Ed Delahanty	12	42	Earl Averill	6	73	Mickey Cochrane	3
14	Frankie Frisch	11	42	George Kelly	6	73	Monte Irvin	3
14	Nap Lajoie	11	42	Jimmie Foxx	6	73	Billy Williams	3
14	Al Simmons	11	42	Earle Combs	6	73	King Kelly	3
14	Joe Medwick	11	42	Jackie Robinson	6	85	Lou Boudreau	2
14	Edd Roush	11	42	Freddie Lindstrom	6	85	Ernie Banks	2
19	Arky Vaughan	10	53	Fred Clarke	5	85	Frank Robinson	2
19	Bill Terry	10	53	Roger Connor	5	85	Tommy McCarthy	2
19	Tris Speaker	10	53	Hank Aaron	5	85	Rick Ferrell	2
19	Eddie Collins	10	53	Mickey Mantle	5	85	Travis Jackson	2
19	Jesse Burkett	10	53	Sam Rice	5	91	Monte Ward	0
19	Buck Ewing	10	53	Hugh Jennings	5	91	Joe Tinker	0
19	Hugh Duffy	10	53	Hack Wilson	5	91	Yogi Berra	0
26	Luke Appling	9	53	Jim Bottomley	5	91	Rabbit Maranville	0
26	George Sisler	9	53	Enos Slaughter	5	91	Ray Schalk	0
28	Babe Ruth	8	62	Sam Crawford	4	91	Luis Aparicio	0
28	Charlie Gehringer	8	62	Sam Thompson	4	91	Brooks Robinson	0
28	Joe Cronin	8	62	Frank Baker	4	91	Roger Bresnahan	0
28	Johnny Mize	8	62	Jim O'Rourke	4	91	Roy Campanella	0
28	George Kell	8	62	Frank Chance	4	91	Eddie Mathews	0
28	Roberto Clemente	8	62	Billy Herman	4	91	Johnny Evers	0
28	Hank Greenberg	8	62	Duke Snider	4	91	Bobby Wallace	0
35	Joe DiMaggio	7	62	Elmer Flick	4	91	Willie McCovey	0
35	Goose Goslin	7	62	Joe Cronin	4	91	Ralph Kiner	0
35	Willie Mays	7	62	Kiki Cuyler	4	91	Pee Wee Reese	0
35	Chick Hafey	7	62	Joe Kelley	4	91	Harmon Killebrew	0
35	Chuck Klein	7	73	Max Carey	3			
35	Joe Sewell	7	73	Jimmy Collins	3			

ALL-TIME AMERICAN LEAGUE PITCHERS RECORDS LIST

1	Walter Johnson	46	7	Addie Joss	11	13	Catfish Hunter	2
2	Ed Walsh	42	7	Eddie Plank	11	14	Whitey Ford	1
3	Cy Young	37	9	Lefty Grove	10	14	Red Ruffing	1
4	Rube Waddell	24	10	Joe McGinnity	9	14	Early Wynn	1
5	Jack Chesbro	18	11	Bob Feller	6			
6	Chief Bender	12	12	Hoyt Wilhelm	4			

ALL-TIME AMERICAN LEAGUE PITCHERS UNBROKEN RECORDS LIST

1	Walter Johnson	12	3	Jack Chesbro	3	7	Joe McGinnity	1
2	Bob Feller	5	5	Catfish Hunter	2	7	Early Wynn	1
3	Ed Walsh	3	5	Lefty Grove	2	7	Cy Young	1

ALL-TIME NATIONAL LEAGUE PITCHERS RECORDS LIST

1	Grover Alexander	21	8	Sandy Koufax	12	17	Mickey Welch	4
2	Hoss Radbourn	18	8	Monte Ward	12	18	Hoyt Wilhelm	2
3	Pud Galvin	14	11	Christy Mathewson	11	19	Carl Hubbell	1
4	Three Finger Brown	13	12	Kid Nichols	9	19	Jack Chesbro	1
4	Cy Young	13	13	Tim Keefe	8	19	Don Drysdale	1
4	John Clarkson	13	14	Amos Rusie	7	19	Bob Gibson	1
4	Joe McGinnity	13	15	Al Spalding	6			
8	Warren Spahn	12	16	Dazzy Vance	5			

ALL-TIME NATIONAL LEAGUE PITCHERS UNBROKEN RECORDS LIST

1	Sandy Koufax	5	6	Cy Young	2	11	Cy Young	1
2	Grover Alexander	4	6	Three Finger Brown	2	11	Hoyt Wilhelm	1
3	Christy Mathewson	4	6	Hoss Radbourn	2	11	Tim Keefe	1
3	Warren Spahn	4	6	Amos Rusie	2	11	Joe McGinnity	1
5	Pud Galvin	3	6	Dazzy Vance	2	11	Al Spalding	1

ALL-TIME MAJOR LEAGUE PITCHERS RECORDS LIST

1	Cy Young	25	10	Lefty Grove	9	19	Christy Mathewson	3
2	Walter Johnson	20	11	Grover Alexander	8	19	Mickey Welch	3
3	Hoss Radbourn	18	11	Hoyt Wilhelm	8	21	Rube Waddell	2
4	Joe McGinnity	15	13	Warren Spahn	7	21	Catfish Hunter	2
5	Pud Galvin	14	13	Sandy Koufax	7	23	Whitey Ford	1
6	John Clarkson	13	15	Al Spalding	6	23	Bob Feller	1
7	Monte Ward	12	15	Amos Rusie	6	23	Carl Hubbell	1
8	Tim Keefe	11	15	Kid Nichols	6	23	Early Wynn	1
8	Three Finger Brown	11	18	Ed Walsh	4			

ALL-TIME MAJOR LEAGUE PITCHERS
UNBROKEN RECORDS LIST

1	Cy Young	8	4	Walter Johnson	2	10	Tim Keefe	1
2	Hoyt Wilhelm	5	4	Ed Walsh	2	10	Amos Rusie	1
3	Sandy Koufax	4	4	Catfish Hunter	2	10	Al Spalding	1
4	Grover Alexander	2	4	Lefty Grove	2	10	Joe McGinnity	1
4	Warren Spahn	2	10	Hoss Radbourn	1			

ALL-TIME ALL-STAR GAME PITCHERS
RECORDS LIST

1	Lefty Gomez	5	5	Lefty Grove	3	10	Juan Marichal	1
2	Whitey Ford	4	5	Red Ruffing	3	10	Catfish Hunter	1
2	Carl Hubbell	4	5	Don Drysdale	3	10	Bob Feller	1
2	Robin Roberts	4	9	Warren Spahn	2			
5	Dizzy Dean	3	10	Early Wynn	1			

ALL-TIME ALL-STAR GAME PITCHERS
UNBROKEN RECORDS LIST

1	Whitey Ford	4	3	Carl Hubbell	2	5	Juan Marichal	1
2	Don Drysdale	3	5	Warren Spahn	1	5	Catfish Hunter	1
3	Lefty Gomez	2	5	Dizzy Dean	1			

ALL-TIME WORLD SERIES PITCHERS
RECORDS LIST

1	Christy Mathewson	37	10	Sandy Koufax	8	18	Bob Lemon	4
2	Three Finger Brown	31	10	Rube Marquard	8	20	Grover Alexander	3
3	Chief Bender	17	12	Red Ruffing	7	20	Red Faber	3
4	Whitey Ford	15	13	Eddie Plank	6	22	Joe McGinnity	2
5	Cy Young	14	13	Stan Coveleski	6	22	Dizzy Dean	2
6	Waite Hoyt	13	13	Ed Walsh	6	22	Lefty Grove	2
7	Walter Johnson	10	16	Don Drysdale	5	25	Carl Hubbell	1
8	Burleigh Grimes	9	16	Bob Gibson	5	25	Jesse Haines	1
8	Herb Pennock	9	18	Lefty Gomez	4	25	Warren Spahn	1

ALL-TIME WORLD SERIES PITCHERS
UNBROKEN RECORDS LIST

1	Whitey Ford	14	4	Chief Bender	6	8	Waite Hoyt	4
2	Christy Mathewson	13	6	Walter Johnson	5	8	Bob Gibson	4
3	Three Finger Brown	8	6	Don Drysdale	5	11	Red Ruffing	3
4	Sandy Koufax	6	8	Bob Lemon	4	11	Lefty Gomez	3

11	Stan Coveleski	3	14	Ed Walsh	2	19	Grover Alexander	1
14	Eddie Plank	2	14	Rube Marquard	2	19	Lefty Grove	1
14	Red Faber	2	19	Carl Hubbell	1	19	Burleigh Grimes	1
14	Herb Pennock	2	19	Joe McGinnity	1			

ALL-TIME PITCHERS LEAGUE LEADERS LIST*

1	Walter Johnson	53	16	Burleigh Grimes	20	33	Catfish Hunter	8
2	Grover Alexander	44	18	Dazzy Vance	18	33	Red Ruffing	8
3	Bob Feller	41	18	Early Wynn	18	33	Bob Gibson	8
4	Joe McGinnity	35	20	Tim Keefe	17	33	Eddie Plank	8
4	Lefty Grove	35	21	Three Finger Brown	15	33	Eppa Rixey	8
6	Warren Spahn	34	21	Rube Waddell	15	38	Pud Galvin	7
6	Ed Walsh	34	21	Whitey Ford	15	38	Stan Coveleski	7
8	Cy Young	31	24	Jack Chesbro	14	40	Waite Hoyt	6
8	Robin Roberts	31	24	Lefty Gomez	14	41	Mickey Welch	5
10	Christy Mathewson	30	26	Don Drysdale	13	42	Chief Bender	4
11	John Clarkson	29	27	Carl Hubbell	12	42	Jesse Haines	4
12	Amos Rusie	24	27	Ted Lyons	12	42	Rube Marquard	4
13	Sandy Koufax	21	27	Kid Nichols	12	42	Addie Joss	4
13	Dizzy Dean	21	30	Juan Marichal	11	46	Herb Pennock	3
13	Bob Lemon	21	31	Red Faber	10	47	Al Spalding	2
16	Hoss Radbourn	20	31	Hoyt Wilhelm	10			

ALL-TIME PITCHERS WITH MOST 20-PLUS WINS SEASONS LIST

1	Cy Young	16	15	Herb Pennock	7	28	Addie Joss	4
2	Christy Mathewson	13	17	Three Finger Brown	6	28	Lefty Gomez	4
2	Warren Spahn	13	17	Bob Feller	6	28	Red Faber	4
4	Walter Johnson	12	17	Robin Roberts	6	28	Dizzy Dean	4
5	Pud Galvin	10	17	Juan Marichal	6	28	Ed Walsh	4
5	Kid Nichols	10	21	Jack Chesbro	5	36	Sandy Koufax	3
7	Grover Alexander	9	21	Stan Coveleski	5	36	Jesse Haines	3
7	Hoss Radbourn	9	21	Catfish Hunter	5	36	Dazzy Vance	3
7	Mickey Welch	9	21	Early Wynn	5	36	Rube Marquard	3
10	Lefty Grove	8	21	Carl Hubbell	5	36	Ted Lyons	3
10	Joe McGinnity	8	21	Burleigh Grimes	5	41	Whitey Ford	2
10	John Clarkson	8	21	Bob Gibson	5	41	Herb Pennock	2
10	Tim Keefe	8	28	Rube Waddell	4	41	Waite Hoyt	2
10	Amos Rusie	8	28	Red Ruffing	4	41	Chief Bender	2
15	Bob Lemon	7	28	Eppa Rixey	4	45	Al Spalding	1

* Pitching categories include games, games started, games completed, wins, losses, winning percentage, ERA, innings, hits allowed, bases on balls, strikeouts, shutouts, relief appearances, relief wins, relief losses, and saves.

ALL-TIME PITCHERS WITH MOST CONSECUTIVE 20-PLUS WINS SEASONS LIST

#	Name		#	Name		#	Name		#	Name	
1	Cy Young	14	12	Robin Roberts	6	26	Bob Feller	3			
2	Christy Mathewson	12	12	Warren Spahn	6	26	Rube Marquard	3			
3	Walter Johnson	10	16	Catfish Hunter	5	26	Bob Lemon	3			
3	Kid Nichols	10	16	Carl Hubbell	5	30	Sandy Koufax	2			
5	Amos Rusie	8	16	Grover Alexander	5	30	Ed Walsh	2			
5	John Clarkson	8	19	Jack Chesbro	4	30	Red Faber	2			
5	Joe McGinnity	8	19	Stan Coveleski	4	30	Lefty Gomez	2			
8	Lefty Grove	7	19	Dizzy Dean	4	30	Burleigh Grimes	2			
8	Tim Keefe	7	19	Addie Joss	4	30	Jesse Haines	2			
8	Hoss Radbourn	7	19	Eddie Plank	4	30	Waite Hoyt	2			
8	Mickey Welch	7	19	Red Ruffing	4	30	Eppa Rixey	2			
12	Three Finger Brown	6	19	Rube Waddell	4	30	Early Wynn	2			
12	Pud Galvin	6	26	Bob Gibson	3	30	Dazzy Vance	2			

ALL-TIME PITCHERS WITH MOST WINS OVER LOSSES LIST

#	Name		#	Name		#	Name	
1	Cy Young	198	17	Joc McGinnity	103	33	Dazzy Vancc	57
2	Christy Mathewson	185	18	Juan Marichal	101	34	Early Wynn	56
3	Sandy Koufax	178	19	Carl Hubbell	99	35	Waite Hoyt	55
4	Grover Alexander	165	20	Lefty Gomez	87	36	Jesse Haines	52
5	Lefty Grove	159	21	Chief Bender	83	37	Pud Galvin	51
6	Kid Nichols	158	21	Amos Rusie	83	38	Rube Waddell	46
7	John Clarkson	149	23	Bob Lemon	79	39	Don Drysdale	43
8	Walter Johnson	137	24	Herb Pennock	78	40	Red Faber	42
9	Eddie Plank	134	25	Bob Gibson	77	41	Robin Roberts	41
10	Whitey Ford	130	26	Stan Coveleski	73	42	Al Spalding	35
11	Tim Keefe	119	27	Ed Walsh	69	43	Ted Lyons	30
12	Warren Spahn	118	28	Dizzy Dean	67	44	Rube Marquard	24
13	Hoss Radbourn	117	29	Jack Chesbro	66	45	Hoyt Wilhelm	21
14	Three Finger Brown	110	30	Addie Joss	63	46	Eppa Rixey	15
15	Bob Feller	104	31	Catfish Hunter	58			
15	Mickey Welch	104	31	Burleigh Grimes	58			

ALL-TIME PITCHERS COMPOSITE RECORDS LIST*

#	Name		#	Name		#	Name	
1	Cy Young	93	6	Joe McGinnity	39	10	Pud Galvin	28
2	Walter Johnson	76	7	Hoss Radbourn	36	12	Sandy Koufax	27
3	Three Finger Brown	55	8	Grover Alexander	32	13	John Clarkson	26
4	Ed Walsh	52	9	Chief Bender	30	14	Rube Waddell	26
5	Christy Mathewson	51	10	Clark Griffith	28	15	Tim Keefe	25

* Composite List includes all leagues (AL, NL, & ML) plus World Series and All-Star games.

16	Lefty Grove	24	26	Red Ruffing	11	36	Bob Gibson	6
16	Monte Ward	24	26	Addie Joss	11	38	Catfish Hunter	5
16	Warren Spahn	22	28	Lefty Gomez	9	38	Dizzy Dean	5
18	Whitey Ford	21	28	Don Drysdale	9	38	Dazzy Vance	5
19	Jack Chesbro	17	28	Burleigh Grimes	9	41	Bob Lemon	4
19	Eddie Plank	17	28	Herb Pennock	9	41	Robin Roberts	4
21	Kid Nichols	14	32	Rube Marquard	8	43	Early Wynn	3
21	Hoyt Wilhelm	14	32	Bob Feller	8	43	Red Faber	3
23	Amos Rusie	13	34	Mickey Welch	7	45	Jesse Haines	1
23	Waite Hoyt	13	34	Carl Hubbell	7	45	Juan Marichal	1
25	Al Spalding	12	36	Stan Coveleski	6			

ALL-TIME PITCHERS COMPOSITE UNBROKEN RECORDS LIST

1	Walter Johnson	19	14	Bob Feller	5	22	Carl Hubbell	3
2	Christy Mathewson	17	14	Catfish Hunter	5	28	Dazzy Vance	2
3	Whitey Ford	16	14	Lefty Gomez	5	28	Red Faber	2
4	Sandy Koufax	15	14	Lefty Grove	5	28	Rube Marquard	2
5	Cy Young	10	18	Bob Lemon	4	28	Herb Pennock	2
5	Three Finger Brown	10	18	Joe McGinnity	4	28	Al Spalding	2
5	Don Drysdale	10	18	Waite Hoyt	4	28	Eddie Plank	2
8	Clark Griffith	9	18	Bob Gibson	4	28	Tim Keefe	2
9	Grover Alexander	8	22	Hoss Radbourn	3	35	Burleigh Grimes	1
10	Ed Walsh	7	22	Pud Galvin	3	35	Dizzy Dean	1
10	Warren Spahn	7	22	Amos Rusie	3	35	Early Wynn	1
12	Hoyt Wilhelm	6	22	Jack Chesbro	3	35	Juan Marichal	1
12	Chief Bender	6	22	Red Ruffing	3			

ALL-TIME MANAGERS RECORDS LIST

1	John McGraw	24	7	Charlie Comiskey	15	12	Clark Griffith	10
2	Connie Mack	22	7	Fred Clarke	15	14	Al Spalding	9
3	Cap Anson	20	7	Frank Chance	15	15	Al Lopez	2
4	Miller Huggins	19	10	Joe McCarthy	13	15	George Wright	2
4	Jimmy Collins	19	11	Harry Wright	11	17	Hugh Duffy	1
6	Casey Stengel	16	12	Hugh Jennings	10	17	Nap Lajoie	1

ALL-TIME MANAGERS UNBROKEN RECORDS LIST

1	Casey Stengel	16	5	Joe McCarthy	7	8	Cap Anson	1
2	John McGraw	13	6	Frank Chance	3	8	Fred Clarke	1
3	Charlie Comiskey	10	7	Al Lopez	2			
4	Connie Mack	8	8	Miller Huggins	1			

ALL-TIME CLUB RECORDS LIST*

1	Babe Ruth	246	37	Ed Delahanty	43	73	Chuck Klein	22
2	Lou Gehrig	150	38	Al Simmons	40	74	Luis Aparicio	21
3	Willie Keeler	125	38	Jimmie Foxx	40	74	Lloyd Waner	21
4	Roger Connor	121	40	Honus Wagner	38	76	Johnny Bench	20
5	Cap Anson	110	40	Hank Aaron	38	77	Ralph Kiner	19
6	Zack Wheat	106	40	Bill Terry	38	77	Carl Yastrzemski	19
7	Jim O'Rourke	96	43	Roy Campanella	37	79	Gabby Hartnett	18
8	Bill Dickey	95	44	Charlie Gehringer	37	79	Dan Brouthers	18
9	Joe DiMaggio	93	45	Billy Herman	36	81	Ross Youngs	17
10	Nap Lajoie	92	46	Jimmy Collins	35	81	Edd Roush	17
11	Tris Speaker	91	46	Hank Greenberg	35	83	Tommy McCarthy	16
12	Pee Wee Reese	87	48	Fred Clarke	34	84	Pie Traynor	15
13	Frank Baker	86	49	Earl Averill	33	85	Bobby Wallace	14
14	Billy Hamilton	82	50	Ray Schalk	32	85	Roger Bresnahan	14
15	Earle Combs	81	50	Joe Sewell	32	85	Johnny Evers	14
16	Jackie Robinson	79	52	Willie Mays	31	85	Joe Kelley	14
17	Duke Snider	77	52	Stan Musial	31	85	Frank Chance	14
18	Mickey Mantle	75	52	Enos Slaughter	31	85	Joe Tinker	14
18	Harmon Killebrew	75	55	Rabbit Maranville	30	91	Billy Williams	13
20	Ty Cobb	74	56	Joe Medwick	29	91	Roberto Clemente	13
21	Sam Crawford	73	56	Luke Appling	29	91	Dave Bancroft	13
22	Monte Ward	72	58	George Kelly	28	91	Chick Hafey	13
23	Jake Beckley	65	59	Johnny Mize	27	91	Arky Vaughan	13
24	Rogers Hornsby	63	59	Eddie Mathews	27	96	Travis Jackson	12
25	Brooks Robinson	61	59	Hack Wilson	27	97	Lou Brock	11
26	King Kelly	59	59	Paul Waner	27	97	Ernie Lombardi	11
27	Eddie Collins	57	59	Jesse Burkett	27	99	Mickey Cochrane	10
28	Yogi Berra	55	64	Hugh Duffy	26	100	Willie Stargell	8
29	Harry Hooper	52	64	Ernie Banks	26	101	Lou Boudreau	7
30	Ted Williams	51	66	Al Kaline	25	102	Joe Cronin	6
30	Elmer Flick	51	66	Bobby Doerr	25	102	Freddie Lindstrom	6
32	Max Carey	48	66	George Kell	25	104	Willie McCovey	5
33	Buck Ewing	46	66	Jim Bottomley	25	105	Rick Ferrell	3
34	Frank Robinson	44	70	Kiki Cuyler	23	106	Monte Irvin	2
34	Sam Thompson	44	70	Frankie Frisch	23	106	George Sisler	2
34	Mel Ott	44	70	Harry Heilmann	23	108	Heinie Manush	1

ALL-TIME UNBROKEN CLUB RECORDS LIST

1	Babe Ruth	75	7	Willie Mays	28	15	Stan Musial	18
2	Lou Gehrig	66	9	Ty Cobb	25	15	Zack Wheat	18
3	Mickey Mantle	58	10	Ted Williams	23	17	Al Kaline	17
4	Joe DiMaggio	52	10	Bill Dickey	23	17	Ernie Banks	17
5	Yogi Berra	37	12	Hank Aaron	22	19	Johnny Mize	16
6	Duke Snider	30	13	Pee Wee Reese	21	19	Harmon Killebrew	16
7	Brooks Robinson	28	14	Luke Appling	19	19	Earle Combs	16

* Represents records set for all teams a player has been on.

19	Cap Anson	16	44	Bobby Doerr	9	80	Tommy McCarthy	3
23	Tris Speaker	15	52	Billy Hamilton	8	80	Dave Bancroft	3
23	Earl Averill	15	52	Jackie Robinson	8	80	George Kell	3
23	Max Carey	15	52	Willie Stargell	8	80	Frankie Frisch	3
23	Frank Robinson	15	52	George Kelly	8	80	Sam Crawford	3
27	Ray Schalk	14	52	Gabby Hartnett	8	80	Harry Heilmann	3
27	Al Simmons	14	57	Eddie Collins	7	80	Buck Ewing	3
29	Chuck Klein	13	57	Jim Bottomley	7	80	Luis Aparicio	3
29	Johnny Bench	13	57	Jesse Burkett	7	88	Roger Connor	2
29	Nap Lajoie	13	57	Willie Keeler	7	88	Bobby Wallace	2
29	Carl Yastrzemski	13	57	Joe Sewell	7	88	Jake Beckley	2
33	Lloyd Waner	12	57	Hugh Duffy	7	88	King Kelly	2
33	Ed Delahanty	12	57	Charlie Gehringer	7	88	Monte Irvin	2
35	Jimmie Foxx	11	57	Mel Ott	7	93	Roger Bresnahan	1
35	Billy Herman	11	57	Kiki Cuyler	7	93	Johnny Evers	1
35	Bill Terry	11	57	Pie Traynor	7	93	Arky Vaughan	1
38	Billy Williams	10	67	Joe Tinker	6	93	Monte Ward	1
38	Paul Waner	10	67	Roy Campanella	6	93	Joe Cronin	1
38	Ralph Kiner	10	67	Edd Roush	6	93	Frank Chance	1
38	Hack Wilson	10	67	Elmer Flick	6	99	Chick Hafey	0
38	Rabbit Maranville	10	71	Jimmy Collins	5	99	Jim O'Rourke	0
38	Eddie Mathews	10	71	Sam Thompson	5	99	Dan Brouthers	0
44	Frank Baker	9	71	Joe Medwick	5	99	George Sisler	0
44	Enos Slaughter	9	71	Travis Jackson	5	99	Heinie Manush	0
44	Rogers Hornsby	9	71	Fred Clarke	5	99	Ross Youngs	0
44	Lou Brock	9	76	Harry Hooper	4	99	Joe Kelley	0
44	Hank Greenberg	9	76	Lou Boudreau	4	99	Freddie Lindstrom	0
44	Honus Wagner	9	76	Willie McCovey	4	99	Rick Ferrell	0
44	Roberto Clemente	9	76	Mickey Cochrane	4	99	Ernie Lombardi	0

ALL-TIME COMPOSITE RECORDS LIST BY POSITION*†

FIRST BASEMEN

1	Cap Anson	100	7	Bill Terry	9	13	Johnny Mize	4
2	Dan Brouthers	78	8	George Kelly	8	14	Jim Bottomley	3
3	Lou Gehrig	51	9	Jimmie Foxx	7	15	Hank Greenberg	2
4	Jake Beckley	31	10	George Sisler	6	15	Harmon Killebrew	2
5	Roger Connor	29	10	Ernie Banks	6			
6	Frank Chance	18	12	Willie McCovey	5			

SECOND BASEMEN

1	Nap Lajoie	74	5	Charlie Gehringer	23	9	Red Shoendienst	10
2	Eddie Collins	46	6	Bucky Harris	16	10	Bobby Doerr	8
2	Frankie Frisch	46	7	Billy Herman	15	11	Jackie Robinson	5
4	Rogers Hornsby	39	8	Johnny Evers	11			

* Players are listed according to the position where they played the most games.
† Includes all league, All-Star, and World Series records, but not club records.

SHORTSTOPS

1	Monte Ward	78	5	Luis Aparicio	14	11	Bobby Wallace	8
2	Honus Wagner	64	7	Arky Vaughan	11	12	Luke Appling	7
3	Joe Tinker	29	7	Dave Bancroft	11	13	Joe Sewell	6
4	Rabbit Maranville	20	7	Hugh Jennings	11	14	Pee Wee Reese	3
5	Joe Cronin	14	10	Lou Boudreau	9	15	Travis Jackson	1

THIRD BASEMEN

1	Frank Baker	42	4	Brooks Robinson	15	7	George Kell	4
2	Jimmy Collins	33	5	Joe Medwick	11	7	Freddie Lindstrom	4
3	Pie Traynor	19	5	Eddie Mathews	11			

CATCHERS

1	Yogi Berra	22	3	Bill Dickey	14	9	Johnny Bench	6
2	Ray Schalk	18	6	Gabby Hartnett	13	10	Mickey Cochrane	5
3	Roger Bresnahan	14	7	Wilbert Robinson	9	11	Rick Ferrell	1
3	Buck Ewing	14	8	Roy Campanella	8	11	Ernie Lombardi	1

OUTFIELDERS

1	Babe Ruth	205	17	Jim O'Rourke	22	34	Elmer Flick	9
2	Ty Cobb	129	19	Willie Mays	20	34	Ross Youngs	9
3	Sam Crawford	52	19	Willie Keeler	20	37	Carl Yastrzemski	8
4	Tris Speaker	51	21	Hugh Duffy	19	38	Chuck Klein	7
5	Stan Musial	50	21	Al Simmons	19	38	Earle Combs	7
6	Sam Thompson	47	21	Harry Hooper	19	40	Kiki Cuyler	6
7	Billy Hamilton	45	24	Paul Waner	16	41	Ralph Kiner	5
8	Fred Clarke	38	25	Zack Wheat	15	42	Enos Slaughter	4
9	Max Carey	37	25	Lou Brock	15	43	Frank Robinson	3
10	Jesse Burkett	30	27	Chick Hafey	13	44	Heinie Manush	2
11	Ted Williams	29	27	Mickey Mantle	13	44	Roberto Clemente	2
12	Mel Ott	27	29	Sam Rice	12	44	Willie Stargell	2
13	Joe DiMaggio	26	30	Al Kaline	11	44	Tommy McCarthy	2
14	King Kelly	25	30	Duke Snider	11	44	Joe Kelley	2
15	Ed Delahanty	24	32	Earl Averill	10	44	Monte Irvin	2
16	Goose Goslin	23	32	Edd Roush	10	50	Billy Williams	0
17	Hank Aaron	22	34	Hack Wilson	9			

ALL-TIME COMPOSITE UNBROKEN RECORDS
LIST BY POSITION

FIRST BASEMEN

1	Lou Gehrig	12	5	Ernie Banks	4	7	Johnny Mize	2
2	Cap Anson	10	5	George Kelly	4	10	Jim Bottomley	1
3	Jake Beckley	6	7	Frank Chance	2	10	Bill Terry	1
4	Willie McCovey	5	7	George Sisler	2			

SECOND BASEMEN

1	Eddie Collins	16	4	Billy Herman	3	7	Nap Lajoie	2
2	Rogers Hornsby	11	4	Charlie Gehringer	3	7	Jackie Robinson	2
3	Frankie Frisch	9	4	Bucky Harris	3	8	Bobby Doerr	1

SHORTSTOPS

1	Honus Wagner	11	4	Dave Bancroft	5	8	Lou Boudreau	2
1	Luis Aparicio	11	6	Monte Ward	4	10	Joe Tinker	1
3	Hugh Jennings	6	7	Joe Cronin	3			
4	Rabbit Maranville	5	8	Arky Vaughan	2			

THIRD BASEMEN

1	Brooks Robinson	15	3	Joe Medwick	4	4	Eddie Mathews	3
2	Frank Baker	9	4	Jimmy Collins	3	6	Pie Traynor	1

CATCHERS

1	Yogi Berra	12	4	Gabby Hartnett	2	5	Mickey Cochrane	1
2	Ray Schalk	6	5	Bill Dickey	1			
3	Johnny Bench	5	5	Rick Ferrell	1			

OUTFIELDERS

1	Babe Ruth	65	14	Fred Clarke	8	28	Mel Ott	3
2	Ty Cobb	20	14	Billy Hamilton	8	28	Al Simmons	3
2	Tris Speaker	20	14	Harry Hooper	8	28	Carl Yastrzemski	3
4	Ted Williams	18	14	Ross Youngs	8	28	Frank Robinson	3
5	Stan Musial	17	18	Edd Roush	6	32	Paul Waner	2
5	Willie Mays	17	18	Willie Keeler	6	32	Earle Combs	2
7	Hank Aaron	14	20	Sam Thompson	5	32	Ralph Kiner	2
8	Zack Wheat	11	21	Max Carey	4	32	Hugh Duffy	2
8	Lou Brock	11	21	Ed Delahanty	4	36	Chuck Klein	1
10	Joe DiMaggio	10	21	Lloyd Waner	4	36	Earl Averill	1
10	Goose Goslin	10	21	Duke Snider	4	36	Roberto Clemente	1
10	Al Kaline	10	21	Hack Wilson	4	36	Monte Irvin	1
13	Sam Crawford	9	21	Chick Hafey	4	36	Willie Stargell	1
13	Mickey Mantle	9	21	Sam Rice	4			

ALL-TIME COMPOSITE RECORDS LIST

This list is the total of records taken from the American, National, and Major League Lists. It also includes all records from All-Star and World Series games and managers' records. It does not include club records.

1	Babe Ruth	192	4	Cy Young	93	7	Dan Brouthers	68
2	Ty Cobb	123	5	Walter Johnson	76	8	Monte Ward	63
3	Cap Anson	120	6	Nap Lajoie	71	9	Honus Wagner	56

Rank	Name	Value	Rank	Name	Value	Rank	Name	Value
10	Three Finger Brown	55	57	Rabbit Maranville	20	108	Burleigh Grimes	9
11	Fred Clarke	53	61	King Kelly	19	108	Herb Pennock	9
12	Jimmy Collins	52	61	Al Simmons	19	108	Lou Boudreau	9
12	Ed Walsh	52	61	Hank Aaron	19	108	Hack Wilson	9
14	Christy Mathewson	51	61	Harry Hooper	19	108	Elmer Flick	9
14	Lou Gehrig	51	61	Pie Traynor	19	108	Ross Youngs	9
16	Sam Crawford	50	66	Ray Schalk	18	116	Roy Campanella	8
17	Tris Speaker	49	66	Al Spalding	18	116	Rube Marquard	8
18	Eddie Collins	48	68	Eddie Plank	17	116	Bobby Wallace	8
19	Frankie Frisch	47	68	Jack Chesbro	17	116	Bob Feller	8
20	Stan Musial	45	68	Hugh Duffy	17	116	George Kelly	8
21	Sam Thompson	44	71	Paul Waner	16	121	Luke Appling	7
22	Charlie Comiskey	42	71	Casey Stengel	16	121	Chuck Klein	7
23	Billy Hamilton	41	73	Zack Wheat	15	121	Carl Hubbell	7
23	Frank Baker	41	73	Lloyd Waner	15	121	Earle Combs	7
25	Joe McGinnity	39	73	Lou Brock	15	121	Mickey Welsh	7
26	Hoss Radbourn	36	73	Billy Herman	15	121	Jimmie Foxx	7
27	Frank Chance	33	73	Brooks Robinson	15	127	Carl Yastrzemski	6
27	Rogers Hornsby	33	78	Joe Cronin	14	127	Ernie Banks	6
29	Grover Alexander	32	78	Hoyt Wilhelm	14	127	Johnny Bench	6
30	Max Carey	31	78	Luis Aparicio	14	127	Kiki Cuyler	6
31	Jake Beckley	30	78	Kid Nichols	14	127	George Sisler	6
32	Joe Tinker	29	78	Roger Bresnahan	14	127	Bob Gibson	6
32	Jesse Burkett	29	78	Bill Dickey	14	127	Joe Sewell	6
32	Connie Mack	29	84	Amos Rusie	13	127	Stan Coveleski	6
32	Chief Bender	29	84	Chick Hafey	13	135	Al Lopez	5
36	Clark Griffith	28	84	Luis Aparicio	13	135	Dazzy Vance	5
36	Pud Galvin	28	84	Gabby Hartnett	13	135	Jackie Robinson	5
38	Sandy Koufax	27	84	Waite Hoyt	13	135	Catfish Hunter	5
38	Roger Connor	27	84	Mickey Mantle	13	135	Willie McCovey	5
40	Joe DiMaggio	26	84	Joe McCarthy	13	135	Dizzy Dean	5
40	Ted Williams	26	91	Sam Rice	12	135	Mickey Cochrane	5
40	George Wright	26	92	Arky Vaughan	11	142	Enos Slaughter	4
40	John Clarkson	26	92	Red Ruffing	11	142	Ralph Kiner	4
40	Rube Waddell	26	92	Joe Medwick	11	142	George Kell	4
45	Tim Keefe	25	92	Harry Wright	11	142	Robin Roberts	4
45	Mel Ott	25	92	Dave Bancroft	11	142	Johnny Mize	4
45	Miller Huggins	25	92	Addie Joss	11	142	Bob Lemon	4
48	Lefty Grove	24	92	Hugh Jennings	11	142	Freddie Lindstrom	4
48	John McGraw	24	92	Johnny Evers	11	149	Pee Wee Reese	3
50	Charlie Gehringer	23	92	Al Kaline	11	149	Early Wynn	3
50	Goose Goslin	23	92	Don Drysdale	11	149	Jim Bottomley	3
52	Warren Spahn	22	92	Duke Snider	11	149	Red Faber	3
52	Jim O'Rourke	22	92	Eddie Mathews	11	149	Frank Robinson	3
52	Ed Delahanty	22	104	Clark Griffith	10	154	Heinie Manush	2
55	Whitey Ford	21	104	Earl Averill	10	154	Harmon Killebrew	2
55	Hugh Jennings	21	104	Buck Ewing	10	154	Roberto Clemente	2
57	Willie Mays	20	104	Edd Roush	10	154	Willie Stargell	2
57	Yogi Berra	20	108	Bill Terry	9	154	Hank Greenberg	2
57	Willie Keeler	20	108	Lefty Gomez	9	154	Tommy McCarthy	2

154	Joe Kelley	2	162	Travis Jackson	1	166	Billy Williams	0
154	Monte Irvin	2	162	Juan Marichal	1	166	Eppa Rixey	0
162	Rick Ferrell	1	166	Ernie Lombardi	0	166	Harry Heilmann	0
162	Jesse Haines	1	166	Ted Lyons	0			

ALL-TIME COMPOSITE UNBROKEN RECORDS LIST

1	Babe Ruth	53	40	Edd Roush	6	71	Jack Chesbro	3
2	Walter Johnson	19	40	Hoyt Wilhelm	6	71	Frank Robinson	3
3	Tris Speaker	18	40	Willie Keeler	6	71	Red Ruffing	3
4	Christy Mathewson	17	40	Jake Beckley	6	71	Eddie Mathews	3
4	Willie Mays	17	40	Hugh Jennings	6	87	Dazzy Vance	2
4	Charlie Comiskey	17	40	Chief Bender	6	87	Paul Waner	2
7	Eddie Collins	16	48	Catfish Hunter	5	87	Mel Ott	2
7	Ted Williams	16	48	Bob Feller	5	87	Frank Chance	2
7	Whitey Ford	16	48	Rabbit Maranville	5	87	Red Faber	2
10	Ty Cobb	15	48	Johnny Bench	5	87	Earle Combs	2
10	Brooks Robinson	15	48	Sam Thompson	5	87	Rube Marquard	2
10	Sandy Koufax	15	48	Lefty Grove	5	87	Gabby Hartnett	2
13	Stan Musial	13	48	Dave Bancroft	5	87	Herb Pennock	2
14	Lou Gehrig	12	48	Lefty Gomez	5	87	George Sisler	2
15	Rogers Hornsby	11	48	Willie McCovey	5	87	Al Spalding	2
15	Zack Wheat	11	57	Monte Ward	4	87	Johnny Mize	2
15	Hank Aaron	11	57	Joe McGinnity	4	87	Eddie Plank	2
15	Yogi Berra	11	57	Max Carey	4	87	Ralph Kiner	2
15	Lou Brock	11	57	Waite Hoyt	4	87	Tim Keefe	2
20	Joe DiMaggio	10	57	Ernie Banks	4	87	Arky Vaughan	2
20	Three Finger Brown	10	57	Bob Gibson	4	87	Nap Lajoie	2
20	Goose Goslin	10	57	Ed Delahanty	4	87	Lou Boudreau	2
20	Don Drysdale	10	57	Bob Lemon	4	87	Hugh Duffy	2
20	Cy Young	10	57	Joe Medwick	4	87	Jackie Robinson	2
20	Al Kaline	10	57	George Kelly	4	107	Burleigh Grimes	1
20	Luis Aparicio	10	57	Duke Snider	4	107	Pie Traynor	1
27	Clark Griffith	9	57	Hack Wilson	4	107	Dizzy Dean	1
27	Frank Baker	9	57	Sam Rice	4	107	Jim Bottomley	1
27	Frankie Frisch	9	57	Chick Hafey	4	107	Early Wynn	1
27	Mickey Mantle	9	71	Carl Hubbell	3	107	Joe Tinker	1
31	Cap Anson	8	71	Hoss Radbourn	3	107	Juan Marichal	1
31	Fred Clarke	8	71	Carl Yastrzemski	3	107	Chuck Klein	1
31	Ross Youngs	8	71	Billy Herman	3	107	Earl Averill	1
31	Billy Hamilton	8	71	Al Lopez	3	107	Roberto Clemente	1
31	Grover Alexander	8	71	Jimmy Collins	3	107	Mickey Cochrane	1
31	Harry Hooper	8	71	Lloyd Waner	3	107	Bill Dickey	1
37	Warren Spahn	7	71	Joe Cronin	3	107	Rick Ferrell	1
37	Ed Walsh	7	71	Pud Galvin	3	107	Monte Irvin	1
37	Sam Crawford	7	71	Charlie Gehringer	3	107	Bill Terry	1
40	Ray Schalk	6	71	Amos Rusie	3	107	Willie Stargell	1
40	Honus Wagner	6	71	Al Simmons	3			

UNBROKEN OUTSTANDING RECORDS BY NON–HALL OF FAME MEMBERS

SEASON RECORDS

Most At Bats, Willie Wilson, KC–AL, 1980	705
*Most Hits, Lefty O'Doul, Phi–NL, 1929	254
**Most Singles, Wade Boggs, Bos–AL, 1985	187
Most Doubles, Earl Webb, Bos–AL, 1931	67
Most Triples, Owen Wilson, Pit–NL, 1912	36
Most Home Runs, Roger Maris, NY–AL, 1961	61
Most Stolen Bases, Rickey Henderson, NY–AL, 1982	130
Most Pinch Hit At Bats, Rusty Staub, NY–NL, 1983	81
Most Pinch Hits, José Morales, Mon–AL 1976	25
Most Relief Games, Mike Marshall, LA–NL, 1974	106
Most Starts, Will White, Cin–NL, 1879	75
Most Complete Games, Will White, Cin–NL, 1879	75
Highest Winning Percentage (Starters), Johnny Allen, Cle–AL, 1937	.938 (15-1)
Most Innings Pitched, Will White, Cin–NL, 1879	680
Lowest ERA, Dutch Leonard, Bos–AL, 1914	1.01
Most Strikeouts, Matt Kilroy, Bal–AA, 1886	513
Most Shutouts, George Bradley, StL–NL, 1876	16
Most Relief Wins, Elroy Face, Pit–NL, 1959	18
Highest Winning Percentage (Relievers), Elroy Face, Pit–NL, 1959	.947 (18-1)
Most Saves, Dave Righetti, NY–AL, 1986	46
Most Wins Plus Saves, Dave Righetti, NY–AL, 1986	54

CAREER RECORDS

Most Games, Pete Rose, Cin–NL, 1961–86	3,562
Most At Bats, Pete Rose, Cin–NL, 1961–86	14,053
Most Hits, Pete Rose, Cin–NL, 1961–86	4,256
Most Singles, Pete Rose, Cin–NL 1961–86	3,310
Highest Winning Percentage, Bob Caruthers, StL–AA, 1884–92 (218–97)	.690
Most Strikeouts, Nolan Ryan, Hou–NL (still active), 1966–89	5,076
Most Saves, Rollie Fingers, Oak–AL, 1968–84	324
Most Wins plus Saves, Rollie Fingers, Oak–AL, 1968–84	430

TITLES RECORDS

Most Singles Titles, Nellie Fox, Chi–AL	9
Most Fewest Hits Allowed Titles, Nolan Ryan, Hou–NL	8

* National League record only.
** American League record only.
   No asterisk indicates a Major League record.

Most Saves Titles, Tony Mullane, Bal–AL 5
Firpo Marberry, Was–AL 5
Bruce Sutter, StL–NL 5

HIGHEST CAREER BATTING AVERAGE

Pete Browning, Lou–AA, 1882–94 .343 (10th)
Riggs Stephenson, Chi–NL, 1921–34 .336
Rod Carew, Min–AL, 1967–84 .330
Tip O'Neill, StL–AA, 1883–92 .326
Babe Herman, Bkn–NL, 1926–45 .324

4

HALL OF FAME RULES AND MEMBERS

THE NATIONAL BASEBALL HALL OF FAME
Eligibility Rules

Candidates eligible for election by the Baseball Writers Association of America must meet the following requirements:

1. Must be a major league player for a minimum of ten years.
2. These ten years must be during a 20-year period ending five years prior to nomination.
3. The player must be retired from major league baseball at least five years.
4. A player who died and who had been retired from baseball for less than five years is eligible in the next regular election six months after the date of death or after the five-year waiting period, whichever occurs first.

The rules further state: "Any candidate receiving votes on 75 percent of the ballots cast shall be elected to the baseball Hall of Fame." All the voting is based "upon the player's record, playing ability, integrity, sportsmanship, character, and contribution to the team(s) on which the player played and not on what he may have done otherwise in baseball."

Hall of Fame admission can also come through the 18-member Committee on Baseball Veterans. This group consists of former players who are members of the Hall of Fame, members of the Baseball Writers Association, and executives now or formerly officially connected with baseball.

Candidates to be eligible must be selected from:

1. Those players retired from the majors prior to 1946. Additionally, those retired after 1945 for at least 23 years. These players must have received 100 or more votes in at least one election of the Baseball Writers Association of America. It is required that they must have competed in at least ten major league championship seasons as players.
2. Baseball executives and/or managers and/or umpires who have been retired from those positions for at least five years prior to election. Those who have reached the age of 65 have their five-year waiting period reduced to six months.
3. Players who performed in the Negro Leagues for at least ten years prior to 1946 or those whose major league and Negro League service totals at least ten years. Additionally, those who are not otherwise eligible for election to the Hall of Fame.

The Veterans Committee is allowed to elect two candidates each year. To be elected, a candidate must have 75 percent of the vote of the quorum of 12 members of the committee.

NATIONAL BASEBALL HALL OF FAME MEMBERS
Cooperstown, N.Y.

ELECTED BY BASEBALL WRITERS ASSOCIATION OF AMERICA (73)

1936   Tyrus R. Cobb
Walter P. Johnson
Christopher Mathewson
George H. Ruth
John P. Wagner

1937   Napoleon Lajoie
Tristram E. Speaker
Denton T. Young

1938   Grover C. Alexander

1939   Edward T. Collins
Henry L. Gehrig
William H. Keeler
George H. Sisler

1942   Rogers Hornsby

1947   Gordon S. Cochrane
Frank F. Frisch
Robert M. Grove
Carl O. Hubbell

1948   Herbert J. Pennock
Harold J. Traynor

1949   Charles L. Gehringer

1951   James E. Foxx
Melvin T. Ott

1952   Harry E. Heilmann
Paul G. Waner

1953   Jay Hanna Dean
Aloysius H. Simmons

1954   William M. Dickey
Walter J. Maranville
William H. Terry

1955   Joseph P. DiMaggio
Charles L. Hartnett
Theodore A. Lyons
Arthur C. Vance

1956   Joseph E. Cronin
Henry B. Greenberg

1962   Robert W. Feller
Jack R. Robinson

1964   Lucius Appling

1966   Theodore S. Williams

1967   Charles H. Ruffing

1968   Joseph M. Medwick

1969   Roy Campanella
Stanley F. Musial

1970   Louis Boudreau

1972   Lawrence P. Berra
Sanford Koufax
Early Wynn

1973   Warren E. Spahn
Roberto W. Clemente

1974   Edward C. Ford
Mickey C. Mantle

1975   Ralph M. Kiner

1976   Robert G. Lemon
Robin E. Roberts

1977   Ernest Banks

1978   Edwin L. Mathews

1979   Willie H. Mays

1980   Albert W. Kaline
Edwin D. "Duke" Snider

1981   Robert Gibson

1982   Henry L. Aaron
Frank Robinson

1983   Juan A. Marichal
Brooks C. Robinson, Jr.

1984   Luis E. Aparicio
Donald S. Drysdale
Harmon C. Killebrew

1985   Louis C. Brock
James Hoyt Wilhelm

1986   Willie L. "Stretch"
McCovey

1987   James A. "Catfish"
Hunter
Billy L. Williams
Willie Stargell

1988   Johnny Bench
Carl Yastrzemski

ELECTED BY BASEBALL HALL OF FAME COMMITTEE
ON BASEBALL VETERANS (117)

1937   Morgan G. Bulkeley
Byron B. Johnson
John J. McGraw
Cornelius McGillicuddy
    (Connie Mack)
George Wright

1938   Alexander J.
    Cartwright, Jr.
Henry Chadwick

1939   Adrian C. Anson
Charles A. Comiskey
William A. Cummings
William B. Ewing
Charles Radbourne
Albert G. Spalding

1944   Kenesaw M. Landis

1945   Roger P. Bresnahan
Dennis Brouthers
Frederick C. Clarke
James J. Collins
Edward J. Delahanty
Hugh Duffy
Hugh A. Jennings
Michael J. Kelly
James H. O'Rourke
Wilbert Robinson

1946   Jesse C. Burkett
Frank L. Chance
John D. Chesbro
John J. Evers
Clark C. Griffith
Thomas F. McCarthy
Joseph J. McGinnity
Edward S. Plank
Joseph B. Tinker
George E. Waddell
Edward A. Walsh

1949   Mordecai P. Brown
Charles A. Nichols

1953   Edward G. Barrow
Charles A. Bender
Thomas H. Connolly
William J. Klem
Roderick J. Wallace
William H. Wright

1955   John F. Baker
Raymond W. Schalk

1957   Samuel E. Crawford
Joseph V. McCarthy

1959   Zachariah D. Wheat

1961   Max G. Carey
William R. Hamilton

1962   William B. McKechnie
Edd J. Roush

1963   John G. Clarkson
Elmer H. Flick
Edgar C. Rice
Eppa Rixey

1964   Urban C. Faber
Burleigh A. Grimes
Miller J. Huggins
Timothy J. Keefe
Henry E. Manush
John Montgomery Ward

1965   James F. Galvin

1966   Charles D. Stengel

1967   Wesley Branch Rickey
Lloyd J. Waner

1968   Hazen S. Cuyler
Leon A. Goslin

1969   Stanley A. Coveleski
Waite C. Hoyt
Robert Cal Hubbard

1970   Earle B. Combs
Ford C. Frick
Jesse J. Haines

1971   David J. Bancroft
Jacob P. Beckley
Charles J. Hafey
William Harridge
Harry B. Hooper
Joseph J. Kelley
Richard W. Marquard
George M. Weiss

1972   Vernon L. Gomez
Ross Youngs

1973   William G. Evans
George L. Kelly
Michael F. Welch

1974   James L. Bottomley
John B. Conlan
Samuel L. Thompson

1975   H. Earl Averill
Stanley R. Harris
William J. Herman

1976   Roger Connor
Fred C. Lindstrom

1977   Alfonso R. Lopez
Amos W. Rusie
Joseph W. Sewell

1978   Adrian Joss
Leland S. "Larry"
    MacPhail

1979   Warren C. Giles
Lewis R. "Hack" Wilson

1980 Charles H. Klein
Thomas A. Yawkey

1981 Andrew "Rube" Foster
John R. Mize

1982 A. B. "Happy" Chandler
Travis C. Jackson

1983 Walter E. Alston
George C. Kell

1984 Richard B. Ferrell
Harold H. "Pee Wee"
Reese

1985 Enos B. "Country"
Slaughter
Joseph F. "Arky"
Vaughan

1986 Robert Doerr
Ernest N. Lombardi

1987 Raymond E. Dandridge

1988 Albert Barlick
Albert "Red"
Schoendienst

ELECTED BY BASEBALL HALL OF FAME COMMITTEE
ON NEGRO BASEBALL LEAGUES (9)

1971 Leroy R. Paige

1972 Joshua Gibson
Walter F. Leonard

1973 Monford Irvin

1974 James T. Bell

1975 William J. Johnson

1976 Oscar M. Charleston
John H. Lloyd

1977 Martin DiHigo

Total Members—203

Bibliography

Carter, Craig, ed. *The Complete Baseball Record Book*. St. Louis, Mo.: The Sporting News, 1987.

Holway, John B. *Blackball Stars*. Westport, Conn.: Meckler Books, 1988.

Lincoln Library of Sports Champions, The. Columbus, Ohio: Sports Resource Co., 1986.

Mercurio, John A. *Chronology of Major League Baseball Records*. New York: Harper & Row, 1989.

Murray, Tom. *Sport Magazine's All-Time All-Stars*. New York: Atheneum, 1977.

Porter, David L. *The Biographical Dictionary of American Sports—Baseball*. Westport, Conn.: Greenwood Press, 1987.

Reichler, Joseph L., ed. *The Baseball Encyclopedia: The Complete & Official Record of Major League Baseball*. New York: Macmillan, 1987.

Rust, Art, Jr. *"Get That Nigger Off The Field!"* New York: Delacorte Press, 1976.

Seymour, Harold. *Baseball: The Early Years*. Toronto: Oxford University Press, 1960.

Siwoff, Seymour. *The Book of Baseball Records*. New York: Sterling, 1981.

Smith, Robert. *The Pioneers of Baseball*. Boston: Little, Brown, 1978.

Thorn, John, and Palmer, Pete, eds. *Total Baseball*. New York: Warner Books, 1989.

Turkin, Hy, and Thompson, S. C. *The Official Encyclopedia of Baseball,* 10th ed. South Brunswick, N.J.: A. S. Barnes, 1979.